Soviet and Post-Soviet Politics and S
ISSN 1614-3515

General Editor: Andreas Umland,
Institute for Euro-Atlantic Cooperation, Kyiv, umland@stanfordalumni.org

EDITORIAL COMMITTEE*

DOMESTIC & COMPARATIVE POLITICS
Prof. **Ellen Bos**, *Andrássy University of Budapest*
Dr. **Ingmar Bredies**, *FH Bund, Brühl*
Dr. **Andrey Kazantsev**, *MGIMO (U) MID RF, Moscow*
Prof. **Heiko Pleines**, *University of Bremen*
Prof. **Richard Sakwa**, *University of Kent at Canterbury*
Dr. **Sarah Whitmore**, *Oxford Brookes University*
Dr. **Harald Wydra**, *University of Cambridge*

SOCIETY, CLASS & ETHNICITY
Col. **David Glantz**, *"Journal of Slavic Military Studies"*
Dr. **Marlène Laruelle**, *George Washington University*
Dr. **Stephen Shulman**, *Southern Illinois University*
Prof. **Stefan Troebst**, *University of Leipzig*

POLITICAL ECONOMY & PUBLIC POLICY
Prof. em. **Marshall Goldman**, *Wellesley College, Mass.*
Dr. **Andreas Goldthau**, *Central European University*
Dr. **Robert Kravchuk**, *University of North Carolina*
Dr. **David Lane**, *University of Cambridge*
Dr. **Carol Leonard**, *Higher School of Economics, Moscow*
Dr. **Maria Popova**, *McGill University, Montreal*

Dr. **Peter Duncan**, *University College London*
Prof. **Andreas Heinemann-Grüder**, *University of Bonn*
Dr. **Taras Kuzio**, *Johns Hopkins University*
Prof. **Gerhard Mangott**, *University of Innsbruck*
Dr. **Diana Schmidt-Pfister**, *University of Konstanz*
Dr. **Lisbeth Tarlow**, *Harvard University, Cambridge*
Dr. **Christian Wipperfürth**, *N-Ost Network, Berlin*
Dr. **William Zimmerman**, *University of Michigan*

HISTORY, CULTURE & THOUGHT
Dr. **Catherine Andreyev**, *University of Oxford*
Prof. **Mark Bassin**, *Södertörn University*
Prof. **Karsten Brüggemann**, *Tallinn University*
Dr. **Alexander Etkind**, *University of Cambridge*
Dr. **Gasan Gusejnov**, *Moscow State University*
Prof. em. **Walter Laqueur**, *Georgetown University*
Prof. **Leonid Luks**, *Catholic University of Eichstaett*
Dr. **Olga Malinova**, *Russian Academy of Sciences*
Prof. **Andrei Rogatchevski**, *University of Tromsø*
Dr. **Mark Tauger**, *West Virginia University*

ADVISORY BOARD*

Prof. **Dominique Arel**, *University of Ottawa*
Prof. **Jörg Baberowski**, *Humboldt University of Berlin*
Prof. **Margarita Balmaceda**, *Seton Hall University*
Dr. **John Barber**, *University of Cambridge*
Prof. **Timm Beichelt**, *European University Viadrina*
Dr. **Katrin Boeckh**, *University of Munich*
Prof. em. **Archie Brown**, *University of Oxford*
Dr. **Vyacheslav Bryukhovetsky**, *Kyiv-Mohyla Academy*
Prof. **Timothy Colton**, *Harvard University, Cambridge*
Prof. **Paul D'Anieri**, *University of Florida*
Dr. **Heike Dörrenbächer**, *Friedrich Naumann Foundation*
Dr. **John Dunlop**, *Hoover Institution, Stanford, California*
Dr. **Sabine Fischer**, *SWP, Berlin*
Dr. **Geir Flikke**, *NUPI, Oslo*
Prof. **David Galbreath**, *University of Aberdeen*
Prof. **Alexander Galkin**, *Russian Academy of Sciences*
Prof. **Frank Golczewski**, *University of Hamburg*
Dr. **Nikolas Gvosdev**, *Naval War College, Newport, RI*
Prof. **Mark von Hagen**, *Arizona State University*
Dr. **Guido Hausmann**, *University of Munich*
Prof. **Dale Herspring**, *Kansas State University*
Dr. **Stefani Hoffman**, *Hebrew University of Jerusalem*
Prof. **Mikhail Ilyin**, *MGIMO (U) MID RF, Moscow*
Prof. **Vladimir Kantor**, *Higher School of Economics*
Dr. **Ivan Katchanovski**, *University of Ottawa*
Prof. em. **Andrzej Korbonski**, *University of California*
Dr. **Iris Kempe**, *"Caucasus Analytical Digest"*
Prof. **Herbert Küpper**, *Institut für Ostrecht Regensburg*
Dr. **Rainer Lindner**, *CEEER, Berlin*
Dr. **Vladimir Malakhov**, *Russian Academy of Sciences*

Dr. **Luke March**, *University of Edinburgh*
Prof. **Michael McFaul**, *Stanford University, Palo Alto*
Prof. **Birgit Menzel**, *University of Mainz-Germersheim*
Prof. **Valery Mikhailenko**, *The Urals State University*
Prof. **Emil Pain**, *Higher School of Economics, Moscow*
Dr. **Oleg Podvintsev**, *Russian Academy of Sciences*
Prof. **Olga Popova**, *St. Petersburg State University*
Dr. **Alex Pravda**, *University of Oxford*
Dr. **Erik van Ree**, *University of Amsterdam*
Dr. **Joachim Rogall**, *Robert Bosch Foundation Stuttgart*
Prof. **Peter Rutland**, *Wesleyan University, Middletown*
Prof. **Marat Salikov**, *The Urals State Law Academy*
Dr. **Gwendolyn Sasse**, *University of Oxford*
Prof. **Jutta Scherrer**, *EHESS, Paris*
Prof. **Robert Service**, *University of Oxford*
Mr. **James Sherr**, *RIIA Chatham House London*
Dr. **Oxana Shevel**, *Tufts University, Medford*
Prof. **Eberhard Schneider**, *University of Siegen*
Prof. **Olexander Shnyrkov**, *Shevchenko University, Kyiv*
Prof. **Hans-Henning Schröder**, *SWP, Berlin*
Prof. **Yuri Shapoval**, *Ukrainian Academy of Sciences*
Prof. **Viktor Shnirelman**, *Russian Academy of Sciences*
Dr. **Lisa Sundstrom**, *University of British Columbia*
Dr. **Philip Walters**, *"Religion, State and Society", Oxford*
Prof. **Zenon Wasyliw**, *Ithaca College, New York State*
Dr. **Lucan Way**, *University of Toronto*
Dr. **Markus Wehner**, *"Frankfurter Allgemeine Zeitung"*
Dr. **Andrew Wilson**, *University College London*
Prof. **Jan Zielonka**, *University of Oxford*
Prof. **Andrei Zorin**, *University of Oxford*

* While the Editorial Committee and Advisory Board support the General Editor in the choice and improvement of manuscripts for publication, responsibility for remaining errors and misinterpretations in the series' volumes lies with the books' authors.

Soviet and Post-Soviet Politics and Society (SPPS)
ISSN 1614-3515

Founded in 2004 and refereed since 2007, SPPS makes available affordable English-, German-, and Russian-language studies on the history of the countries of the former Soviet bloc from the late Tsarist period to today. It publishes between 5 and 20 volumes per year and focuses on issues in transitions to and from democracy such as economic crisis, identity formation, civil society development, and constitutional reform in CEE and the NIS. SPPS also aims to highlight so far understudied themes in East European studies such as right-wing radicalism, religious life, higher education, or human rights protection. The authors and titles of all previously published volumes are listed at the end of this book. For a full description of the series and reviews of its books, see www.ibidem-verlag.de/red/spps.

Editorial correspondence & manuscripts should be sent to: Dr. Andreas Umland, c/o DAAD, German Embassy, vul. Bohdana Khmelnitskoho 25, UA-01901 Kyiv, Ukraine. e-mail: umland@stanfordalumni.org

Business correspondence & review copy requests should be sent to: *ibidem* Press, Leuschnerstr. 40, 30457 Hannover, Germany; tel.: +49 511 2622200; fax: +49 511 2622201; spps@ibidem.eu.

Authors, reviewers, referees, and editors for (as well as all other persons sympathetic to) SPPS are invited to join its networks at www.facebook.com/group.php?gid=52638198614 www.linkedin.com/groups?about=&gid=103012 www.xing.com/net/spps-ibidem-verlag/

Recent Volumes

162 Natalya Ryabinska
Ukraine's Post-Communist Mass Media
Between Capture and Commercialization
With a foreword by Marta Dyczok
ISBN 978-3-8382-1011-7

163 Alexandra Cotofana, James M. Nyce (eds.)
Religion and Magic in Socialist and Post-Socialist Contexts
Historic and Ethnographic Case Studies of Orthodoxy, Heterodoxy, and Alternative Spirituality
With a foreword by Patrick L. Michelson
ISBN 978-3-8382-0989-0

164 Nozima Akhrarkhodjaeva
The Instrumentalisation of Mass Media in Electoral Authoritarian Regimes
Evidence from Russia's Presidential Election Campaigns of 2000 and 2008
ISBN 978-3-8382-1013-1

165 Yulia Krasheninnikova
Informal Healthcare in Contemporary Russia
Sociographic Essays on the Post-Soviet Infrastructure for Alternative Healing Practices
ISBN 978-3-8382-0970-8

166 Peter Kaiser
Das Schachbrett der Macht
Die Handlungsspielräume eines sowjetischen Funktionärs unter Stalin am Beispiel des Generalsekretärs des Komsomol Aleksandr Kosarev (1929-1938)
Mit einem Vorwort von Dietmar Neutatz
ISBN 978-3-8382-1052-0

167 Oksana Kim
The Effects and Implications of Kazakhstan's Adoption of International Financial Reporting Standards
A Resource Dependence Perspective
With a foreword by Svetlana Vlady
ISBN 978-3-8382-0987-6

168 Anna Sanina
Patriotic Education in Contemporary Russia
Sociological Studies in the Making of the Post-Soviet Citizen
ISBN 978-3-8382-0993-7

Timm Beichelt, Susann Worschech (eds.)

TRANSNATIONAL UKRAINE?

Networks and Ties that Influence(d) Contemporary Ukraine

ibidem-Verlag
Stuttgart

Bibliografische Information der Deutschen Nationalbibliothek
Die Deutsche Nationalbibliothek verzeichnet diese Publikation in der Deutschen Nationalbibliografie; detaillierte bibliografische Daten sind im Internet über http://dnb.d-nb.de abrufbar.

Bibliographic information published by the Deutsche Nationalbibliothek
Die Deutsche Nationalbibliothek lists this publication in the Deutsche Nationalbibliografie; detailed bibliographic data are available in the Internet at http://dnb.d-nb.de.

Cover map © Christoph Breit / MASZSTAB cartography (www.maszstab.eu)
Created using QGIS 2.14.11 Essen;
Geodata: Natural Earth. Free vector and raster map data @ naturalearthdata.com.

∞
Gedruckt auf alterungsbeständigem, säurefreien Papier
Printed on acid-free paper

ISSN: 1614-3515

ISBN-13: 978-3-8382-0944-9

© *ibidem*-Verlag
Stuttgart 2017

Alle Rechte vorbehalten

Das Werk einschließlich aller seiner Teile ist urheberrechtlich geschützt. Jede Verwertung außerhalb der engen Grenzen des Urheberrechtsgesetzes ist ohne Zustimmung des Verlages unzulässig und strafbar. Dies gilt insbesondere für Vervielfältigungen, Übersetzungen, Mikroverfilmungen und elektronische Speicherformen sowie die Einspeicherung und Verarbeitung in elektronischen Systemen.

All rights reserved. No part of this publication may be reproduced, stored in or introduced into a retrieval system, or transmitted, in any form, or by any means (electronical, mechanical, photocopying, recording or otherwise) without the prior written permission of the publisher. Any person who does any unauthorized act in relation to this publication may be liable to criminal prosecution and civil claims for damages.

Printed in Germany

Contents

Acknowledgements 7

List of Contributors 9

Part I:
Introduction

Timm Beichelt and Susann Worschech
Transnational Networks in and around Ukraine: Theories and Practices 15

André Härtel
**The "Novorossiya" Project and National Affiliations in Ukraine's
Southeast: A Failed Attempt at Transnational Community Reconstruction?** 39

Part II:
Symbolic Transnationalism

Mikhail Minakov
Novorossiya and the Transnationalism of Unrecognized Post-Soviet Nations 65

Yuliya Yurchuk
**Global Symbols and Local Meanings:
The "Day of Victory" after Euromaidan** 89

Part III:
Practice-related Transnationalism

Alexander Clarkson
**Coming to Terms with Odessa Ukraine:
The Impact of the Maidan Uprising on the Ukrainian Diaspora** 115

Andriy Korniychuk, Magdalena Patalong and Richard Steinberg
**The Influence of Protest Movements on the Development
of Diasporic Engagement: The Case of Euromaidan
and its Impact for the Ukrainian Diaspora in Poland and Germany** 137

Part IV:
Socio-structural Transnationalism

Heiko Pleines
The International Links of Ukrainian Oligarchs.
Business Expansion and Transnational Offshore Networks 161

Susanne Spahn
Ukraine in the Russian Mass Media:
Germany as an Example of Russian Information Policy 179

Simon Schlegel
Ukrainian Nation Building and Ethnic Minority Associations:
The Case of Southern Bessarabia 203

Veronika Borysenko, Mascha Brammer and Jonas Eichhorn
The Transnational "Neo-Eurasian" Network
and its Preparation of Separatism in Ukraine 2005–2014 225

Part V: Conclusion

Susann Worschech and Timm Beichelt
Ukraine and Beyond: Concluding Remarks on Transnationalism 251

Acknowledgements

This book arose from a conference in November 2015 that was based on a challenging idea. Only shortly after the Euromaidan protests, the annexation of Crimea, the start of the war in Eastern Ukraine, scholars from various disciplines gathered at European University Viadrina in Frankfurt (Oder), just a few steps away from the German-Polish border. Against this scenery of a symbolically charged border, about twentyfive scholars discussed how to conceptualize and analyze contemporary Ukraine. Our ambition was to acknowledge the huge and courageous societal change within that country, but also to include the multifold and ambivalent external links of a space that by definition seems to be a borderland: «україна».

In this context, the idea was born to edit some of the papers presented at the conference under the heading "Transnational Ukraine". We chose transnationalism as an analytical starting point because of a core research area at European University Viadrina on the interplay of borders and orders in contemporary Europe (https://www.borders-in-motion.de/). Transnationalist perspectives seem to be appropriate in constellations in which nation states and their borders retain importance, but are challenged and transgressed by actors, practices, and ideas. The conference led us to the insight that Ukraine represents a paradigmatic case when thinking about the porosity of borders in a world where some actors have more powers or resources than others to question these borders.

The conference was co-financed by the German Association for East European Studies and European University Viadrina. We like to thank both institutions greatly for having facilitated that debate. In particular, we want to express our special thanks to Ulrike Sapper and Gabriele Freitag for their excellent preparation and organization of the conference. We really enjoyed this great cooperation.

Further, we would like to thank Karoline Winter for her wonderful and diligent support in preparing the manuscript. Also, we would like to thank Maria Ugoljew for helping us to deploy a correct and coherent transliteration. Special thanks go to the editorial team at *ibidem*, in particular to the editor Andreas Umland and to Valerie Lange who steered us through the publication process.

List of Contributors

Timm Beichelt is a professor for European Studies at European University Viadrina. His research interests are related to regime developments in countries of Eastern, Central, and Western Europe. Among many other trips to Ukraine, he has undertaken a series of scientific field trips which are documented in a blog (https://viadrinagoesukraine.wordpress.com/). Recent publications cover German European policy, Civil Society and Democracy Promotion in Eastern Europe, and Legitimate Authoritarianism in Russia.

Veronika Borysenko is a master student of the program "European Studies" at European University Viadrina, Germany. She holds a bachelor's and master's degree in International Relations from Kyiv National Taras Shevchenko University. Since 2016 she is working as Project Assistant in *European Exchange* within the project European Platform for Democratic Elections. Her main areas of research interests are political developments in Post-Soviet countries and democracy support for countries in transition.

Mascha Brammer obtained her BA in Social Science and Literature Studies from the University of Erfurt. She is currently enrolled in the MA European Studies at European University Viadrina in Frankfurt/Oder. During her studies she spent two semesters at the Bosphorus University, Istanbul and gained working experience at the German Bundestag, a political youth education program and several NGOs.

Dr Alexander Clarkson is Lecturer for German and European Studies at King's College London. He holds a PhD in Modern History (University of Oxford). His research focuses on the politics of immigrant communities including the Ukrainian diaspora, the impact of immigration on German society as well as European security. He is author of *Fragmented Fatherland: Immigration and Cold War Conflict in the Federal Republic of Germany* (2013).

Jonas Eichhorn is a master student of the program *Culture and History of Central and Eastern Europe* at the European University Viadrina in Frankfurt (Oder) and at Charles University in Prague. Previously, he studied Slavic Studies and History in

Heidelberg and St. Petersburg. Jonas Eichhorn was as a volunteer for Action Reconciliation Service for Peace and worked in the archive of Memorial in Moscow for one year. He holds a scholarship of the Heinrich Böll Foundation.

Dr André Härtel (born in 1979) currently works as DAAD Associate Professor for *German and European Studies* at the National University Kyiv-Mohyla Academy in Ukraine. Before, he has been Political Advisor at the Council of Europe's Directorate of Policy Planning (Strasbourg, France) and a Lecturer in International Relations at Friedrich-Schiller-University Jena, Germany. He was educated in Political Science and International Relations at Friedrich-Schiller-University Jena, the University of Virginia (US) and Oxford Brookes University (UK). Aside from being a regional specialist for the Post-Soviet space his research interests cover foreign policy analysis, international organizations, democratization, and state-building.

Andriy Korniychuk is an Analyst in European, Migration Policy, Democracy and Civil Society Programs at the Institute of Public Affairs (Warsaw, Poland). He graduated in European Public Affairs (M.A.) from Maastricht University and Society and Politics from Lancaster University/Centre for Social Sciences (M.A.). Currently, he is doing his doctoral research as a member of the European Studies Unit at the Graduate School of Social Research of the Institute of Philosophy and Sociology of the Polish Academy of Sciences (research area: democratic legitimacy beyond nation-state, case of EU).

Mikhail (Mykhailo) Minakov is an Associate Professor of the Department of Philosophy and Religious Studies of the National University of Kyiv-Mohyla Academy (Ukraine) and Editor-in-Chief of the Ideology and Politics Journal. He graduated in Philosophy (M.A.) from Kiev-Mohyla Academy, defended his Candidate (2000) and Doctoral (2007) dissertations at the Kiev Institute of Philosophy. Mikhail's main interest is dedicated to political modernization, theories and practices of revolutions, political imagination and ideologies.

Magdalena Patalong is Research Assistant at the Institut für Europäische Politik (IEP) Berlin. She studied political science at the Ludwig-Maximilians-University in Munich and Eastern European Studies at the Free University of Berlin. Magdalena

Patalong's academic focus includes civil society and think tanks in Ukraine, the Eastern Partnership and EU-Russia Relations.

Heiko Pleines is head of the Department of Politics and Economics, Research Centre for East European Studies and Professor of Comparative Politics at the University of Bremen. He has been conducting research on the political role of Ukrainian oligarchs since 2004, leading to numerous publications.

Simon Schlegel obtained his PhD in Social Anthropology from the Martin Luther University in Halle, Germany in 2016. His doctoral research was funded by the Max Planck Institute for Social Anthropology, where Simon Schlegel is part of the research group *Historical Anthropology in Eurasia*. His thesis is based on fifteen months of fieldwork in rural south-western Ukraine during which he experimented with combining research methods from ethnography and historiography. His main research interests are the Post-Socialist transition, new forms of nationalism, clientelism, and emerging civil societies. He currently teaches social anthropology at the Martin Luther University.

Susanne Spahn (PhD) is an East European historian, politologist and journalist based in Berlin. Spahn completed her degree in East European History, Slavonic Studies and Political Sciences in St. Petersburg and Cologne. In 2011, she received her doctor's degree and published her thesis on the topic *State Independence—the End of the East Slavonic Unity? Russia's Foreign Policy towards Ukraine and Belarus since 1991*. In 2010 and 2011, Spahn worked in Moscow with, among others, Dow Jones News, die Welt, Deutsche Welle, Zeit online, Magazin Außenwirtschaft. She conducts research on Russia's foreign policy in the post-Soviet area and Russian information policy. Her latest book *The Image of Ukraine in Germany: The Role of Russian Mass Media. How Russia Influences the German Public Opinion* was published in July 2016.

Richard Steinberg is Research Associate at the University of Hamburg and the Institut für Europäische Politik (IEP) Berlin. He studied recent history and social sciences at the University of Erfurt, the Humboldt University of Berlin and the Université II—Le Mirial. He is currently working on his PhD on *Crises in European Integration*. Further research interests are the history of the European integration process, social European integration and EU-Ukraine-relations. Richard Steinberg is alumnus of the Foundation of German Business (sdw) and of the Woodrow Wilson International Center for Scholars in Washington, D.C. (Junior Scholarship 2010).

Susann Worschech is a post-doc research associate at European University Viadrina. Her research interests include political sociology of Central and Eastern Europe, civil society and social movements, as well as methods of empirical research. She graduated from the Humboldt University of Berlin with a diploma in Social Sciences. Her doctorate at European University Viadrina focused on networks of external democracy promotion and the structuring of civil society in Ukraine.

Yuliya Yurchuk got her PhD in History from Stockholm University. Her dissertation *Reordering of Meaningful Worlds: Memory of the Organization of Ukrainian Nationalists and the Ukrainian Insurgent Army in Post-Soviet Ukraine* was defended in 2015. She is currently working at Södertörn University, Sweden. Her main field of interest includes memory politics in East European countries, remembering of the Second World War, nationalism, state- and nation-building in Ukraine. Her current research is focused on popular history writing in post-Maidan Ukraine, the role of religion and churches' activities in formation of public representations of history and the applicability of post-colonial theory in the analysis of cultural memory. She is currently working on the project *Information Management in Ukraine-Russia Crisis* and *Religion and Memory in Ukraine*, both funded by the Baltic Sea Foundation.

Part I:
Introduction

Transnational Networks in and around Ukraine: Theories and Practices

Timm Beichelt and Susann Worschech

The text deals with different objects and perspectives of transnationalism research and their attribution to Ukraine. Starting from a typology from Steven Vertovec, we identify three approaches to border-transgressing phenomena: socio-structural, symbolic, and practice related transnationalism. These approaches are then crossed with spatial, social, and temporal aspects of transnationalism and applied to the Ukrainian case. From this framework of analysis, several expectations with regard to the character of transnationalism in Ukraine are developed. First, we expect that migration will most likely bear the character of transmigration, which fuels a re-nationalization of identities. This means, second, that national symbols will become even more relevant, but in contested ways. Third, we expect practices of transnationalism to be fuzzy, volatile, and liquid. The chapter closes with an outlook on the other manuscripts of this book.

1. Introduction

The so-called *Revolution of Dignity* and the subsequent events in Southern and Eastern Ukraine propelled a new self-perception of Ukraine as a nation of unity and togetherness, on the one hand. On the other, the de-facto break-off process of some Donbass regions fuels a different a narrative of Ukraine as a nation between two alternative orientations: Europe or Russia. Within the first narrative, the European Union (EU), and sometimes NATO, are portrayed as guarantors of Ukrainian independence. The counter-picture presents Ukraine as an entity with limited self-determination because of the country's intertwinement with Slavonic culture and, ultimately, because of its subordination to Russian power. Both narratives of unity and bipolarity, we argue, are far too schematic to grasp the character of the huge transformation of Ukrainian society since 2014.

The contributions to this volume have the aim to break with both narratives. The manuscripts were first presented at a conference at European University Viadrina in Frankfurt/Oder (Germany) that focused on Ukraine's historical and contemporary interlockings. During this conference, a nuanced perspective on Ukraine during and after Euromaidan evolved. The argument was developed that Ukraine, despite its status as a nation with newly gained political independence, is characterized by multiple fragmentations and belongings that link the country—its society, its regions, its culture—to different areas and powers at different points in time. These fragmentations and belongings underline Ukraine's long-standing and multiple ties beyond its borders. In this book, the conference's findings are reformulated into the argument that contemporary Ukraine can be better understood by focusing on its transnational characteristics. Accordingly, concepts and theories of transnationalism are used to analyze a country that is not situated between two blocks but that draws its richness from roots that go beyond national categories.

For many scholars of contemporary Europe, these findings should not come as a surprise. For several decades, the political structure of Europe has been characterized as part of a postnational constellation in which nation states alone lack autonomy and are subject to both European integration and globalization (Habermas 1998). This situation was and is not a property solely of Western Europe or member states of the EU. Many sources indicate that Eastern Europe has also become a part of globalization in cultural, economic, and social terms since 1989 (Kovacs 1999; Janos 2000). Therefore, on the one hand, placing Ukraine within the context of a Europe of increasing permeability of national borders and reference areas does not constitute a scientific breakthrough.

On the other hand, at least since the rise of the inner-soviet independence movements in the late 1980s, scholarship on Ukraine has constantly referred to a national framework. Major contributions regarding post-soviet developments in Ukraine turned to issues that contrasted with the idea of an ever closer Europe as—idealistically—attributed to the European Union. Ukraine was analyzed with regard to nation building and to the dilemmas in Ukrainian-Russian relations that followed from that nation building (Wolchik & Zviglyanich 2000; Kuzio 1998; Motyl 1993). The Orange Revolution of 2004 was celebrated as a landmark that separated a Ukrainian way of transformation from most, if not all, other post-soviet transitions (Christensen et al. 2005; Karatnycky 2005). The hitherto largest protest movement of independent Ukraine highly benefitted from training and organizational support provided by Western civil society organizations. This fact was interpreted by many observers as a legitimate form of international cooperation that strengthened

Ukrainian independence vis-à-vis Russia and its ambitions of influencing Ukrainian politics (Wilson 2006; McFaul 2007).

Since Ukrainian independence, the geographic area outlined by Lviv, Prypyat, Kharkiv, Luhansk, Sevastopol, and Odessa has been characterized as a 'nation', although this 'nation' has been portrayed as an entity with varying sources, aspects, and serious ruptures. In social and economic terms, Ukraine has been analyzed as an area that is heavily interlinked with Russian history. Political developments, however, only partially reflect these cultural and economic overlaps. Political and economic elites in the EU as well as in the United States advocated a simultaneous democratization and capitalist marketization of Ukraine—a political aim that has become increasingly incompatible with the course Russia has taken since Putin's coming to power in 1999/2000.

In the years after the Orange Revolution, Ukrainian elites tried to close ranks with the West and fostered the narrative of Ukraine as an independent nation in order to facilitate Western support, following the pattern of the Central European transition countries. The argument of a coherent Ukrainian nation turned into a political tool to secure the success of democratization. It would be an interesting endeavor to analyze to what extent scholars have been part of the epistemic drift from (inherently open) democratization to (inherently teleological) nation building. We have the impression that very few experts on Ukrainian politics and its transformation have not—at one time or another—been part of the supervising business around Ukraine, its democratization and/or Western integration. Many scholars involved in this discourse are part of civil society organizations, think tanks or agencies that depend on grants from the EU, the USA or other Western governments.

However, it is not our main point to criticize scholars for an alleged lack of impartiality.[i] Politically, we sympathize with the argument that an aggressive and authoritarian Russia plays a destructive game of destabilization in Ukraine. At the same time, we also want to argue that this normative position bears the danger of an epistemological dead corner. While sympathizing with the political goals of most elites and civil society organizations, we run into the danger of overlooking important conjunctions in Ukraine. Within the context of this book, this means that while it may be politically questionable to adopt (Russian) narratives that cast doubt on the teleology of coherent nation building in Ukraine, it is scientifically necessary to insist that the heterogeneity of Ukraine may also point to different directions than a stable nation state. This heterogeneity mainly concerns Ukraine's contemporary and historical intertwinement with Russia, but also Poland, Lithuania, the Austro-Hungarian Empire, and the Soviet Union.

In this book, we try to replace the narratives of nation building, democratization, and capitalist marketization by perceiving contemporary Ukraine as a transnationalist entity. Applying transnationalism as a scientific paradigm is not without problems because of its inherent fuzziness and its one-concept-fits-all appeal. However, while the approach "seems to be everywhere, at least in social science" (Vertovec 2009: 1), a coherent transnational perspective on Ukraine has not really been established yet. Transnationalism generally refers to situations or processes in which borders of nation states are transcended by social activities (Pries 2010: 9). A major motivation of transnationalism studies is and was to escape the "methodological nationalism" inherent in much social science (Amelina et al. 2012). By applying categories that have been developed to analyze social practices taking place within nation states, there is a danger of tacitly taking over assumptions that are exclusively linked to nation states. One such assumption, for instance, is to imagine political activities and practices predominantly in relation to national governments or institutions that depend on central governments. In this introduction and the subsequent texts, we want to show that a more open view on political, economic and societal practices and their interrelations can further our understanding of contemporary Ukraine.

2. Transnationalism as a Tool for Regime Analysis: Three Different Methodological Perspectives

Transnationalism serves many scientific goals simultaneously. It has served as a real-world diagnosis to overcome the focus on nations (Marjanen 2009), it has been used as a political tool in order to give a voice to persons who do not fit neatly within the framework of methodological nationalism (Brettell 2003), and it has been employed as a mind-map to differentiate economic, political and societal globalization (Pries 2008). With regard to Ukraine, all these approaches seem useful and maybe even necessary. Ukraine is both less and more than a nation because of its long-term, intense and formative historical entanglements with Russia in the north, east, and south, with Poland in the west, with Romania in the southwest, and with miscellaneous empires in the past. Contemporary political processes are transnational as well. The internal refugees from the *trans-border* war in Donbas and the millions of semi-forced Ukrainian migrants heading to the EU or North America during the post-soviet economic crises certainly deserve more attention. Hence, there is more to Ukraine's blurring of boundaries than mere globalization—in fact, the country could serve as a blueprint for societies that have for one reason or another transcended politically given borders.

Yet, how can we proceed to systematize the various approaches of transnationalism? Steven Vertovec has suggested differentiating six different "takes" on transnationalism (Vertovec 2009). The first is the most general and concerns "social formation[s] spanning borders" (ibid.: 4). This approach focuses on networks of various kinds: social, cultural, economic, and political. The strengthening of border-transgressing networks goes along with an alteration of pre-existing interactions, thus "calling into question the traditional definition of the state" (ibid.: 5). Some authors who follow this way of defining transnationalism seem to be quite confident that the evolving networks lead to new transnational communities (see some contributions in Schiffauer et al. 2005). In this case, the state would somehow be replaced by one or several alternative entities that develop or even enforce new societal rules. However, there are other authors who are more pessimistic and insist on the necessity of building up genuine transnational, international or supranational institutions in order to compensate for the loss of political steering capacities (Castells 2000; Zürn 1998).

In the second dimension, Vertovec (2009: 5) identifies transnationalism as a "type of consciousness" that is specifically linked to diasporas. Diasporas show that border transgression alone is only one necessary condition of transnationalism. Another condition is the persistence of a reference community, for example, Jewish or Armenian. While such communities are formed by social ties, there also exists a strong subjective element that perpetuates the idea of the givenness of a community. As Brubaker (2005) argues, diaspora communities often share hybrid collective identities, thus blurring boundaries. Therefore, transnationalism as consciousness goes along with terms such as identity, collective memory, and shared imagination. Insofar as identities are open and live in limited conflict with their respective environments, the term "cosmopolitanism" is used to characterize a productive approach to consciousness creation (Vertovec & Cohen 2002; Beck & Grande 2004).

Third, transnationalism can be seen as a "mode of cultural reproduction" (Vertovec 2009: 7). This take focuses on practices that are employed to create or uphold the new transnational imagined communities—to paraphrase the title of Benedict Anderson's famous book on nationalism (Anderson 1983). Such practices consist in the memory-enriched creativity of fashion, movies, fiction, and visual arts. The digital age is held liable for the emerging intensity of the new transnational culture production. Easy access to transnational communication and networks is seen as one precondition for multiple practices of mixing elements from different cultures, leading to "syncretism, creolization, bricolage, cultural translation, and hybridity" (Vertovec 2009: 7). Transnationalism in this mode is therefore marked by creativity of the unexpected.

The fourth dimension of transnationalism refers to economics. Specifically, economic transnationalism is associated with corporations that operate massively beyond borders. It is therefore quite closely linked to economic globalization and its inherent transnational business companies, such as Google, Goldman Sachs and eBay. The difference from international business consists in focus: Transnational corporations have developed routines that cannot be reduced to the national origins of a company and that involve practices rooted in a "transnational capitalist class" (ibid., 8) of its own right. Economic transnationalism is driven by economic motives and comprises actors involved in petty trade, micro-transactions and temporary labor migration. In a way, the approach is used as a sociology of border-transgressing economic activities and is demarcated against the approach of global economics that deals with open financial markets, international flows of trade, and foreign investment (a scholar who uses the globalization paradigm in this sense is Scholte 2000).

Fifth, Vertovec speaks of transnationalism as a site of political engagement (Vertovec 2009: 10). This dimension refers to actors that have political aims and pursue them by operating beyond borders. Again, the dimension is best understood by thinking of competing concepts. Transnational politics are not international politics (this would be the arena of international organizations like the United Nations), and they are not supranational politics (these would involve a powerful political center like in the EU). Transnational political actors are international NGOs, but they are also the often self-claimed political representations of diasporas or other sub- and transnational social groups. All kinds of nationalisms without a given "homeland" (Brubaker 1997) can be addressed within the framework of political transnationalism. Because of the lack of a central political authority in this highly politicized field, transnationalism is closely linked to the paradigm of international governance (Rosenau & Czempiel 1992).

The sixth and final take on transnationalism concerns a "(re)construction of 'place' or locality" (Vertovec 2009: 12). This reconstruction is, in the first place, undertaken by persons who move between places and face difficulties with a "growing disjuncture between territory, subjectivity and collective social movement" (ibid.). In contrast to the third type developed by Vertovec ("cultural reproduction"), transnationalism can also be associated with a kind of homelessness—a state that can creatively be transformed into new kinds of identities but also into a consciousness of lacking completeness. Persons or groups that live under the auspices of transnationalism may develop actions that relate to an (imagined) past or future in which collective consciousness was allegedly more coherent. As can be seen with regard to Kurds in contemporary times, such a feeling of incompleteness may well relate back to traditional nationhood and, therefore, to stateness (Østergaard-Nielsen 2003). This example shows that transnationalism is, after all, a concept that is marked by ambivalence. While the mind map of nationalism may be too narrow to understand certain contemporary developments of blurred boundaries, the framework of transnationalism may sometimes be re-focused on nations after all.

The discussion of Vertovec's work has revealed that scholarship on transnationalism may be useful for the focus of this book in several regards. It has been shown that the term transnationalism is used in demarcation against other competing concepts—particularly the concepts of globalization (Scholte 2000), cosmopolitanism (Vertovec & Cohen 2002), and approaches of state-driven international politics (Keohane & Nye 1977). Transnationalism does not refer to anonymous forces that drive globalization but to clearly identifiable actors as subjects who are *doing* transnationalism. In this perspective, Vertovec's accounts of transnationalism can be systematized into two categories: transnational interaction patterns on the one hand and actors of transnationalism on the other.

Transnational interaction patterns, on the one hand, include networks as social formations that span borders, the construction of border-transgressing identities such as diasporas, the practices of transnational cultural reproduction, and the symbolic construction of certain transnational localities. These interactions may consist of symbolic or communicative interactions, the exchange of resources or information, or direct cooperation. Hence, one aspect of transnationalism studies is a focus on border-transgressing or border-blurring interaction patterns. Within these patterns or networks, cultural codes, interpretations, roles and positions of actors are negotiated and attributed. Thus, transnational interaction patterns open up new social spaces.

On the other hand, actors of such transnational sociation processes are identifiable subjects that may switch to new roles and positions in a transnational social space. These actors exist in different spheres of action—Vertovec mentions culture, economics, and politics. These may shift when issues are transferred from a regional or national to a transnational dimension. In the process of *being transnationalized*, actors may undergo significant transformation when they seek to adapt to new roles and positions in a transnational network.

The emerging transnational spaces are thus built upon interaction patterns that already exist on national, regional or local levels but that create new institutions, orders and norms once they are transferred to a cross-border dimension. Hence, transnationalism can be referred to as processes of constructing normative, institutional, economic, political or social orders beyond rather than between nation states (Bernhard & Schmidt-Wellenburg 2014: 137). These interactions of groups, persons, social movements, companies and other individual or corporative actors thus constitute emerging transnational fields as "recognized areas of institutional life" (DiMaggio & Powell, 1991: 65). Consequently, transnational fields are made up of social ties and interlinkages between the actors in the field; the symbolic meanings and interpretations actors contribute to the field; and finally, the agency of actors that generates new symbolic orders and frames.

Within these demarcations, we can see that transnationalism focuses on different dimensions of analysis and, hence, requires different methodological approaches. The making of transnational spaces or fields (and the respective analysis thereof) may rest on social ties, on symbolic interpretations, or on active practices of (re)construction, each focusing on transnational actors, interaction patterns, and meanings. While we underline that social analysis may well pursue a strategy of methodological triangulation, we suggest distinguishing among three broad approaches in order to attain conceptual clarity. These approaches of transnationalism are socio-structural, symbolic, and practice-related transnationalism:

- *Socio-structural transnationalism studies* are interested in detectable social linkages, particularly within networks that reach beyond borders. One goal of pertinent research consists in spotting and characterizing such networks. Due to an inherent lack of formal institutions of transnationalism (if they existed, we would be employing an international politics approach), research is oriented at communication and at the emergence of informal institutions and networks (Wellman & Berkowitz 1988; Mayntz 1998: 56; McAdam et al. 1996; Bröchler & Grunden 2014). Methodologically, this means that actors, their discursive practices and the re-structuring of social patterns need to be taken into consideration.

- *Symbolic transnationalism studies* concentrate on the symbols and codes that hold together communities that cannot be clearly placed with regard to nation states. These codes, which can be transported through all sorts of cultural artifacts, are in need of symbolic interpretation (Berger & Luckmann 1966; Esser 2001). Interpreters are not to be found solely within diasporas or other forms of transnational communities. Rather, a statement of belonging to a transnational community depends on differential cultural codes. For example, "Russians" or "Ukrainians" have *different* views on Crimea as a symbol: both entities can bring forward meaningful reasons for the claim that the region belongs "to us, not them". Symbolic transnationalism is interested in such symbols and enquires into the different and dynamic meanings attributed to them across borders.

- *Practice-related transnationalism studies* reflect on the production side of symbols and culture in interaction. The creation of symbol-carrying artifacts such as movies and art bears a strategic element; an example would be the political engagement of the Ukrainian diaspora in Berlin during and after Euromaidan. Therefore, the approach can never disregard questions of agency. It does not come along in a latently post-structural form; rather, it tries to be aware of transnational actors and their motives. Since agency is included, practice-related transnationalism is also accompanied by the question of to what extent intentional action is successful or not. Thus, ideational frames that define the conditions of rationality are of importance as well (Goffman 1980; Benford & Snow 1988; Apter 2006; Polletta & Ho 2006). In that sense, symbolic and practice-related transnationalism stand in a complementary position to each other: border-transgressing practices only make sense with regard to the symbols demarcating these boundaries, but symbols need to be produced in order to unfold their relevance.

3. Three Dimensions of Transnationalism

In which way can these three approaches be made fruitful for the analysis of contemporary Ukraine? Certainly, socio-structural, symbolic and practice-related elements of transnationalism can be found in many areas of Ukrainian regime development. Pertinent research has already identified several of them. For example, the socio-structural composition of Ukraine has been profoundly analyzed with regard to elections (Kurth & Kempe 2004) and to the geography of language speakers (Kulyk 2010). In addition, migration flows have been studied systematically (Chindea et al. 2008). The symbolic composition of Ukraine and its diverse regions has been researched with a special focus on state symbols (Jilge 1998, 2014). Practices of transnationalism have been addressed as well, for example, in terms of the establishment of (state and non-state) institutions of the EU's Eastern Partnership (Stegniy 2012), the bonding potential of football (Halling 2013) and the making of national identities in a transnational space (Brudny & Finkel 2011).

While it is possible to subsume much research on Ukraine under our different approaches of transnationalism, we still have to deal with the problem that the categories seem quite incoherent—they contain very different research objects. We therefore propose an additional differentiation that is sometimes used in border research (Bossong & Carrapico 2016; Bossong et al. 2016). It builds on a comprehensive research framework developed at European University Viadrina Frankfurt/Oder and deals with the permeability, durability and liminality of borders in contemporary Europe (Schiffauer 2011).[ii] One aspect of this framework distinguishes among spatial, temporal, and social aspects of orders and their limitations. We propose that this additional distinction should be included to isolate different aspects of transnationalism in Eastern Europe and beyond.

Spatial elements concern all aspects of transnationalism that relate to territory. Obviously, migration—often across borders—is one major object of territorial transnationalism. Nevertheless, the relevance of borders is not restricted to persons or groups crossing them, in the sense that different territories are involved. Today, we know of the existence of borders in collective memories: "phantom borders" continue to exist in people's minds long after their territorial existence has ceased (Löwis 2015; Janczak 2015). Spatial belonging therefore derives from two sources: (1) from places where social beings actually live, have lived or have passed by and (2) from imaginations of affiliation that are inspired by symbols. This points toward the necessity of taking into consideration (3) the production of territorial symbols through which intermediate—transnational instead of national—spaces are created.

Social, or better: *societal* aspects have to do with social affiliations, cultural codes and/or practices of community creation within transnational contexts. Again, these three elements are marked by different properties. (1) Social affiliations concern population strata of transnational groups, for example, with regard to certain professions or age groups. (2) These transnational communities are held together not only by the space they settle in (or through which they pass) but also by symbols that (re-)constitute them as cultural entities. With regard to the imaginational dimension of societal belonging across borders, (3) the process of the construction of transnational consciousness again deserves special attention.

Temporal aspects form a third dimension for research on transnationalism. Time-related elements are important to understand the transformation of social groups, symbols and/or practices that evolve around border transgressions. In fact, the whole terminus of transnationalization points to the fact that transnational networks are, as a rule, instable rather than stable (Pries 2008). Again, we can make distinctions using the approaches developed in the previous section. (1) Minorities or diasporas may change their social position within their host societies. The typical representative of this or that group may turn from a dishwasher to a white collar employee, or the simple fact of ageing in transnational networks may change the configuration of certain social groups (Pries 2010: 48–56). Furthermore, (2) the symbols accompanying such change may be subject to change. One example would be the relevance of the Koran to Muslim communities in Western Europe (Schiffauer 2002; Kaya 2012). Again, the configuration of such symbols and their meaning as well as (3) their construction should be seen as an integral field of research in transnationalism studies.

If we take the discussion in sections 2 and 3 and then apply it to contemporary Ukraine, we arrive at table 1. With a focus on theory and methodology, three approaches have evolved that stand for different meta-perspectives of the social sciences: societies and their structure, cultures and their meanings, and practices and their consequences. These meta-perspectives can be combined with different properties of boundaries: in our context, with the territorial, societal, and temporal aspects of the (partial) dissolution of these boundaries. Transnationalism is, in this perspective, both an implication and a result of a growing fluidity of different kinds of lines of distinction between territories, cultures, and practices.

Table 1: Objects and phenomena in transnationalism research

	Dimensions of transnationalism		
	Spatial/Territorial	**Societal**	**Temporal**
(1) Socio-structural approach			
Scholarly object	Migration of individuals or groups across (state) borders	Social affiliations of persons/groups living in more than one national context	Dynamic social developments in (trans)migrant groups
Expected phenomenon within the context of Ukraine	Transmigration	Equal distribution of migration experience across social classes	Increase of "national" affiliation (de-sovietization)
(2) Symbolic approach			
Scholarly object	State- or geography-related symbols of belonging and their interpretations	Cultural codes of transmigrant communities	Dynamics of (geographic or cultural) symbols and their meanings over time
Expected phenomenon within the context of Ukraine	Importance of symbols that delimit Ukraine from other Slavonic entities	New codes of (post-imperial or national) belonging	Reconfiguration of formerly Soviet codes
(3) Practice-oriented approach			
Scholarly object	Creation of intermediate spaces through border transformation	Practices of transnational community re-construction	Emergence of diasporas and/or minorities
Expected phenomenon within the context of Ukraine	Emergence of liminal zones and/or clearly visible diasporas	Diaspora politics	Growing visibility of post-soviet diasporas over time

While much of the literature on Ukraine deals with the conditions of constructing a nation against the background of a previously non-national context, we suggest analyzing Ukraine as an object with very relevant transnational properties that go along with the country's intermingled society, culture, and practices.

This, however, does not lead to a general hypothesis of contemporary Ukraine evolving into an all-liquid, all-relational, or all-transcending entity. There is no such general proposition. Instead, the transnational properties of Ukrainian society and politics have to be seen within the specific context of post-soviet transformation. Ukraine, with regard to both its territory and its population, is strongly embedded in a post-imperial setting in the aftermath of the Russian Empire and the Soviet Union. The properties of multi-ethnic empires are quite specific: they are marked by a mix of ethnic populations, by a confrontation of cross-national public affairs in relation to national or regional identities, and by asymmetric relations of different sub-entities to the imperial center (Leonhard & Hirschhausen 2010). With a perspective on Ukraine as part of the post-soviet world, this translates into a few specific expectations with regard to Ukrainian transnationalism (again, see table 1):

- A long-lasting history of permeable borders between the sub-regions of the Russian empire and/or the Soviet Union makes linear processes of migration less probable than transmigratory processes. Migration is—again, because of the long-lasting legacy of ethnic and national mixture—likely to include persons from all strata of society. Migration is not restricted to labor and/or poverty migration but includes other motives, such as education or private bonds. Conflicts over the autonomy and independence of its national republics not only marked the end of the Soviet Union but were present during its entire history (Carrère d'Encausse 1978). Since the breakup, a socio-structural expectation is that the tendencies of (re-)nationalization will break their ground, at least in the initial phase. Newly patriotic or nationalist movements and politics are, in that sense, a typical post-imperial phenomenon.

- Therefore, the importance of symbols representing "new" nationalisms is likely to increase rapidly during and after regime transformations and the decomposition of multi-national states. Nationalism is needed in its function to clarify cultural and political identities. However, the fact that national symbols increase in relevance does not determine their interpretation. Nation-related symbols can become very strong in their demarcating function (for example, with regard to the Ukrainian flag during Euromaidan), but they do not have to (examples would be the shared pride in Soviet sports or the Soviet space program).

- In light of transmigration (instead of linear migration) and of multi-vectoral symbols (instead of a clear symbolism of demarcation), the practices of transnationalism in post-soviet Ukraine should be expected to be fuzzy, volatile, and liquid. Border zones, whether with Russia or neighboring EU member states, are likely to be liminal rather than offer clear-cut "Ukrainian" or "non-Ukrainian" social action. Transmigration is likely to lead to diasporas (with a transnational identity) rather than to minorities (with a national identity).

As our discussion in section 2 has shown, all these expectations go along with central findings of transnationalism research (again, see Vertovec 2007; Pries 2008; Schiffauer 2011). They add up to a central argument of the given book—contemporary Ukraine is not only better understood by including a transnational focus, it also presents a most interesting case to understand fragmented and multi-vectoral processes in a world of (post-soviet) transformations.

4. Structure of the Book

The proposed analytical framework of transnationalism as a group of socio-structural, symbolic and practice-related phenomena in its spatial, societal and temporal manifestations will be illustrated and implemented in the following chapters. The specific compilation of the following chapters in this volume emphasizes two analytical aspirations: First, by selecting a broad range of empirical issues and aspects of Ukraine's cross-border interrelations, we seek to underline our presumption that state building and the formation of society in Ukraine are characterized by transnational processes. Again, our presumption does not fall in line with the claim of recent Russian political propaganda, which declares that "Ukraine is not even a state".[iii] Quite the contrary, we argue that Ukraine's stateness and society can be seen as an emergent product of border-transgressing entanglements and interdependencies in history and the present. Second, the empirical studies of this volume exemplify how transnationalism as an analytical concept and tool can be spelled out and deployed in order to reveal the making of structures, symbols and practices of societies beyond methodological nationalism.

Directly following this introduction, the contribution by ANDRÉ HÄRTEL titled *The "Novorossiya"-Project and National Affiliations in Ukraine's Southeast: A Failed Attempt at Transnational Community Reconstruction?* gives background information on the most important aspects of spatial, societal and temporal transnationalism in Ukraine. Härtel focuses on the role of conflicts and crises in the emergence of new symbols, boundaries and collective self-conceptions, especially in the wake of the events of Euromaidan in 2013/2014. The author sketches Novorossiya as a counterframe (see Benford & Snow 2000) to Ukrainian national identity that sets free latent disloyalties. At the same time, however, the Russian attack on Crimea and Eastern Ukraine gave birth to Ukraine as a civil nation, including identity narratives based on political inclusion. These findings shed light on Ukrainian society as being made up of identical transnational interlinkages and diverse, if not fluid, loyalties.

Part 2: Symbolic Transnationalism
The second part of the volume presents our symbolic transnationalism approach by focusing on the narrative and symbolic construction of the nation and national myths.

The first article of this section sheds light on the famous ideational concept of "Novorossiya". MIKHAIL MINAKOV discusses the re-framing of national myths and belongings in a manuscript titled *Novorossiya and the Transnationalism of Unrecognized Post-Soviet Nations*. Focusing on the evolution of the concept of Novorossiya, Minakov analytically disentangles its myth from the political installation of the so-called people's republics of Donetsk and Luhansk. The text deploys a content and intention analysis of debates within web-based pro-separatist communities with regard to the motives for supporting the separatist forces. The author argues that the myth of Novorossiya is accepted and supported by local people because of its utopian strength, which makes possible demands for social and political change. In the analysis, Minakov finds evidence that the Novorossiyan myth is shared and supported by two russophone groups: "transnationalists" and "imperialists". The first group imagines Novorossiya as a socio-political utopian alternative to the existing political order, while the imperialists hope for a re-establishment of Soviet rule and glory.

A second contribution that addresses symbolic transnationalist practices is YULIYA YURCHUK's essay on the realignments of Ukrainian national remembrance and symbols to strengthen a new transnationally oriented collective identity. In her text *Global Symbols and Local Meanings: "Day of Victory" after Euromaidan*, Yurchuk explains the shift within Ukrainian official remembrance politics of World War II and the discursive conjunction with the recent political communication regarding Ukraine's state sovereignty prospects and the war in the east. The reformulation of symbols and meanings as well as the introduction of new holidays dedicated to more-genuine Ukrainian historical interpretations indicate an intrinsic reframing of national and regional history, emphasizing Ukraine's autonomy within the post-soviet space.

Taken together, these two contributions underline our argument that the importance of symbols and meanings for the formation of new identities increases in times of transformation and crisis. However, the very manner of how actor groups tackle, promote or counter these symbols in their everyday life and how multi-vectoral symbol systems are translated into practices remains in question. Therefore, the third part will shed light on practice-oriented approaches of transnationalism.

Part 3: Practice-related Transnationalism
In the third part of the book, two essays provide insights into transnational diaspora dynamics and the making of the Ukrainian diaspora with respect to different identity narratives and protest mobilization.

ALEXANDER CLARKSON describes the evolution of distinctive predominant identity narratives within Ukrainian diasporas in Western Europe and Northern America. In his contribution, *Coming to Terms With Odessa Ukraine: The Impact of the Maidan Uprising on the Ukrainian Diaspora*, he presents an overview of the different diasporic waves since the early 20th century and their specific manifestations of national identities. The analysis highlights how the identity construction of diasporas is heavily linked to transnational social interaction. The example of the Canadian Ukrainian Diaspora demonstrates the difficulties and potential cleavages diasporas face when they are insulated from cultural shifts in their country of origin: The entanglement of identity, (West-)Ukrainian language and culture made it difficult for the diaspora to accept the more recent russophone foundation of modern Ukrainian identity. However, the active support of the Euromaidan protests accelerated a cultural and political process of realignments within the global Ukrainian diaspora—showing that transnational interaction is most relevant for reframing processes.

The contribution of ANDRIY KORNIYCHUK, MAGDALENA PATALONG and RICHARD STEINBERG displays how Ukrainian diaspora structures changed during Euromaidan. Based on a large empirical study, their manuscript, titled *The influence of protest movements on the development of diasporic engagement: the case of Euromaidan and its impact for the Ukrainian diaspora in Poland and Germany*, shows that Ukrainian communities outside Ukraine were unified and largely homogenized during their active support for the protest events in the 'homeland'. Following a broad and open understanding of relations and networks, the authors present both digital and non-digital media as social hubs that helped establish a transnational diasporic civil society. In this perspective, digital and social platforms contributing to diaspora structuration can be regarded as locations and facilitators of externalization processes of social conflicts and protest movements, as Della Porta and Tarrow (2004) have shown in another context.

Both studies present empirical evidence for our main argument on practice-related transnationalism: the liminal and permeable character of boundaries (rather than borders) is mirrored in the evolution of diaspora groups with multiple transnational roots and influences. This points to the fourth part of our book, which addresses some of those networks and agency patterns that deploy symbols to establish new groups and forms of cooperation across borders.

Part 4: Socio-structural Transnationalism
The fourth part of the volume focuses on networks and transnational agency in the economy, in local patronage systems based on ethnicity, in the media and in the formation of conflict groups in Eastern Ukraine.

HEIKO PLEINES presents a detailed analysis of the transnational embeddedness of oligarchic business empires. In his text on *The international links of Ukrainian oligarchs. Business expansion and transnational offshore networks*, he displays the entanglements of Ukrainian Big Business with offshore networks and international economic structures. The transnational ties of Ukrainian oligarchs are not as established and diverse as one would expect, but they follow a specific rational, goal-oriented pattern that corresponds to the peculiarities of the Ukrainian macro-economic situation. In fact, the transnational engagement of Ukrainian oligarchs' business is not targeted at making money in international affairs. Rather, it aims to secure competitive advantages and improve rent seeking in the domestic market. Thus, the internationalization strategy of Ukraine's Big Business stands for re-domestication and adaptation to local rules.

Patterns of transnational action targeted at local advantages and adaptions are also the subject of SUSANNE SPAHN's analysis of Ukraine-related Russian media campaigns in Germany. Her contribution on *Ukraine in the Russian Mass Media: Germany as an example of Russian information policy* reveals the multitude of Russian media outlets in Russia and Germany, including prominent individual persons in certain positions of trust within the German public. The analysis unfolds relevant actors in this transnationally orchestrated media landscape and their contribution to the creation of a biased image of Ukraine.

The essay written by SIMON SCHLEGEL differs from the other contributions in that it addresses the boundaries of ethnic minorities rather than the transgression of national borders. His text, titled *Ukrainian Nation Building and Ethnic Minority Associations: The Case of Southern Bessarabia*, discusses transnationalism in the sense of a multi-ethnic composition of the society. The study focuses on the Ukrainian region of Southern Bessarabia, a region of extraordinary ethnic diversity. Here, clientelism based on ethnic affiliations, loyalties and stories of identity that refer to the heartland can be observed as a proactive strategy of mobilizing political support. Thereby, national identities are being created and promoted in a setting that allows for multi-ethnicity.

The link among identity creation, the promotion of new affiliations, and political mobilization through purposive action is also analyzed in the empirical study presented by JONAS EICHHORN, MASCHA BRAMMER and VERONIKA BORYSENKO. Based on the theories on Transnational Advocacy Networks (Keck & Sikkink 1999), the authors focus on mobilization processes that preceded the establishment of the Donetsk and Luhansk People's Republics. Supported by a network analysis, the text discloses organizations, debates, ideological alignments and trainings that happened in Eastern Europe long before the conflict in Eastern Ukraine began. The analysis provides evidence that the idea of and the political mobilization for Novorossiya had a long and explicitly transnational forerun.

Conclusion

Is transnationalism in its symbolic, practice-related and socio-structural perspectives a seminal analytical concept? Does it contribute new approaches and offer new insights into complex processes of nation building and societal evolution in the post-soviet space in general and in Ukraine in particular? Is Ukraine—although probably unintentionally—a role model for transnational state formation? At the least, transnationalism is an empirical phenomenon that has shaped the dynamics of the post-soviet societies after 1989/91, when it became much easier for citizens to cross borders than ever before.

In their *conclusion*, SUSANN WORSCHECH and TIMM BEICHELT try to sum up the empirical findings of how transnationalism occurs as a real-world phenomenon in Ukraine. We also intend to refine our above-discussed concept and look for findings which might hold beyond the Ukrainian case. The example of Ukraine may provide hints regarding the benefits, dangers or unintended effects of the transnationalization of societies, and it will hopefully encourage further studies to apply the concept of transnationalism.

5. Bibliography

Amelina, Anna; Devrimsel D. Nergiz; Thomas Faist and Nina Glick Schiller. 2012. *Beyond methodological nationalism. Social science research methods in transition.* London: Routledge (Routledge research in transnationalism).

Anderson, Benedict. 1983. *Imagined Communities. Reflections on the Origin and Spread of Nationalism.* London: Verso.

Apter, David E. 2006. "Duchamp's Urinal: Who Says What's Rational When Things Get Tough?" In *The Oxford Handbook of Contextual Political Analysis*, edited by Robert E. Goodin and Charles Tilly, 767–796. Oxford: Oxford University Press.

Beck, Ulrich and Edgar Grande. 2004. *Das kosmopolitische Europa.* Frankfurt am Main: Suhrkamp Verlag.

Benford, Robert D. and David A. Snow. 1988. "Ideology, frame resonance, and participant mobilization." *International Social Movement Research* 1: 197–217.

Benford, Robert D. and David A. Snow. 2000. "Framing Processes and Social Movements: An Overview and Assessment." *Annual Review of Sociology* 26 (1): 611–39.

Berger, Peter and Thomas Luckmann. 1966. *Die gesellschaftliche Konstruktion der Wirklichkeit. Eine Theorie der Wissenssoziologie.* Frankfurt am Main: Suhrkamp Verlag.

Bernhard, Stefan and Christian Schmidt-Wellenburg. 2014. "Editorial." *Berliner Journal für Soziologie* 24: 137–140.

Bossong, Raphael and Helena Carrapico. 2016. *EU borders and shifting internal security. Technology, externalization and accountability.* Cham: Springer.

Bossong, Raphael; Dominik Gerst; Imke Kerber; Maria Klessmann; Hannes Krämer and Peter Ulrich. 2016. *Complex Borders: Analytical Problems and Heuristics.* Frankfurt (Oder): Manuscript under review.

Brettell, Caroline. 2003. *Anthropology and migration. Essays on transnationalism, ethnicity, and identity.* Lanham: AltaMira Press.

Bröchler, Stephan and Timo Grunden. 2014. *Informelle Politik. Konzepte, Akteure und Prozesse.* Wiesbaden: Springer VS.

Brubaker, Rogers. 1997. *Nationalism reframed. Nationhood and the National Question in the New Europe.* Cambridge: Cambridge University Press.

Brubaker, Rogers. 2005. "The 'diaspora' diaspora." *Ethnic and Racial Studies* 28: 1–19.

Brudny, Yitzhak M. and Evgeny Finkel. 2011. "Why Ukraine Is Not Russia. Hegemonic National Identity and Democracy in Russia and Ukraine." *East European Politics & Societies* 25 (4): 813–833.

Carrère d'Encausse, Hélène. 1978. *L'empire eclaté. La révolte des nations en URSS.* Paris: Flammarion.

Castells, Manuel. 2000. *The rise of the network society.* Oxford, Malden, Mass.: Blackwell Publishers (Information age, v. 1).

Chindea, Alin; Magdalena Majkowska-Tomkin; Heikki Mattila and Isabel Pastor. 2008. *Migration in Ukraine. A Country Profile 2008.* Geneva: International Organization for Migration.

Christensen, Robert K.; Edward R. Rakhimkulov; Charles R. Wise. 2005. "The Ukrainian Orange Revolution brought more than a new president. What kind of democracy will the institutional changes bring?" *Communist and Postcommunist Studies* 38: 207–230.

Della Porta, Donatella and Sidney Tarrow. 2004. *Transnational Protest and Global Activism.* Lanham, Md.: Rowman & Littlefield.

DiMaggio, Paul J. and Walter W. Powell. 1991. *The New Institutionalism in Organizational Analysis.* Chicago: University of Chicago Press.

Esser, Hartmut. 2001. *Soziologie. Spezielle Grundlagen. Band 6: Sinn und Kultur.* Frankfurt am Main: Campus-Verlag.

Fuhse, Jan A. and Sophie Mützel. 2010. *Relationale Soziologie. Zur kulturellen Wende der Netzwerkforschung.* Wiesbaden: VS Verlag für Sozialwissenschaften (Netzwerkforschung, 2).

Fuhse, Jan A. 2016. *Soziale Netzwerke. Konzepte und Forschungsmethoden.* Konstanz: UTB; UVK.

Goffman, Erving. 1980. *Rahmen-Analyse: Ein Versuch über die Organisation von Alltagserfahrungen.* Frankfurt am Main: Suhrkamp Verlag.

Habermas, Jürgen. 1998. *Die postnationale Konstellation. Politische Essays.* Frankfurt am Main: Suhrkamp Verlag.

Halling, Steffen. 2013. "Integrationsmotor Fußball? Russland, die Ukraine und die 'Vereinigte Liga'." *Osteuropa* 63 (9): 79–98.

Janczak, Jaroslaw. 2015. "Phantom borders and electoral behaviour in Poland. Historical legacies, political culture and their influence on contemporary politics." *Erdkunde* 69 (2): 125–138.

Janos, Andrew C. 2000. *East Central Europe in the Modern World. The Politics of the Borderland from Pre- to Postcommunism.* Stanford: Stanford University Press.

Jilge, Wilfried. 1998. "Staatssymbolik und nationale Identität in der postkommunistischen Ukraine." *Ethnos-Nation* 6: 85–113.

Jilge, Wilfried. 2014. "Geschichtspolitik auf dem Majdan. Politische Emanzipation und nationale Selbstvergewisserung." *Osteuropa* 64 (5-6): 239–258.

Karatnycky, Adrian. 2005. "Ukraine's Orange Revolution." *Foreign Affairs* 84 (2): 35–52.

Kaya, Ayhan. 2012. *Islam, Migration and Integration: The Age of Securitization.* Basingstoke: Palgrave Macmillan.

Keck, Margaret E. and Kathryn Sikkink. 1999. "Transnational advocacy networks in international and regional politics." *International Social Science Journal* 51(159): 89–101.

Keohane, Robert O. and Joseph S.Nye. 1977. *Power and Independence.* New York: Longman.

Kovacs, Janos Matyas. 1999. "Turbulenzen im Vakuum. Anmerkungen zur kulturellen Globalisierung in Osteuropa." *Transit 1* 17: 33–45.

Kulyk, Volodymyr. 2010. "Gespaltene Zungen. Sprache und Sprachenpolitik in der Ukraine." *Osteuropa* 60 (2-4): 391–402.

Kurth, Helmut and Iris Kempe. 2004. *Presidential Election in Ukraine. Implications for the Ukrainian Transition.* Kiew: Friedrich-Ebert-Stiftung.

Kuzio, Taras. 1998. *Ukraine. State and nation building.* London: Routledge.

Leonhard, Jörn and Ulrike von Hirschhausen. 2010. *Empires und Nationalstaaten im 19. Jahrhundert.* Göttingen: Vandenhoeck & Ruprecht.

Löwis, Sabine von. 2015. "Phantom borders in the political geography of East Central Europe: an introduction." *Erdkunde* 69 (2): 99–106.

Marjanen, Hayo. 2009. "Undermining Methodological Nationalism. Histoire Croisée of Concepts as Transnational History." In *Transnational political spaces. Agents, structures, encounters*, edited by Mathias Albert, Gesa Bluhm, Jan Helmig, Andreas Leutzsch and Jochen Walter, 239–263. Frankfurt, New York: Campus (History of political communication).

Mayntz, Renate. 1998. "Informalisierung politischer Entscheidungsprozesse." In *Informale Verfassung*, edited by Axel Görlitz and Peter Burth, 55–65. Baden-Baden: Nomos.

McAdam, Doug; John D. McCarthy and Mayer N. Zald. 1996. *Comparative perspectives on social movements. Political opportunities, mobilizing structures, and cultural framings*. Cambridge [England], New York: Cambridge University Press.

McFaul, Michael. 2007. "Ukraine Imports Democracy. External Influences on the Orange Revolution." *International Security* 32 (2): 45–83.

Mohr, John W. and Harrison C. White. 2008. "How to Model an Institution." *Theory and Society* 37: 485–512.

Motyl, Alexander. 1993. *Dilemmas of Independence: Ukraine after Totalitarianism*. New York: Council on Foreign Relations.

Østergaard-Nielsen, Eva. 2003. *Routledge research in transnationalism. Transnational politics/ Turks and Kurds in Germany*. London: Routledge.

Polletta, Francesca and M. Kai Ho. 2006. "Frames and Their Consequences." In *The Oxford Handbook of Contextual Political Analysis*, edited by Robert E. Goodin and Charles Tilly, 187–209. Oxford: Oxford University Press.

Pries, Ludger. 2008. *Die Transnationalisierung der sozialen Welt. Sozialräume jenseits von Nationalgesellschaften*. Frankfurt am Main: Suhrkamp Verlag.

Pries, Ludger. 2010. *Transnationalisierung. Theorie und Empirie grenzüberschreitender Vergesellschaftung*. Wiesbaden: VS-Verlag.

Rosenau, James N. and Ernst-Otto Czempiel. 1992. *Governance without Government: Order and Change in World Politics*. Cambridge: Cambridge University Press.

Schiffauer, Werner. 2002. *Die Gottesmänner. Türkische Islamisten in Deutschland.* Frankfurt am Main: Suhrkamp Verlag.

Schiffauer, Werner. 2011. *B/Orders in Motion.* Frankfurt (Oder): Unpublished manuscript.

Schiffauer, Werner; Riva Kastoryano and Steven Vertovec. 2005. *Civil enculturation. Nation-state, school and ethnic difference in the Netherlands, Britain, Germany and France.* Oxford: Berghahn Books.

Scholte, Jan Aart. 2000. *Globalization. A critical introduction.* Basingstoke: Palgrave Macmillan.

Stegniy, Oleksandr. 2012. "Ukraine and the Eastern Partnership. 'Lost in Translation'?" In *Eastern Partnership: A New Opportunity for the Neighbors*, edited by Elena Korosteleva, 52–74. New York: Routledge.

Vertovec, Steven. 2009. *Transnationalism.* London, New York: Routledge.

Vertovec, Steven and Robin Cohen. 2002. *Conceiving cosmopolitanism. Theory, context and practice.* New York: Oxford University Press.

Wellman, Barry and Stephen D. Berkowitz. 1988. *Social structures. A network approach.* Cambridge, New York: Cambridge University Press.

White, Harrison C. 2008. *Identity and control. How social formations emerge.* Princeton, NJ: Princeton University Press.

Wilson, Andrew. 2006. "Ukraine's Orange Revolution, NGOs and the Role of the West." *International Affairs* 19 (1): 21–32.

Wolchik, Sharon L. and Volodymyr Zviglyanich. 2000. *Ukraine. The Search for a National Identity.* Lanham: Rowman & Littlefield.

Zürn, Michael. 1998. *Regieren jenseits des Nationalstaates.* Frankfurt am Main: Suhrkamp Verlag.

---

i   Both authors of this text have heavily profited from the support of several German "Stiftungen" (foundations). These are 100% financed by the German state, which has an explicit agenda of supporting the democratization and market reforms in Ukraine. The conference at which the papers of this volume were gathered was indirectly financed by the German Auswärtiges Amt.

ii See [https://www.borders-in-motion.de/en/center-en], visited 23 June 2016.

iii This statement is attributed to Vladimir Putin, who said it to George W. Bush at the NATO Bucharest Summit, April 4, 2008. See, for example, [http://content.time.com/time/world/article/0,8599,1900838,00.html].

The "Novorossiya" Project and National Affiliations in Ukraine's Southeast: A Failed Attempt at Transnational Community Reconstruction?[i]

André Härtel

In early 2014, despite having declared its independence almost a quarter-century earlier, Ukraine's existence hung by a thread. Russia had annexed the Crimean Peninsula in the aftermath of the "Revolution of Dignity" in Kyiv and was about to initiate the "Russian Spring" and a hybrid war in eastern Ukraine. At this decisive moment, the buzzwords "Novorossiya" and Moscow's "reconquering" of southeastern Ukraine (or at least its separation from Kyiv) gained popularity with pro-Russian separatists, nationalists who favored a "Greater Russia" and elements of the Kremlin. Their hopes were nourished by the widespread belief in Russia that a large majority of those living in south-eastern Ukraine were ethnic Russians and that their belonging to present-day Ukraine was merely a historical accident. Ultimately, the failure of Novorossiya, as both an idea and as a transnational community of south-eastern Ukrainians and "mainland" Russians, can be attributed mainly to developments within Ukraine that have involved a renegotiation—since 1991—not of ethno-national self-ascriptions but of national and political loyalties.

1. Introduction

The Minsk Agreement of February 2015 ("Minsk 2") marked the start of a tenuous ceasefire in the territorial conflict over parts of the Donbass region. Nonetheless, fundamental questions concerning the status of the occupied territories remained and remain unanswered. In this respect, the prevailing public and academic debate concerning the background of the conflict (referred to as a civil war, "imported separatism", and as an interstate dispute) (Wilson 2014; Mitrokhyn 2015a; Buzgalin 2015) conceals another central question: why did the "Russian Spring" (*russkaya vesna*), in other words the "reconquering" of the entirety of south-eastern Ukraine (which had been the declared objective of pro-Russian separatists along with cohorts of Russian volunteers and also some leaders within the Russian Federation) end precisely on the contact line that we see today? Why were the other campaigns of terror and destabilization carried out by pro-Russian forces unsuccessful in Odessa and Kharkiv and also in Dnipropetrovsk, Mariupol, Zaporizhia, Kherson and Mykolaiv, as well as in large parts of the Donbass?

In seeking answers to these questions, we inevitably confront the far more significant issue of how, just twenty-five years after independence, the Ukrainian nation and national consciousness or affiliations within Ukraine have developed. Especially outside of Ukraine, there has long been a rather uncritical agreement on this question. While an alleged ethno-cultural divide in Ukraine along the Dnieper has, to date, enjoyed paradigmatic importance in Western and especially German discourses (Schneider 2007; Hildebrandt 2015), and has partly guided actions and policies, the question of Ukraine is much clearer to the Russian elite. As early as 2008, during a meeting with former American President George W. Bush, Vladimir Putin claimed that "Ukraine is not even a state" (Moscow Times 2008). After the conflict with Ukraine began in early 2014, Putin became even more unequivocal. Approximately one third of Ukraine's population is deemed to be ethnically Russian by the Russian President; thus, according to Putin, Russia's strong interest in this population's fate is only natural. Furthermore, Putin insisted that the southeastern regions around the centers of Kharkiv, Luhansk, Donetsk, Kherson und Mykolaiv (for which Vladimir Putin explicitly uses the term *Novorossiya*) were only been handed over to the former Ukrainian Soviet Republic in the twentieth century, and this was by chance more than anything else ("why, God only knows").[ii] This is also the reason why, according to the Russian President's comments in January 2016, the present-day border between Ukraine and Russia has an "artificial and gratuitous character".[iii]

If one accepts this argument of strong socio-cultural (ethnic) transnational bonds between Russia and Ukraine's southeast, the division of Ukraine should not have come as a surprise back in early 2014 and throughout that summer, when a virtual power vacuum had been created due to Kyiv's Revolution of Dignity and the subsequent disintegration of the Donetsk elite in the country's south-east. In reality, this did not come about. Moreover, the supporters of Novorossiya had to be content with a much smaller territory that was not uniformly governed and that revolved around the self-proclaimed Donetsk and Luhansk "People's Republics" ("DNR" and "LNR"). This situation points either to a serious mistake in how Vladimir Putin and others understood national allegiances and transnational ties in the Post-Soviet region, or to a significant change in the identity of the inhabitants of Ukraine's south-eastern regions[iv]. How strong is the loyalty to the Ukrainian state twenty-five years after independence or, asked differently, how strong are alternative loyalties, such as transnational social affiliations and identities? Is there any significant relationship between ethno-national types of self-identification in Ukraine's southeast and the commitment to statehood? And finally, what influence did the turning points of the Revolution of Dignity, the annexation of Crimea, and the war in Donbass, have on the political attitudes of the people living there, on their imaginations of territorial belonging?

2. The "Unexpected Nation"

Ukraine's emergence as an independent state in 1991 was mainly a consequence of the dissolution of the Soviet Union (USSR), driven by republican elites who succeeded in asserting their individual republic's borders. Similar to the situations in other emergent republics, the republican communist elite was also the main force behind independence in the Ukrainian Soviet Socialist Republic (UkSSR). As for truly nationally conscious actors, the Ukrainian "Rukh" movement also established a political power base, yet it only had significant numbers of supporters in western and central Ukraine. The Communist Party of Ukraine, whose members had transformed themselves into national communists led by Leonid Kravchuk, later the first President of independent Ukraine, pulled the strings in the state's foundation, which was for them an instrument that allowed them to remain in power and take control of economic assets (Wittkowsky 1998).

However, among elite circles within Ukraine's eastern neighbor, and among many western observers, the foundation of an independent Ukrainian state within the borders of the former Soviet republic took some getting used to. Because there were allegedly significant ethnic, linguistic and religious differences in Ukraine, some observers liked to call the new state "artificial" and later described the Ukrainian nation as "unexpected" (Wilson 2002). Doubts were raised regarding Ukraine's ability to survive and, mainly among politically motivated critics, about the legitimacy of the new project. This was due to the large proportion of inhabitants identifying themselves as ethnic Russians (22.1% according to the 1989 census, see below) as well as to the widespread uncertainty at the time concerning the new state's constitutive elements, community spirit and the borders of the Ukrainian nation.

However, here one must consider that, after seven decades of Soviet communism, ethnic or national criteria could have only a limited identity-defining effect not only in Ukraine but throughout the Post-Soviet region. While the question of nationalities indeed served as a political instrument (cf. the "*korenisaciya*" policy (Simon 1986)), especially during the founding period of the USSR, work on the new "Soviet Man" and internationalism propagated from above had been internalized in many cases. This meant that for the majority of the population, ethnic and national affiliations receded into the background. The year 1991 was thus in many ways another foundational moment in terms of how people living in the territory of Ukraine identified themselves. From this point on—as Fredrik Barth once wrote—ethnic and also national allegiances were to be renegotiated once again between external attribution and self-identification (Barth 1998).

3. Ukrainians, Russians and People with Hybrid Identities— On the Complexity of the Nationality Question

As a fledgling independent state, Ukraine was suspected of being a divided nation. This suspicion was due to the rigid criteria that foreign countries—for different reasons—applied to the question of nationalities in Ukraine, and yet it was also due to the nature of the questions posed within Ukraine concerning ethnic or national affiliations well up to the most recent official 2001 census (see Table 1). Because a large majority of those who described themselves as "Russian" in the extremely simplified official census were also concentrated in Crimea and in the country's south-eastern region, the alleged divide also acquired a sensitive geopolitical significance.

Table 1: National affiliation in Ukraine according to the official census

NATIONAL AFFILIATION / YEAR OF CENSUS	1989	2001
Ukrainian	72.7 (as a percentage of the overall population)	77.8
Russian	22.1	17.3
Belarusian	0.9	0.6
Moldavian	0.6	0.5
Crimean Tatar	0.0	0.5

Source: State Statistics Committee of Ukraine, accessed 30 January 2016 [http://2001.ukrcensus.gov.ua/eng/results/general/nationality/].

However, critics stressed early on that the simplistic way of comparing only the numbers of self-described ethnic Ukrainians and Russians was hardly useful (Pogrebinskij 2015). First, in the absence of other criteria, this distinction was predominantly made purely on grounds of language as an "identity marker". In this respect, it is often overlooked that a sizeable majority of Ukrainians are essentially bilingual or speak mixed forms such as "Surzhyk"; the boundaries between languages are therefore not clear cut. Hence, if language is seen as a key distinguishing characteristic of the "national communities" living in Ukraine and is weighed against the obvious existence of a large group of multi-lingual people, the ethnic divide argument already loses impact (see Figures 1 and 2 as well as Table 2). Furthermore, it must be remembered that in regions such as the Donbass (the oblasts of Donetsk and Luhansk), which are characterized by a particularly high concentration of native Russian speakers and ethnic Russians (according to the 2001 census, 38.2% or 39%), there is a clear urban–rural split. In other words, the "Russian"-dominated towns and cities are often surrounded by majority "Ukrainian" rural areas (Wilson 2002). This circumstance also contradicts the generally accepted divide paradigm.

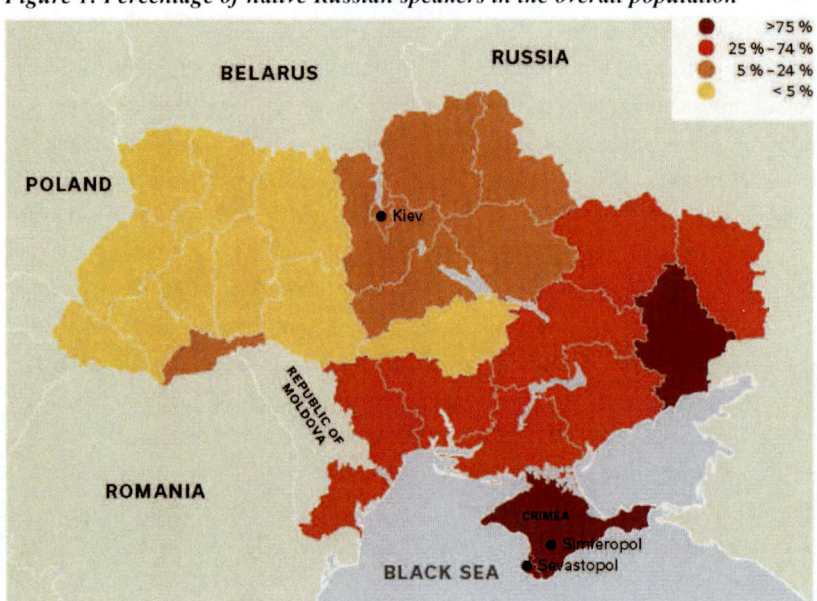

Figure 1: Percentage of native Russian speakers in the overall population

Source: Illustration: racken GmbH, Berlin, based on CNN 2014: "A Divided Ukraine", 3 March 2014, in: [http://edition.cnn.com/interactive/2014/02/world/ukraine-divided] (17 February 2016); Natural Earth, [http://naturalearthdata.com] (10 March 2016).

Table 2: A historical and comparative perspective on language use in Ukraine

LANGUAGE GROUPS	1991 to 1994	1995 to 1999	2000 to 2003
Ukrainian-speaking Ukrainians	41.2	46.3	45.4
Russian-speaking Ukrainians	32.6	28.2	30.9
Russian-speaking Russians	19.7	17	16.5
Other	6.5	8.5	7.2

Source: Khmelko (2004)

Figure 2: Languages spoken at home in Ukraine

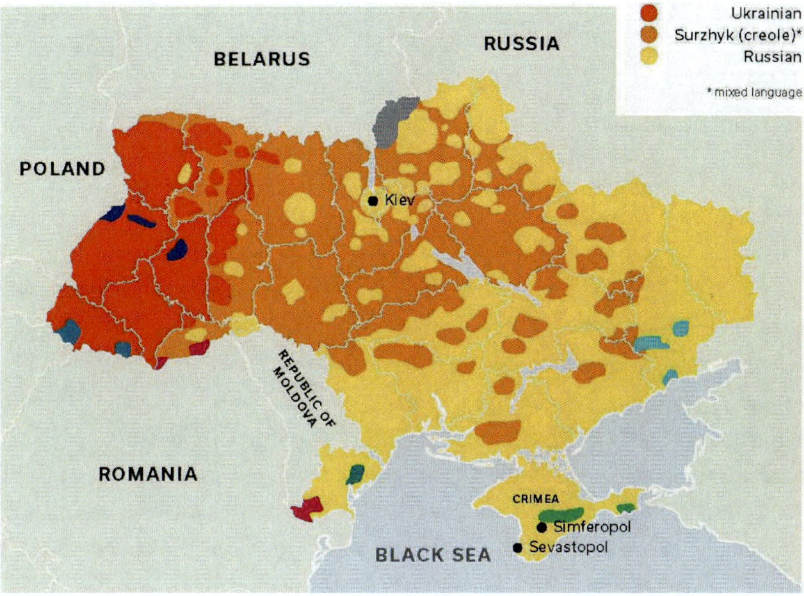

Source: Illustration: racken GmbH, Berlin, based on National Linguistic University Kiev 2009; Natural Earth, [http://naturalearthdata.com] (10 March 2016).

The territorial division of "Ukrainians" and "Russians" thus assumes more complex dimensions than language alone. Therefore, since the early 2000s it has been the custom in Ukraine to include another criterion as a supplement to these two general categories: namely, a further category of ethnic self-identification as so-called "bi-ethnors" (Khmelko 2004), or, to adopt a relevant term in this context, "people with hybrid identities". The introduction of this so-called hybrid identity, that is, the possibility of describing oneself as both "Ukrainian" and "Russian", can be traced to the observation that large groups of people with such a "hybrid identity" live in the towns and cities of south-eastern Ukraine in particular. As a result, opinion polls (see Table 3) reveal a highly differentiated picture with regard to Ukrainians' self-identification, and it is notable that the group of "pure" ethnic Russians is, consequently, almost reduced by half.

Table 3: A historical and comparative perspective on the ethnic structure of Ukraine

IDENTITY	1994 to 1999	2001 to 2003
Only Ukrainian	59.8	62.9
Russian and Ukrainian	24.4	22.5
Only Russian	11.3	10.0
Other	4.5	4.6

Source: Khmelko (2004)

Therefore, the ethno-national structure of Ukraine is shown to be much more complex than is suggested by the official census, with its simplified Ukrainian-Russian dichotomy. However, what conclusions can actually be drawn from this, especially if we recall what were referred to above as the evidently limited meanings of ethnic and national references in approximately 1991? Did the self-ascription of "ethnic Russian", for example, also imply that one was defining oneself more in terms of belonging to a transnational community of Russians than as a Ukrainian citizen? Did it imply that one belonged to a Russian diaspora living in Ukraine, or even to a phantom Soviet transnational community? These questions require, first, an assessment of what Ukraine was and wanted to be as a state and community before 2013/2014. Were there significant debates on the national question and related issues, such as the orientation of cultural and foreign policies, in the first two decades of Ukraine's independence? Were the results of the opinion polls on self-assigned group identities therefore actually reflected in the political reality of Ukraine as well as in the actions of political elites?

4. The Amorphous Ukraine: On the Importance of Ethnicity and the Nation Before the Maidan

The Ukrainian analyst Oleksandr Sushko recently described this reality in the most telling manner when he spoke of the "amorphous identity" of Ukraine before the Euromaidan and the Revolution of Dignity in 2013 and 2014.[v] He suggests that ethnic and national self-identification could have had only limited political effectiveness in a post-1991 society that was mostly preoccupied with adapting to new and, for most social groups, difficult, economic conditions. Moreover, this society was still caught up in the Soviet tradition and therefore, to a large extent, subject to the political elite. Like those with hybrid identities, groups describing themselves simply as "Ukrainian" or "Russian" were, with the exception of marginalized nationalistic fringe groups, hardly nationally aware and distinct in the years following independence; they could not have had a genuine incentive to be mobilized on the grounds of ethnic dividing lines. How was this amorphous identity affected by Ukraine's development as a polity later on? Both the political-societal dynamic and policy makers' actions become the primary sources for renegotiating identities, particularly if one leaves behind the classic primordial perspective of basically predetermined and rigid ethnic group allegiances and instead accepts a constructivist view of the concepts of ethnicity and nation.

Against this background, all Ukrainian presidents, with one notable exception, deliberately decided against the role of ethnic or national entrepreneurs and conformed to the amorphous national identity of Ukraine with regard to both their domestic and foreign policies. The major issues here were the—to some extent unavoidable—Ukrainization policy domestically as well as the country's general foreign policy toward the West and its institutions on the one hand and toward Russia on the other. Although Ukrainian became the national language in the new Constitution of 1996 and in specific legislation in 1998, the elites only implemented this central part of the Ukrainization policy in a "lax" manner (Guttke & Rank 2012). This was a consequence of the delicate politicization of the issue: Under Viktor Ianukovych, a law on regional languages was introduced, albeit controversially, in the form of the Kivalov-Kolesnichenko Law (2012). In the area of the politics of memory, President Leonid Kuchma, who was in office from 1994 to 2004, was happy to state simply that "Ukraine is not Russia" (Kuchma 2004).

Yet, like Viktor Ianukovych later (2010 to 2013), Kuchma otherwise refrained from constructing a dedicated national Ukrainian view of history. Only Viktor Iushchenko (2005 to 2010) very consciously deviated from this policy and attempted a more explicit form of nation-building using numerous initiatives related to the "politics of memory". Furthermore, with his foreign policy geared towards joining the European Union (EU) and the North Atlantic Treaty Organization (NATO), Iushchenko discontinued the "multi-vector" or "block-free" policy that Kuchma and, until 2013, Ianukovych had been pursuing. This foreign policy, in both their views, was in accordance with Ukrainian interests as well as with the people's allegedly "hybrid" attitudes concerning this question (Härtel 2012).

Hence, a type of amorphous political narrative became firmly established in Ukrainian politics—with, at its core, a notable unwillingness to make clear commitments. The approach was neither to work too deliberately towards the Ukrainization of the state nor to focus on deciding on a clear foreign policy direction. Ukraine was therefore always implicitly caught in the middle between its Ukrainian and Russian identities, and between the West and Russia geopolitically (see the frequently used "bridge metaphor" (ibid.: 304)). "Amorphous" here means, first of all, that Ukrainian elites largely avoided or postponed the expected (re-)nationalization and de-sovietization,[vi] resulting in a lack of distinctiveness and therefore a reduced potential for domestic and international conflicts. This policy also ensured—at least on the surface—relative connectivity with both the EU and Russia. The degree to which this amorphous character (and related policies) has been a consequence of transnational socio-cultural ties or even a source of them is debatable: Although the specter of separatism was present during the early phase of the new state (mostly in Crimea, much less so in the Donbass (Kuzio 2007)) and thus needed to be acted upon, once it had been overcome, the fact that the majority of elites refrained from creating progressive policies on nationality and deciding on foreign policy orientations can be largely explained by their interest in retaining the status quo. That way, they risked losing neither the carefully constructed balance between the regional power structures that ultimately characterized Ukrainian politics nor the considerable benefits of shady Russian-Ukrainian business networks, especially in the energy sector (e.g. Balmaceda 2013).

5. Revolution, Annexation, War: A Change of Narrative and Mobilization Along Ethno-National Lines

The restraint shown by political actors therefore partially explains the relative stability of ethno-national attitudes in Ukraine's first two decades after independence. The less effort the political actors invested in the construction and consolidation of a national identity or identities, the lower their potential for change, mobilization and therefore also for danger. However, the pivotal question now was what would happen if the existing balance—made up of amorphous identity and narrative—were to be challenged or completely upset by specific internal and external developments.

The loyalty issue had already emerged briefly in Ukraine in the wake of the "Orange Revolution" in late autumn 2004 (cf. the Separatist Congress in Severodonetsk). Yet, at that time any concerns about separatism had largely been removed from the agenda by an elite consensus that essentially put an end to the "revolution"

(Wilson 2006) and to related concerns about Moscow's eventual response. The situation that arose in late autumn 2013 and winter 2014 was, however, a novelty. Viktor Ianukovych had only realized too late that the Association Agreement negotiated over a long period of time with the EU was, certainly from the point of view of his own people, yet also in the Kremlin's eyes, forcing him, as the first leader of independent Ukraine, to clearly decide on a foreign policy direction. This made a retreat to the amorphous narrative—dominating until then—impossible. In choosing to appease Moscow by not signing the agreement, Ianukovych triggered a protest movement, the Euromaidan, which slipped out of his control and, in January 2014, morphed into a genuine revolution. The Revolution of Dignity resulting from the Euromaidan was then crucial in terms of policies relating to nationality. This was because the revolution—in contrast to 2014—brought about the implosion of the elite network of the Party of Regions, which had almost wholly monopolized power in south-eastern Ukraine since the early 2000s, thus creating a power vacuum that the Russian government used to intervene both in Crimea and later also in the Donbass.

In relation to the question of nationalities and to the so-far unknown mobilization of people along ethno-national dividing lines in Ukraine, an entirely unprecedented situation had emerged: First, the Euromaidan had been transformed into an ultimately victorious revolutionary movement. Partially due to Russia's role before and after the summit, the revolution strongly resembled a national Ukrainian liberation movement. As a result, along with radicals, large sections of what had, until then, been moderate national camps were mobilized. During this process, and in particular from April 2014 onward, a clearly reciprocal effect was recognizable—a type of mutual mobilization and growing national awareness. Second, the new rulers in Kyiv—partly due to pressure from protesters on the street—quickly abolished the amorphous narrative and now openly committed themselves to a foreign policy course aimed at full integration with the West and to a national Ukrainian narrative that had been badly prepared and was not well thought through.[vii] Third, the Russian Spring, or Russia's policy of intervention and annexation in Crimea and later in the Donbass, which was based on a hybrid type of warfare, had created an option that until that point had almost been unthinkable: the reconquering of south-eastern Ukraine by the Russian Federation, or at least the secession of those territories supported by the Russian government—the so-called *Novorossiya* Scenario.

6. Why *Novorossiya* Failed: The Emergence of a Civil Nation in Ukraine

In early 2014, an event occurred that even people in Russia had not seriously expected: after an illegal referendum, which took place during a de facto occupation, the Crimean Peninsula was officially annexed or, in the language of the Russian President, "incorporated" into the Federation.[viii] Vladimir Putin's decision to integrate a part of the former empire into the Russian Federation for the first time since the break-up of the Soviet Union must, even in light of Moscow's long-standing support of pro-Russian de facto states, be considered a geo-political earthquake of the first order. This earthquake set in motion important revisionist forces in Russia and also had a profound impact on neighboring states.

Although today we still do not know whether Vladimir Putin's personal strategy was actually geared towards the reconquering of what he and a majority of Russian nationalists described as Novorossiya (Gazeta.ru 2014a) (see Figure 3), there is good reason to believe that, had it proceeded successfully, he would not have interfered with such a scenario. Putin's remarks, mentioned at the beginning of this chapter, make it clear that he openly questions the existence of Ukrainian statehood where, in his opinion, a majority of "Russian citizens" is living. Furthermore, the official Kremlin narrative, which contests any direct or official participation by the Russian military as well as any support for the "DNR"/"LNR" separatists,[ix] is to be understood merely as a tactic.[x] This is how it was—and is—possible for pro-Russian forces and forces "imported" from Russia to use hybrid warfare methods, such as targeted experimental moves and month-long massive destabilization campaigns, in the centers of the south-east, particularly in Kharkiv and Odessa but also in Zaporizhia and Mariupol (Korrespondent 2016), without losing face should there be a negative outcome (Gazeta.ru 2014a). There are also numerous indications that these "experimental moves" were centrally controlled and financed by Moscow (Gazeta.ru 2014b). Therefore, Vladimir Putin, based on the notion of a strong socio-cultural (ethnic) transnational bond between Russia and Ukraine's south-east (both in his view being parts of an indivisible Russian world), instrumentalized the hitherto largely historic concept of Novorossiya to not only de-legitimize Ukrainian sovereignty but also to challenge the country's territorial integrity. By turning Novorossiya into a new symbol of belonging, Putin engaged in and encouraged practices going far beyond the reconstruction of an alleged transnational community of south-eastern Ukrainians and mainland Russians. His aim was the re-configuration not only of imagined borders but also of ultimately genuine ones. However, one thing was certain: only a corresponding reaction from the people living in those regions—a materialization of alleged socio-cultural ties—would have facilitated the referendum and subsequent secession policy later successfully implemented in Donetsk and Luhansk.

Figure 3: The claimed territory of Novorossiya

Source: Illustration: racken GmbH, Berlin, based on edmaps.com, Historical Maps of Novorossiya, Federal Republic of Novorossiya (source list), [http://edmaps.com/html/novorossiya.html] (16 June 2016); Natural Earth, [http://naturalearthdata.com] (10 March 2016).

In this situation, the people in the towns and cities of south-eastern Ukraine were assigned a key role, all the more so because large sections of the existing elite had, as mentioned above, discredited themselves, and a power vacuum had emerged in many places. Although the situation varied from one town or city to the next, there was one common thread. Pro-Russian activists failed in their attempts at destabilization wherever it was possible to mobilize broad groups of pro-Ukrainians and wherever the latter were supported by remaining local political elites and businessmen. In particular, the pro-Russian side underestimated the potential of mobilizing the pro-Ukrainian peoples of south-eastern Ukrainian towns and cities, and even pro-Ukrainian observers and analysts were surprised by the magnitude of the phenomenon.[xi]

What were the underlying causes of this reaction? Did pro-Russian and Russian forces at the time overestimate the mobilizing potential of the Russian diaspora? How did south-eastern Ukrainians evaluate the offer of "brotherly" support by Russia and what perspective did they develop towards an eventual territorial solution to their alleged "betrayal" by the "junta coup" in Kyiv? Although opinion polls conducted in these regions—with a majority of Russian-speaking inhabitants and a high percentage of ethnic Russians—had always revealed little sympathy for separatist projects or for annexation by Russia, it is important to note that for the first time the option of a change in the territorial status quo now appeared within the realm of possibility. When investigating the underlying causes of the ultimate failure of the Novorossiya Project, a particularly revealing picture is therefore provided by opinion polls (see Tables 4, 5, and 6) from April 2014, when the window of opportunity for such a development was wide open. The following conclusions can be drawn from these opinion polls:

1. First, it is interesting that a majority of the inhabitants of the regions in question expressly denied the Russian state the right—claimed by Vladimir Putin (see above)—to represent their interests (see Table 4). Here, we refer to absolute majorities of over 70%, in particular outside the Donbass (Mykolaiv). If we start by assuming that, with his statement about "rights", Vladimir Putin aimed at the groups of ethnic Russians clearly over-represented in these regions and at those with hybrid identities, even the relatively high values in Kharkiv and Odessa are revealed in their true light. However, in Donetsk and Luhansk the trend is reversed although—even here—there are no absolute majorities supporting an intervention to protect "Russian citizens". This statistic is not only the first indication that, excluding the presently occupied areas, the people living in the south-east did not question the territorial status quo despite an often ambivalent attitude toward the revolution in Kyiv and general uncertainty, it makes it nearly impossible to suggest a connection between their ethno-national identification and their attitude toward Ukrainian statehood. Both aspects become clearer in light of the next two sets of statistics.

Table 4: Do you agree that Russia is justifiably protecting the interests of Russian-speaking citizens in south-eastern Ukraine? (April 2014)

REGION OR OBLAST	Yes	No	Difficult to say	I would prefer not to answer
South-east as a whole	32.6	49.9	16.1	1.4
Dnipropetrovsk	21.0	65.6	12.1	1.2
Donetsk	47.0	33.4	19.6	0.0
Zaporizhia	19.5	53.3	23	4.2
Luhansk	44.2	31.8	19.6	4.5
Mykolaiv	14.6	71.5	13.4	0.5
Odessa	30.6	52.3	15.8	1.2
Kharkiv	36.6	53.0	10.1	0.2
Kherson	23.5	61.1	14.9	0.5

Source: Kyiv International Institute of Sociology (2014a)

2. Even in this situation of multiple possibilities, the inhabitants of the south-eastern oblasts—in particular Kharkiv, Odessa, Kherson, Mykolaiv, Dnipropetrovsk and Zaporizhia—were unable to accept the idea of any type of "separation" of their territories from Ukraine or autonomy (see Table 5). The very low values (all three negative options together <15% of those questioned) correspond more closely to those of central Ukraine but diverge significantly from those of the partial region of Donbass (here all three negative options together equal 54.4%, while only approximately one-third of those questioned are in favor of both separation options). Beyond the statistics mentioned above, it is clear that even during the tense situation in April and May 2014, when a change to Ukraine's territorial status quo had already occurred (in Crimea), no significant support for further actions of this type is discernible outside the Donbass. In contrast, these high values in favor of maintaining the status quo point to the significant potential of the possible mobilization of segments of the pro-Ukrainian population—a potential that was also observable in many of the affected towns and cities.

Table 5: Which of the following variations on the status of your region would you choose if such an opportunity were to arise? (according to region, April 2014)

	Donbass	East (others)	South	Centre
Retention of the present status in a united Ukraine with the current jurisdictions	9.3	17.8	23.4	30.5
Retention of the present status in a united Ukraine with expanded jurisdictions	25.7	55.2	58.9	53.8
Autonomy in a federal Ukraine	23.5	9.5	7.0	2.3
Separation from Ukraine and creation of autonomous statehood	8.4	2.1	0.5	0.4
Separation from Ukraine and unification with another state	22.5	3.2	2.3	1.0
Difficult to answer/I don't know/Still haven't made a decision	10.6	12.2	7.9	11.9

Source: Kyiv International Institute of Sociology (2014a)

3. The values shown in Table 6 ultimately make it clear that there is, in contrast to the alleged direct connection postulated by the apologists for *Novorossiya*, only a relatively weak connection between ethno-national self-identification and people's attitudes toward Ukrainian statehood. Among the ethnic Russians in Ukraine in particular, only a fifth of those questioned appeared amenable to the idea of a change to the territorial status quo; however, up to a third of those with a hybrid identity were amenable. If these values are compared with data from similar surveys taken during the time before the Maidan, no direct effect appears to have been produced by the revolution and war. For example, in 2007 only 25.5% of ethnic Russians in Ukraine answered "No" to the question as to whether they would consider Ukraine their homeland.[xii]

Table 6: Which of the following variations on the status of your region would you choose if such an opportunity were to arise? (according to nationality, May 2014)

	Ukrainians	Russians	Ukrainians and Russians	Others
Retention of the present status in a united Ukraine with the current jurisdictions	25.2	7.9	8.8	22.9
Retention of the present status in a united Ukraine with expanded jurisdictions	57.2	34.5	22.8	28.6
Autonomy in a federal Ukraine	4.7	19.7	17.5	14.3
Separation from Ukraine and creation of an autonomous statehood	1.1	6.1	8.8	2.9
Separation from Ukraine and unification with another state	2.3	16.2	24.6	14.3
Difficult to answer/I don't know/Still haven't made a decision	9.5	15.7	17.5	17.1

Source: Kyiv International Institute of Sociology (2014b)

What can we conclude from the mainly negative reactions of the inhabitants of south-eastern Ukraine to the Russian Spring with regard to national self-identification and the general understanding of the concept of nation in the region? First, it can be assumed that the various types of ethno-national self-attribution, which have formed the basis of survey questions since the beginning of the 2000s (in other words, including people with hybrid identities), have remained relatively consistent. However, as of 2014, the number of ethnic Russians has fallen to 6.4% (2013: 8.3%) and the number of people with hybrid identities to 18% (2013: 21.8%),[xiii] though this can be explained above all by the loss of Crimea (no longer included in opinion polls from 2014) and the movement of refugees out of Donbass and into the Russian Federation, among other places.

At the same time, it must be noted that, next to the above-mentioned negative attitude towards Russian support and a change in the territorial status quo, a significant increase in many indicators of patriotism is observable after the events of 2014 among all segments of the south-east's population. This trend is particularly striking among younger cohorts; in this respect, 81% of all 14- to 35-year-olds are proud to be Ukrainian; among teenagers and young adults in the south-eastern oblast of Odessa, the figure is an astonishing 62%.[xiv] In contrast to the overriding identification with one's own region, commune, etc., identification as inhabitants of Ukraine increased by 10% in the country as a whole (Kulyk 2015). Furthermore, in the south-east a long-term trend appears to be continuing. After 2005, when only 32% of the inhabitants of the Eastern regions and 35.8%[xv] of those in the southern regions indicated that they considered themselves first and foremost to be inhabitants of Ukraine, these numbers rose in 2015 to 53.8% and 45.1% respectively.

We should be careful not to overstate numbers and trends. Moreover, considerable caution in light of the continuing unstable and dynamic situation in the affected regions is recommended. Still, it can be stated that external observers in particular have underestimated how tenuous the link was and is between aspects of ethno-national self-identification on the one hand and attitudes toward Ukrainian statehood and nationhood in south-eastern Ukraine on the other. Rather, both phenomena seem to have become even more decoupled from each other in the long term, and this has occurred in an accelerated fashion due to the shock effects of 2014. There is therefore a definite trend towards a "Ukrainian civil nation"[xvi] in south-eastern Ukraine that involves the dissociation of national consciousness from ethnic and linguistic patterns. However, this civil nation should not be confused with a Ukrainian political nation. Although the vast majority of inhabitants of the south-eastern regions identify with Ukrainian statehood, state symbols and the Constitution, they would have a negative view of an aggressive policy of Ukrainization in terms of language and how the country's history is viewed. It can be argued, therefore, that the failure of Novorossiya—as an attempt or practice to reconstruct and instrumentalize a transnational community of Russians and Russian-speakers—is mainly a consequence of a delayed, incremental and eventually accelerated process of nationalization in Ukraine's south-east. We should not deny the existence of certain forms of transnational socio-cultural ties between south-eastern Ukrainians and mainland Russians, but it seems that those bonds lost out in the competition with other imaginations of affiliation and ultimately perceptions of spatial belonging[xvii] (to Ukraine as a community of Ukrainian citizens, not ethnic Ukrainians).

One can only speculate about the reasons for this movement towards a "Ukrainian civil nation". The Russian policy of annexation in Crimea, and the later intervention in the Donbass, obviously triggered a "rally around the flag" effect, which was clearly embraced by many inhabitants of Ukraine whose loyalty to the Ukrainian state had previously been much less than equivocal. This factor is still gaining strength in many ways today, above all in the unoccupied parts of the Donbass[xviii] after it became clear that the Russian government is primarily pursuing geopolitical and few, if any, humanitarian goals on the other side of the contact line. Additionally, a long-term habituation effect as a result of twenty-five years of Ukrainian statehood can be observed. Younger cohorts in particular no longer have any experience of the Soviet Union. Despite what are in many cases complex ethnic patterns of identification, Ukraine is their only reality and experience of their homeland. Last, Ukrainian elites have, despite the amorphous narrative described above, never questioned independence based on their own interests. This also applies to the Party of Regions, which monopolized the south-east for a long time but whose leaders were less inclined toward pro-Russian policies than is often assumed and actually proved more sympathetic to an implicitly defined "pragmatic nationalism" (Härtel 2012).

7. Conclusion and Outlook

The Euromaidan, the 2014 Revolution of Dignity, the annexation of Crimea in March of the same year and the war in Donbass were turning points in the history of independent Ukraine, the Post-Soviet region as such, as well as for European politics. Revolution and war are profound shocks to domestic and international order; both give rise to basic concerns about personal survival but also cast doubt over self-identification and allegiance to a community. In Ukraine, in the wake of the Revolution of Dignity, the previously prevailing amorphous identity could not survive. That identity was propped up by a corresponding elite narrative and allowed a large number of Ukrainians, during the first two decades after independence, to avoid a definitive commitment to Ukrainian statehood and nationhood. Moreover, the revolution rescinded the power pact among the competing regional elite clans that had always been in force up until then, thus creating a power vacuum in the south-east of the country. Here, the subsequent annexation of Crimea and Moscow's intervention had resulted in an alternative option for societal and political allegiance that became known as the Novorossiya Scenario.

Despite the thesis of an ethno-cultural division in Ukraine, which was mainly popular outside of the country, this scenario ultimately enjoyed only limited success in the form of the self-proclaimed "DNR" and "LNR" in the Donbass. This fact can largely be explained by a gradual development, reinforced by the events of 2014, towards a Ukrainian civil nation in the south-east of the country. In this region, where ethnic Russians and people with what may be called hybrid identities are over-represented, ethnic and linguistic identification patterns were decoupled from questions of national allegiance and loyalty to the state. After a quarter century of Ukrainian statehood, a majority of people now identify as citizens of Ukraine and reject a change to the territorial status quo. In Vladimir Putin's view, the revolution and intervention therefore had an unexpected and conflicting effect. Instead of south-eastern Ukrainian citizens rising up against what Russian propaganda portrayed as a fascist coup d'état in Kyiv and siding with the pro-Russian activists, a majority committed themselves to Ukrainian unity, thereby discouraging the apologists for Novorossiya. Obviously, policies directed at the reconstruction of a transnational community of south-eastern Ukrainians and mainland Russians under the symbolic banners of Novorossiya or the Russian world failed.

Despite this undoubtedly positive news for Ukraine, which had been severely affected by the crises of recent years, caution should be urged in several respects. First, the situation in south-eastern Ukraine is anything but consolidated. This is mainly related to the deep economic and political crisis in the country, alongside continued attempts at destabilization from inside the occupied territories and beyond. If Kyiv proves unsuccessful in providing sustained security and economic opportunities in these regions, this could have an adverse effect on identification with and support for Ukrainian statehood in the medium term. Furthermore, the nature of the relationship between the Ukrainian political nation, which is strengthened by the Maidan and the new elite, and the above-mentioned trend towards a civil conception of nationhood in the south-east is still unclear. One must, for example, agree with Nikolai Mitrokhyn (2015b) when he states that a large majority of the citizens in the south-east do not share the official narrative, which manifests itself in policies relating to Ukrainization and the country's history.

After signs that appeared as early as the Maidan essentially pointed to the potential for an all-Ukrainian civil nation, above and beyond the boundaries of language (Kulyk 2015), Kyiv's current policy is more oriented toward a dangerous form of alienation. In other words, if Ukrainian elites fail to see that the construction of a Ukrainian nation based on ethnicity is an impossibility given current borders, future attempts aimed at an instrumentalization or reconstruction of existing transnational bonds in the country's south-east might be more promising. Finally, it should be reiterated that, despite the perspective chosen here with regard to the effectiveness of ethno-national types of self-identification, there are important objective consequences arising from the dynamic of the last two years. In this respect, the group of ethnic Russians in particular has been decimated by annexation, secession and exodus to such an extent that it now effectively represents a national minority due to its small numbers. Protection of this group should not just be of humanitarian interest to Kyiv; it is especially important because of Vladimir Putin's nationalist logic, which was described here in detail.

8. Bibliography

Balmaceda, Margarita. 2013. *The Politics of Energy Dependency: Ukraine, Belarus, and Lithuania Between Domestic Oligarchs and Russian Pressure.* Toronto: University of Toronto Press.

Barth, Fredrik. 1998. *Ethnic Groups and Boundaries: The Social Organization of Cultural Difference.* Long Grove: Waveland Press.

Buzgalin, Alexander. 2015. "Ukraine: Anatomy of a Civil War." *International Critical Thought* 5 (3): 327–347.

Gazeta.ru. 2014a. "Četyre Novorossij i odin Krym." 10 December 2014.

Gazeta.ru. 2014b. "Ne raskačali lodku." 4 December 2014.

Guttke, Matthias and Hartmut Rank. 2012. "Mit der Sprachenfrage auf Stimmenfang: Zur aktuellen Sprachengesetzgebung in der Ukraine." *UkraineAnalysen* 106: 11–15.

Härtel, André. 2012. *Westintegration oder Grauzonen-Szenario? Die EU- und WTO-Politik der Ukraine vor dem Hintergrund der inneren Transformation, 1998–2009.* Münster: LIT.

Hildebrandt, Reinhard. 2015. *Die Ukraine – Grenzland oder Brücke? Reflexionen zum aktuellen Konflikt.* Frankfurt am Main: Peter Lang.

Khmelko, V. 2004. "Linguistic and Ethnic Structure of Ukraine: Regional Differences and Trends of Change Since Independence." *Scientific Notes of Kyiv-Mohyla Academy, Social Science* 32.

Korrespondent. 2016. "Koroli v Isgnanii." 4 March 2016.

Kuchma, Leonid. 2004. Ukraina – ne Rossija. Moscow: Vremja.

Kulyk, Volodymyr. 2015. "One Nation, Two Languages? National Identity and Language Policy in Post-Maidan Ukraine." *PONARS Policy Memo,* No. 389.

Kuzio, Taras. 2007. *Ukraine-Crimea-Russia: Triangle of Conflict*. Soviet and Post-Soviet Politics and Society, Vol. 47. Stuttgart: ibidem.

Kyiv International Institute of Sociology. 2014a. "The Views and Opinions of Southeastern Regions Residents of Ukraine." April 2014. Accessed 2 February 2016. http://www.kiis.com.ua/?lang=eng&cat=news&id=258.

Kyiv International Institute of Sociology. 2014b. "Attitude to the Unitary State and Separatism in Ukraine." Accessed 2 February 2016. http://kiis.com.ua/?lang=eng&cat=reports&id=319.

Mitrokhyn, Nikolaj. 2015a. "Infiltration, Instruction, Invasion: Russia's War in the Donbass." *Journal of Soviet and Post-Soviet Politics and Society* 1 (1): 219–250.

Mitrokhyn, Nikolaj. 2015b. "Zwischen Stabilität und Labilität: Die gesellschaftspolitische Situation im Süden und Osten der Ukraine." *Friedrich-Ebert-Stiftung*, http://library.fes.de/pdf-files/id-moe/11625.pdf.

Moscow Times. 2008. "Putin Hints at Splitting Up Ukraine." 8 April 2008. http://old.themoscowtimes.com/sitemap/free/2008/4/article/putin-hints-at-splitting-up-ukraine/361701.html/.

Peremitin, Georgij. 2015. "Putin priznal naličie v Donbasse 'rešajuščich voennye voprozy' rossijan." 17 December 2015. http://www.rbc.ru/politics/17/12/2015/56728d4c9a7947794fc63cea.

Pogrebinskij, Mikhail. 2015. "Russians in Ukraine: Before and After "Euromaidan." *e-ir.info*. 26 March 2015. http://www.e-ir.info/2015/03/26/russians-in-ukraine-before-and-after-euromaidan/.

Portnov, Andrij. 2015. "Das neue Herz der Ukraine? Dnipropetrovs'k nach dem Euromaijdan." *Osteuropa* 4: 173–185.

Schneider, Eberhard. 2007. "Ukraine – Gespalten zwischen Ost und West." *BpB Informationen zur Politischen Bildung*. http://www.bpb.de/izpb/25087/ukraine-gespalten-zwischen-ost-und-west?p=all

Simon, Gerhard. 1986. *Nationalismus und Nationalitätenpolitik in der Sowjetunion: Von der Diktatur zur nachstalinistischen Gesellschaft*. Baden-Baden: Nomos.

Sutyagin, Igor. 2015. "Russian Troops in Ukraine." *Royal United Services Institute, Briefing Paper.* https://rusi.org/sites/default/files/201503_bp_russian_forces_in_ukraine.pdf.

Wilson, Andrew. 2002. *The Ukrainians: Unexpected Nation.* 2nd edition. New Haven and London: Yale Nota Bene.

Wilson, Andrew. 2006. *Ukraine's Orange Revolution.* New Haven and London: Yale University Press.

Wilson, Andrew. 2014. *Ukraine Crisis: What it Means for the West.* New Haven und London: Yale University Press.

Wilson, Andrew. 2016. "The Donbas in 2014: Explaining Civil Conflict Perhaps, but not Civil War." *Europe-Asia Studies* 68 (4): 631–652.

---

i An earlier, slightly different version of this text has already been published under the title "Where Putin's Russia Ends: 'Novorossija' and the Development of National Consciousness in Ukraine" in KAS International Reports, No. 2 (2016), pp. 107–125.

ii Cf. Putin's utterances of 17 April 2014, known as his "Novorossiya Comments", accessed online on 13 February 2016 on [http://kremlin.ru/events/president/news/20796].

iii This is what Putin said during his appearance at the meeting of the "All-Russian People's Front" on 25 January 2016, accessed online on 14 February 2016 on [http://kremlin.ru/events/president/news/51206].

iv Other factors for the ultimate failure of the Novorossiya-idea such as military resistance or entrenched local identities are discussed in e.g. Portnov (2015).

v Oleksandr Sushko used this formulation in the author's presence at a conference of the Konrad-Adenauer-Stiftung (KAS), entitled "Die Beziehungen EU-Ukraine-Rußland vor dem Hintergrund eines andauernden Konflikts" in August 2015 in Cadenabbia, Italy.

vi See the introduction to this volume.

vii Among others, see the attempted rescinding of the "Kivalov-Kolesnichenko Language Law" in 2014 or the new laws on the "de-communisation" of Ukraine (April 2015), which were criticized, e.g. by the Council of Europe, due to possible restrictions on freedom of speech.

viii Cf. Putin's speech on 18 March 2014, accessed online on 15 February 2016 on [http://en.kremlin.ru/events/president/news/20603].

ix Journalists, independent military experts and researchers have gathered convincing evidence for the presence of regular Russian armed forces in the Donbass since July 2014 (Wilson 2016: 648; Sutyagin 2015).

x Vladimir Putin has, since the start of the conflict in March 2014, gradually revised his communication strategy in regard to the presence of Russian troops on Crimea and the Donbass, while ultimately falling short of openly admitting the presence of regular Russian armed forces. While in December 2014 he insisted that all fighters with a Russian background are "volunteers" and that regular Russian armed forces are in no form part of the conflict, in December 2015 he admitted the presence of Russians as military advisors in the Donbass, "who are deciding certain questions [on behalf of the Russian government], among others also in the military sphere". In October 2016, Putin said that a Russian intervention (without specifically referring to its form) was necessary in order "to protect the Russian-speaking population in the Donbass" (Peremitin 2015; Golos Ameriky 2016).

xi This is according to, e.g., the respected Ukrainian professor at the National Kyiv-Mohyla Academy, Mykhailo Wynnickij, in the "Facebook Diary" he kept during the "Revolution of Dignity".

xii Cf. the opinion poll conducted by the Kyiv-based Razumkov Centre from 31 May to 18 June 2007, accessed online on 13 January 2016 on [http://www.razumkov.org.ua/ukr/poll.p hp?poll_id=775].

xiii The data for 2014 are taken from a survey of the Kyiv International Institute for Sociology, conducted from 29 April 2014 to 11 May 2014, "Attitude to the Unitary State and Separatism in Ukraine", [http://kiis.com.ua/?lang=eng&cat=reports&id=3199]. Comparative data for 2013 can be found in Pogrebinskij (2015).

xiv Cf. GfK Ukraine 2015: Study entitled "Jugend der Ukraine, 2015", accessed online on 15 February 2016 on [http://www.gfk.com/uk-ua/insights/news/doslidzhennja-molod-ukrajini-2015/].

xv Cf. the opinion poll carried out by the Kyiv-based Razumkov Institute in December 2015, accessed online on 2 February 2016 on [http://www.razumkov.org.ua/ukr/poll.php?poll_i d=762].

xvi Mikhail Pogrebinskij (2015) and other authors have already used the term. However, I use it here only in a limited sense for the south-eastern regions because these regions are at the forefront here, and the question of a pan-Ukrainian type of national understanding must be explained elsewhere (see also Conclusion).

xvii For both terms, see the conceptual discussion in the introduction to this volume.

xviii According to an opinion poll carried out by the Kyiv-based Democratic Initiatives Institute, in these areas an increase of 21% (to 63% overall) in the number of people identifying as "citizens of Ukraine" was recorded between 2013 and 2015. Cf. Democratic Initiatives Institute 2015: Ukraine: Two Years After "Maidan", accessed online on 13 March 2016 on [http://dif.org.ua/modules/pages/files/1457009023_4029.pdf].

Part II:
Symbolic Transnationalism

Novorossiya and the Transnationalism of Unrecognized Post-Soviet Nations

Mikhail Minakov

This article is dedicated to the Novorossiyan political myth among the populations of Southeastern Ukraine, Transnistria, Abkhazia, and South Ossetia. The author analyzes this myth in terms of the peculiar transnationalism and political imagination that led to the formation of a utopian alternative to the existing East European order. The author argues that the Novorossiyan myth is the separatists' response to the needs and demands of groups that feel excluded from post-Soviet title nations. Also, the myth is a response to needs and demands of the populations of unrecognized states—the "invisible nations" that are now seeking a new "international order".

1. Introduction

On 20 September 2015, a conference entitled "A Dialogue of Nations: the Right to Self-Determination and the Construction of a Multipolar World" was held in Moscow.[i] The conference brought together distinguished separatists from around the world. As reports from the conference indicate, one of the key issues discussed was "Novorossiya", a term used to describe a hypothetical union of oblasts in southeastern Ukraine and a region of Moldova that would exist either as an independent state or as a part of the Russian Federation. The conference's most important participants were pro-separatist intellectuals from Russia, the "DNR" and the "LNR" (Donetsk People's Republic and Lugansk People's Republic, two separatist polities in the eastern part of the Donetsk Oblast), southeastern Ukraine, Transnistria, and Abkhazia. The discussions about Novorossiya at the conference suggest that some now regard the project to be as legitimate as separatist movements in Puerto Rico, Catalonia, the Basque Country, and elsewhere.

How did Novorossiya, a Russian imperial project dating back to Catherine the Great, become so influential in contemporary Ukraine, Russia, Moldova, and Georgia? What motivated Ukrainian and non-Ukrainian citizens to support the "Novorossiya project" beginning in 2014? Was it the brainwashing effects of propaganda and financial incentives that brought droves of men and women to polling stations in the Donbas oblasts to vote in referenda on the creation of DNR/LNR? Why did a Russian imperial phenomenon play such an important role in the symbolism of the anti-Ukrainian uprisings?

Politicians, experts, and activists who share the Russian national perspective have offered two explanations. In contemporary Russian propaganda and the political imaginations of certain populations in the northern Black Sea lands (in which there are strong elements of conservative, imperial, and colonial thinking), the "Novorossiya project" is a legitimate answer to the unjust nation-building processes taking place in Ukraine, Moldova, and Georgia, which have deprived local populations of their cultural and political rights.[ii] The state-building models in Ukraine, Moldova, and Georgia are presented as having favored their "titular nations" at the expense of ethnic minority groups.[iii] In the context of these models, Novorossiyan separatism is seen as the result of either Russian nationalist/imperialist propaganda (which has made Ukrainian, Moldovan, and Georgian citizens question their loyalty to their respective states), or as the result of separatists being paid by Russia to revolt against their existing governments.[iv]

However, both explanations disregard the ideas and motivations of the local populations that supported or still support the separatist movements in the northern Black Sea lands. People in these regions were not, by and large, active participants in separatist military activities. Yet, they eagerly gave money and other resources to separatist leaders and fighters. These populations participated in the "referenda" on the creation of local peoples' republics in several regions of eastern Ukraine in 2014. They also attended mass gatherings in support of the so-called "peoples' republics" (the DNR and the LNR) that were held in southeastern Ukrainian cities from March to May 2014.

In this article, I analyze the peculiar transnationalism and political imagination that led to the formation of a utopian alternative to the existing Eastern European order. I argue that the "Novorossiyan myth" is the separatists' response to the needs and demands of groups that feel excluded from post-Soviet nations, and it is also a response to the needs and demands of the populations of unrecognized states—the "invisible nations" that are now seeking a new "international order".

2. Transnational Perspective on Novorossiya

A transnational perspective is necessary to understand the interests, motivations, and practices of those involved in Novorossiyan separatism. I use the term "transnationalism" for activities and processes "that take place on a recurrent basis across national borders and that require a regular and significant commitment of time by participants" (Portes 1999: 464). I follow the methodology proposed by Timm Beichelt and Susann Worschech in the introduction to this book by looking at transnationalist practices with a focus on the construction of symbols. In this article, the transnational community is defined as a group of people characterized by its participation in cross-border activities and/or networks with common aims, practices, and symbols (Kastoryano 2000). This essay describes the transnational community that shares a utopian—and hence symbolic—ideology shaped by the Novorossiyan myth.

Another important starting point for my study is the differentiation between political and ideological thinking. I accept the distinction proposed by Michael Freeden (2008: 1). From his perspective, political thinking aims at the implementation of a goal once power has been assumed. Ideological thinking is thinking "about politics" as well as the "central issues and problems... and [the] meaning of words" in which those problems are articulated. The political leaders of the separatist movements, as well as their foreign allies and national rivals, do think and act politically. In contrast, the supporters of these movements have created an ideological substrate that helps legitimize their leaders' political actions; these supporters think ideologically, thereby excluding themselves from political action.

The ideological thinking in question is of a utopian character. Support for the Novorossiyan project does not require active participation in the political construction of the DNR/LNR state, nor does it require active service in separatist forces. The utopian quality is connected with a specific element of the Novorossiyan myth: it demands political and social change here and now while simultaneously denying and/or ignoring political realities in Ukraine, Russia, the separatist republics, and the international legal framework.[v]

The utopian disregard for political reality is connected to the phenomenon of political imagination. As Chiara Bottici (2014: 60) notes, "imaginal politics" is a term that means collective irrational thinking (a mixture of conscious and unconscious processes). This imagination denies past experiences and is based on re-sentiment and the visualization of difficult ideological issues, thus avoiding discursive thinking. Perhaps most importantly, it makes a future collective project possible.

In 2014–15, Donbas was not only a war-torn region but also a post-Soviet laboratory of political ideologies. One of the most visible products of separatist political imagination was the Novorossiyan myth. Its utopian ideas created an environment that facilitated the political and military actions of the separatists. As will be shown below, an analysis of the transnational aspects of this ideological construction sheds light on some post-Soviet political phenomena that easily escape our attention if we stick to a national approach. In particular, a transnational analysis can provide insight into the ideas, visions, and hopes shared among the populations living in the separatist republics and the unrecognized post-Soviet nations (Transnistria and Abkhazia).

To understand the functioning of the Novorossiyan myth during the war in Donbas (April 2014 to the present), I studied political and ideological statements made on social networks by those who support the Novorossiya project (1) for non-economic reasons (they are not mercenaries) and/or (2) for non-institutional reasons (they are not officers in the Russian Army or representatives of other foreign agencies). I studied web-based communities whose members excluded people who openly declared themselves to be mercenaries, as well as officers and soldiers in the Russian Army or any official security agency. To find adequate sources of data, I narrowed my focus to the motivations and beliefs held by pro-Novorossiya populations. In particular, I focused on the use of the history of Novorossiya for political and/or mobilization purposes by pro-separatist activists living in Abkhazia, Transnistria, Crimea, Donbas, and in other regions in southeastern Ukraine.

Because the war is ongoing and I have no direct access to the target group, I further narrowed this group to include only those who actively use social networks (namely, VKontakte and Facebook), publish blogs, or comment on web-sites specifically dedicated to the War in Donbas and/or the Novorossiya project. As a result of this filtering, I identified a set of web resources and internet groups whose participants were eager to openly discuss their beliefs, motivations, experiences, and fantasies about Novorossiya as a political entity, Ukraine as a rival state, and Russia in a multitude of roles (see details in Annex 1).

3. Brief History of Novorossiya

To better understand the speech acts I analyze below, a short discussion of the history of the idea and concept of Novorossiya seems appropriate. Novorossiya was one of many names for the lands between the Danube and the Don from the late 18th to the early 20th centuries. The history of the region known as Novorossiya was well documented in imperial times: Apollon Skalkovskii, Petr Shibalskyi, Gavriil Rozanov, Dmitrii Bagalei, and Dmitrii Miller wrote a number of historical works dedicated to the study of the colonization of Novorossiya.[vi] However, the same lands have also been studied by Dmytro Iavornitskyi (Evornitskyi 1897),[vii] Yakov Novytskyi (1905), and other historians of Ukraine. In a way, imperial historiographies were quite flexible in their understandings of these territories and their cultural-historical contexts.

Soviet historiography, in contrast, was rather limited in its use of the word 'Novorossiya'. Instead, the region was predominantly known as 'southern Ukraine'. However, one important study did use Novorossiya in its title: *Settling into Novorossiya* by Vladimir Kabuzan (1976). Yet, it needed a sub-heading to explain what exactly the author meant by Novorossiya: the Iekaterinoslavskaia and Khersonskaia regions.

In contemporary post-Soviet and Western studies of imperial Russia and Ukraine, Novorossiya is used alongside a large number of other terms, including southern Russia, southern Ukraine, the northern Black Sea lands, Iekaterinoslavskaia guberniia, Khersonskaia guberniia, Novorossiiskaia guberniia, and southern Bessarabia, all of which are used to describe the region to the north and east of the Black Sea from the late 18th to the early 20th century (ibid.).

As a result of the centuries-long wars and armistices between the Ottoman and Russian Empires, the people living between the fortress of Chyhyryn and the slave market of Kaffa, between the pastures of Budzhak and the Azov steppes, lived in a unique environment. Many ethnic and religious groups, including the hordes of Budzhak, Ochakov, and Nogai, had to flee to the territories of the shrinking Ottoman Empire to survive. Turkish and Crimean Tatar towns and fortresses were either deserted or transformed into settlements occupied by different peoples. Bulgarians, Greeks, Serbs and other Christian groups in the Ottoman Empire moved northwards to the emerging cities of Novorossiya. Russians, Ukrainians, Jews, Germans, and other Christian groups came from the north and the west.

Between the 1750s and 1850s, life in the northern Black Sea lands underwent tremendous cultural changes. Many political organizations that had existed between the 15th and early 18th centuries were destroyed, including the *Niz* (or *Viisko Zaporizke,* lands controlled by the organization of Zaporozhian Cossacks), the polities of the Black Sea nomads, the Crimean Tatar Khanate, and the Ottoman imperial trade and security structures. Instead, new Russian Imperial sites emerged. By the middle of the 19th century, people had begun moving to the new cities and towns where economic and cultural life was booming. They were located in the following areas:

- Novaya Serbiia and Slavyanoserbiia (1750–1760);
- Novorossiya (stretching from the city of Taganrog to the Odessa region and the town of Ismail);[viii]
    - Novorossiiskaya guberniia (1764–1775, 1796–1803);
    - Novorossiisko-Bessarabskoye general-gubernatorstvo (1805–1874); and
    - The city of Novorossiisk in the eastern Black Sea region.
- Tavria/Tavrida (whose geography changed considerably between 1730 and 1920);
- The steppes of Kherson (Khersonskiie stepi, 1770-present); and
- The South (Yug) and/or South-West (Yugo-Zapad), a term from the vocabulary of the Empire's administration and the White Movement (1830–1921).

The local population began to develop a modern culture in the 19th century. The cities of Odesa, Nikolayev (later Mykolayiv, in Ukrainian spelling), Kherson, Yekaterinoslav (later Dnipropetrovs'k), Aleksandrovsk (later Zaporizhzhia), and other cities had populations ranging from 75,000 to 300,000 inhabitants by the end of the 19th century.

The desire to live in and dominate the northern Black Sea and Azov lands was based on Christian, Greek, and imperial political and historical myths. According to the Christian myth, Novorossiya was connected to the "source" of Russian Christendom because Vladimir the Great was baptized in Chersonese. This myth also legitimized the "reconquista" of these lands from the Moslems. According to the Greek myth, because the Novorossiyan lands once belonged to Ancient Greece and the Byzantine Empire, it was only "natural" that the Russian Empire, which saw itself as the heir to Byzantium, returned to rule them. Finally, the imperial myth was based on the idea that the construction of Novorossiya was necessary for civilization to triumph over barbarism.

Russian literature in the 19th and early 20th centuries incorporated these lands into Russian cultural geography. Pushkin, Gogol, Tolstoy, Chekhov, Dostoyevsky, and Gorky wrote stories that take place in Novorossiya or mention it by name. Odesa became one of the major centers of Russian cultural production. Here, colonial normalization took place alongside the glorification of local heroes, including Field-Marshal Alexander Suvorov, the heroes of the defense of Sevastopol during the Crimean War, Admiral Pavel Nakhimov, sailors in the Russian Black Sea Fleet, and others.

In addition to Russian Imperial literature, there was also a local literary focus on Novorossiya. There is some little-known literature that specifically describes these lands. For example, Russian writer Grigorii Danilevskii's *Beglyie v Novorossii* (1862), *Beglyiie vorotilis* (1863), and *Novyiie mesta* (1867) describe everyday life in Novorossiya and the specific roles that the people in the region played vis-à-vis the imperial center. Ivan Nechui-Levytskyi's novel *Mykola Dzheria* (1878) included Novorossiya in the context of Ukrainian culture and described the transformation of the Niz in Ukrainian symbolic geography.

For the purposes of this study I will briefly outline the major issues with which Novorossiya was associated in the Russian cultural context of the 19th century. First, Novorossiya was viewed as a place of new beginnings. It was in Novorossiya that Russian capitalism was concentrated and where entrepreneurship flourished in the 19th century. Second, Novorossiya was regarded as a place that lacked order but promised opportunities for daring people. Suvorov, for example, is seen as something of a military entrepreneur, the Duke de Richelieu (governor of Novorossiya and Bessarabia in 1804–15) as an administrative entrepreneur, the Rallie family as economic entrepreneurs, and Gogolian Chichikov as a criminal entrepreneur. Finally, Novorossiya was appreciated as a hideaway for migrants, a relatively free land compared to the northern regions. Thousands of urban losers, sectarians, adventurers, and revolting serfs fled there to start a new life.

Among the cities of the northern Black Sea and the Azov lands, there was a real competition for administrative, economic, and symbolic superiority. Kherson and Nikolayev, Odesa and Yekaterinoslav, Taganrog and Mariupol competed for administrative and economic supremacy. By the beginning of the 20th century, Odesa had emerged as a leader on most of these fronts. Odesa was home to Novorossiya's university (established in 1863) and the region's most important port, and it had become a center for science and the arts. Odesa was the jewel of the Novorossiyan *krai*.

In the Soviet period, the term Novorossiya disappeared from public discourse. Between 1917 and 1924, the northern Black Sea and Azov lands survived many political projects, including "The South", which was a White Army stronghold, and the anarchic republic of Nestor Makhno. By the end of 1918, the Ukrainian People's Republic (UNR) included the region in its maps; UNR forces controlled many cities in the region between 1918 and 1921. The Bolsheviks' projects in the region ultimately led to the creation of the Ukrainian Soviet Socialist Republic (USSR), which included contemporary Transnistria and parts of Moldova.

With the Bolshevik victory and the creation of the USSR in 1922, the northern Black Sea territories were divided among the Russian Socialist Federation, the Ukrainian Socialist Republic and, later, the Moldovan Socialist Republic. The Soviet nationalization project in Ukraine (*korenizatsia*, 1923–33), in combination with the promotion of the Soviet Marxist ideology, turned the northern Black Sea lands into integral parts of proletarian Russia and Ukraine. During those times, the term Novorossiya was mainly to be found in Lenin's *The Development of Capitalism in Russia* (1899). By this time, the Black Sea territories were no longer seen as one land with a common name.

In the 1920s and 1930s, Donetsk, Zaporizhzhya, and Odesa took on symbolic significance in Soviet culture. The industrial utopias of Donbas and DneproGES[ix] were dissociated from their imperial past. Odesa's literature, cinema, and visual arts groups promoted the Soviet avant-garde (partially associated with Russian culture and partially with Ukrainian culture) with no reference to the colonization of the region. From the 1930s to the 1960s, the northern Black Sea and Azov lands had no single name. Still, many images and stories that were important for Soviet ideology focused on the urban and industrial centers in the region. However, these were images of the Soviet political and cultural community and did not reflect any regional identity.

Only during Perestroika did some memories of Novorossiya return, mainly among those interested in Russian Imperial history. Several books dedicated to Novorossiya or to the colonial wars in those lands were re-printed.[x] At the same time, however, the renaming of these lands in the late Soviet period was closely tied to the Ukrainian Soviet tradition of oblast names: Odessa oblast as *Odeshchyna*,

Kherson oblast as *Khersonshchyna*, etc. In local historical literature printed between 1979 and 1989, the northern Black Sea and Azov lands were called either "Southern Ukraine" or "Southeastern Ukraine".

Crimea's experience during this period was unique. At the end of the 1980s, some members of the local "Slav" population contested the Crimean Tatars' repatriation from their Stalinist exile. The Novorossiyan myth was revitalized in 1989–91, when Crimean Slavs and Tatars tried to portray themselves as locals while shunning the so-called "newcomers". Conservative leaders of the Slavic Crimean population invoked the legacy of Novorossiya—despite the fact that Crimea had never been part of any administrative division related to Novorossiya. This historical argument was one of the ideological reasons that people supported the referendum on Crimean autonomy held on January 20, 1991. In the 1990s, the Novorossiyan myth played an active role in Crimean secessionist ideology.

Independent Ukraine's nation-building efforts have also revised collective memories and created and redistributed identities.[xi] Local histories became invisible as narratives about a national Ukrainian identity began to take hold. However, during the 1990s, regional identities became an important factor in local and national political development. During this time, voting patterns changed: whereas there had once been a cleavage between regions that voted predominantly for communists and those that supported nationalists, a new cleavage developed between the Ukrainian-speaking northwest and the Russian-speaking southeast.

The Ukrainian east-west cleavage was not limited to voting patterns. Regional elites were united by the Party of Regions into a single network; different local political organizations joined together, creating a strong network of local elites, mainly in the southeastern oblasts. During the first separatist outbreak in southeastern Ukraine—the Siveronets'k Congress in November 2004—Novorossiyan symbols were on display, as were other ideologically charged separatist expressions (e.g., the slogan "solidarity with the fathers who brought civilization here under Catherine the Great" or St. Andrew's Black Sea flag, etc.). However, the government quashed this movement after the Orange Revolution.

The slogans of the Siverodonets'k Congress were given a second life in the anti-Maidan movements in southeastern Ukraine during the Euromaidan Revolution. However, there was a difference: the new slogans were less connected with local elites and were shared by anti-Maidan activists instead. When the Euromaidan protests turned violent in January 2014, the social networks of anti-Maidan groups teemed with allegations of "American involvement". As one activist wrote in the "Novorossiya" Facebook group in February 2014, it was time "to ask for Russia's defense".

Between the end of February and April 2014, the Novorossiya myth became accepted as one of several guiding ideas behind the separatist movement in southeastern Ukraine. Other ideas included the "Russian Spring" myth and local "people's republics" projects (in Kharkiv, Luhansk, Donetsk, Zaporizhzya, Dnipropetrovsk, Kherson, Mykolaiiv, and Odesa). Unlike the "Russian Spring", which took an ethnic-based approach to nationhood, the Novorossiya myth was supported by a variety of different peoples and ethnic groups, namely the pro-separatist inhabitants of southeastern Ukraine, Transnistria, and Abkhazia (see below).[xii]

4. Data Analysis and Interpretation of the Novorossiyan Myth: Between Social Reality and Historical Justice

The following section presents the results of the empirical study. To enquire into the functioning of the Novorossiyan myth during the Donbas War (beginning in April 2014), I focused on the use of a complex of beliefs connected to the Novorossiyan myth as outlined in Section II. It has become obvious that the myth rests on both geographic and historic symbols that are open to a wide variety of interpretations. I identified uses of the myth for mobilization purposes by pro-separatist activists living in Crimea, Donbas, and other regions in southeastern Ukraine, as well as in Abkhazia and Transnistria. To understand the ideological motivations of the people supporting the revolt and the war against Ukraine, I looked for sources in web-based pro-separatist communities. I identified a set of web resources and groups on social networks, which are displayed in Annex I (Tables 1–3). The material I used is open-source. I gathered over 1,500 texts and discussions about issues related to the Novorossiya myth co-written by approximately 25,000 people.[xiii]

By using content analysis and intention analysis, I was able to identify major ideas as well as specific terms, metaphors, and value-expressions used by pro-separatist activists that supported the basic ideas of the Novorossiyan myth. Through the analysis of a large number of texts (words, sentences and other verbal expressions constituting discussions among the groups on social networks), I was able to identify the following:

- The basic *keywords* of the discussion;
- The meaning of prominently used *terms*, their alleged *intentions*, and the *values* associated with them;
- The major *trends in the usage of key terms* that led to the redefinition of meanings and values; and
- The major issues and *audiences* associated with the dominant trends.

The keywords that were used by participants to provoke and sustain lengthy and popular discussions included "Novorossiya/Novorossiyan", "Ukraine/Ukrainian", "Russia/Russian", "war", "justice", "enemy", "Slavs/Slavic", and "West/Europe/US" (see Annex II, Table 4). In this table, I have provided a description of the most-used words and their meanings. For example, the term "Novorossiya/Novorossiyan" was used at least 1120 times per month in the selected groups. There were at least three meanings ascribed to the word. Above all, it was a name used for the Kharkiv, Luhansk, Donetsk, Zaporizhzhya, Dnipropetrovsk, Kherson, Mykolayiv and Odesa oblasts of Ukraine. In fewer cases, it was the name given to the aforementioned territories *plus* Crimea and Transnistria. Finally, in several cases this name was used to refer to an even larger region that included Abkhazia and parts of southern Russia. In this table, I also outline some other characteristics of the way the term is used. For example, "Novorossiya" was used more for territories than for peoples, and the term had an outright positive meaning in the first half of 2014, whereas it has had a predominantly neutral connotation since September 2014. In this way, the table describes the content and intent of the use of key terms by those who adhered to the Novorossiyan myth.

The analysis of these data made it possible to identify the groups involved in the discussions. Although populations with pro-separatist attitudes seem to be homogenous at first sight, online discussions about key topics reveal differences in how different groups imagine Novorossiya's future status and its relationship with Russia. Two distinct groups can be identified: (1) a group with "imperialist" views (approximately 60% of participants) and (2) groups that have "transnationalist" agendas (approximately 40% of participants).

Among the imperialist group, the most influential collective voice was the one that supported the unification of Russia and Novorossiya. The reason given for this unification was usually the common imperial past of the populations in Russia and the southern oblasts of Ukraine. This agenda was actively promoted by a core group of activists and intellectuals around Konstantin Malofeev, a Russian oligarch and one of Putin's champions of imperialism. The two major figures in this group are Igor Strelkov and Aleksander Borodai. Their Novorossiya is based on images of the past—mainly Soviet and imperial. For them, the dominant context for Novorossiya is the "Russian Spring". The symbolic geography of this group puts Russia and Moscow at the center of the project, with Ukraine's southern oblasts as a part of the Russian Federation.

While this group has received the most media attention, they face opposition in the communities they actually refer to. In some situations, people in the separatist republics, as well as in other oblasts in southeastern Ukraine and Transnistria and Abkhazia, express opinions that differ from those promoted by the imperialists. A sizeable number of people discuss the Novorossiya project as the "people's own" local business, and the locality they refer to does not respect existing national borders. Instead, they talk about a solidarity that can be described as neither imperial/colonial nor ethnic.

This transnationalist group has certain characteristics. First of all, it views Novorossiya as a separate country with very vaguely defined borders. In most discussions, this imagined country includes the southern Ukrainian oblasts, Crimea, and Transnistria. However, as I noted in Table 4, there were several discussions concluding that oblasts in southern Russia, Abkhazia, and even Southern Ossetia should be included in Novorossiya. Group participants pointed more to a common Soviet legacy (twenty-three separate discussions), and less so to an imperial past (eleven discussions) in their arguments for the legitimacy of this constellation of lands. It is important to note here that their Soviet arguments were less "historical" or "temporal" (related to the past). Instead, members of this online separatist community refer to the Soviet Union's social safety net, to a higher quality of life and to the feeling of belonging to a non- or supra-ethnic society.

The power structure of the transnationalist group is much more horizontal and decentralized than its imperialist counterpart. It does not have a core group of leading personalities. Instead, traditionalist views of Novorossiya are shared by participants who refer to themselves as "simple people", "grass-root activists", and "supporters" rather than leaders or intellectuals. They identify themselves as "those living" (*zhyvushchiie, naseleniie*) in southern Ukraine, Transnistria, and Abkhazia.

This transnationalist group has become more visible as the intensity of the war and war-driven mobilization have decreased. In these situations, the "imperialist" group has declared that "Moscow betrayed Novorossiya", lamenting "the closure of the project". However, the transnationalist group saw Novorossiya as their "own project" whose future did not depend on Moscow. I counted at least nine significant discussions that led to a consensus that the Transnistrian and Abkhazian experiences as non-recognized states were models for the separatist republics and/or for a future Novorossiya.

Furthermore, the transnationalist group is less inclined to use militarist symbols. Instead, theirs is a moderate aesthetic: for them, St. Andrew's flag and St. George's ribbon are the major symbols of Novorossiya. The "imperialist" groups, in contrast, have a much richer variety of symbols that often include a mixture of current Russian official and military symbols, Russian Imperial symbols, symbols of the DNR and LNR, and stylized weaponry.

This review of debates among supporters of the "Novorossiyan project" has shown that the "Novorossiyan identity" has been used not only in opposition to the Ukrainian, Moldovan, and Georgian national perspectives but also, to a lesser extent, by moderates opposing the "imperialist" group. The identity in question has clear transnational character. First of all, it links marginalized and/or isolated groups in Georgia, Moldova, and southeastern Ukraine to a cross-border network of people who share certain attitudes towards their national majorities, national governments, and the global order. Second, it provides these activists with an ideological justification for their separatist projects and creates a kind of historical, regional, and ideological solidarity. It also establishes common ground for solidarity across borders in Eastern Europe. Finally, this identity is connected to—but also opposed to—neo-imperialist and ethno-nationalist perspectives in the region.

In studying the aforementioned texts, I found that the word "Novorossiya" is associated with ideological meanings that have legitimized political separatism in the region, as well as with military mobilization and solidarity among populations in the unrecognized polities. When mentioning "Novorossiya", supporters of separatist ideas tended to espouse nativist, anti-Western, and anti-globalist attitudes, as well as to describe the need to "restore historical justice."

- Whenever *nativism* came up, internet users stressed that they have their own "native" and "common" history that is distinct from the nationalized histories of Ukraine, Moldova, and Georgia. Nativist metaphors often contained "blood and soil" arguments, which contrasted with the "foreign" or "alien" histories of the nations of Ukraine, Moldova, and Georgia. While for separatists from Transnistria and the southern Ukrainian oblasts, nativism was based on their Slavic origin, speakers from Abkhazia or South Ossetia referred to "Soviet-era internationalism", which motivated them to oppose Georgia. According to some forum users, Abkhazia's Novorossiyan identity stems from the threat that the Abkhaz population, which "flourished in Soviet times", faces from pro-Western Georgia.

- *Anti-Western motives* are strong and stable among both the imperialist and transnationalist groups. The West, Europe, and the U.S. are seen as presenting an existential threat to the collective identities, values and memories of the Novorossiyan populations. Sometimes, however, "Europe" is used positively, especially when referring to "EU welfare" or to "European allies" in far-right groups and political parties in France, Italy, Austria, and Hungary.
- The issue of "historical justice" for all unrecognized nations—particularly for Russophones in Ukraine—is among the most popular topics. The populations of Donbas, Transnistria, and Crimea are seen as groups whose statehood is historically justified: "we have our own political culture" based on a "non-ethnic statehood" uniting "representatives of all ethnic groups", they say. Russian-speakers are said to be "excluded from state-building" processes and treated as "second-class citizens" in Ukraine and Moldova. This argument is mostly used in debates focusing on the Ukrainian, Georgian, and Moldovan right to statehood. Russian Imperial and Soviet history provide unrecognized nations and pro-separatist activists with the "historical foundation" for new polities in the region. This historical argument is employed to oppose belonging to Ukraine, Georgia, and Moldova.

The Novorossiyan myth refers to the past as a series of events that provides both imperialists and transnationalists with their justifications for their respective visions. Unsurprisingly, the "Golden Age" of Imperial Russia is equally important for both groups. However, there are differences between the visions. The imperialists tend to focus on military history, while the transnationalists are more attentive to the economic and cultural boom of 19th century as well as to the peaceful coexistence of different ethnic and religious groups together with the Russian Orthodox Church. The socialist experience in the construction of the Donbas-Krivorizhzhya Republic stresses that social fairness was important to the transnationalists, too. In contrast, imperialist groups focus more on the Civil War of 1917–1924.

The lost paradise of the Soviet Union is equally relevant to both groups' debates. However, transnationalist discussants focus more on social security and the cultural rights of Russian speakers during the Soviet period. The glory of "the Victory in the Great Patriotic War (Second World War)" is also equally important to both groups. However, the imperialists use this issue in reference to the military confrontation with the West, whereas the transnationalists focus more on the experience of "Heroic Cities" such as Odesa, Sevastopol, and Kerch. Transnationalists are also more inclined to distance themselves from the supposed glorification of Nazis in mainland Ukraine and "Romania Mare" (Great Romania) in Moldova. Following the passage of Ukraine's "de-communization" laws in April 2015, the number of anti-Kyiv comments doubled among residents of Odesa, Mykolayiv, Kherson, Zaporizhzhya, and Dnipropetrovsk. Thus, even though historical arguments are important for all supporters of Novorossiya, they deploy transnationalist and imperialist elements differently. While imperialists tend to focus on unity with Russia, transnationalists focus on the local populations' right to self-determination. Furthermore, they emphasize the extent to which their separatist "nations" are different from Georgia, Moldova, and Ukraine.

Finally, some general comments on the attitudes of members of the transnationalist group should be made. Unlike the imperialists, many transnationalists have experienced life in unrecognized states and are often critical of it. This means that they have different historical reference points when they write about Novorossiya. Transnistrians and Abkhazians often complain about living in unrecognized states. Their anti-Western sentiment is less utopian and more focused on the limitations placed on them by nation-states and international organizations. Often, they criticize their own leaders and political regimes as unjust and corrupt. Those living in the DNR and LNR also increasingly criticize their leadership for ignoring the interests and rights of their citizens. Still, they criticize their own states in different ways than they criticize the political order in Georgia, Moldova and Ukraine. Here, local "bad orders" are seen as home-grown; discussants often joke that "these are bandits, but they're our bandits". In Georgia, Moldova, and Ukraine, however, corrupt elites are denounced as "foreign exploiters". Although the current situation is predominantly described in negative terms, the emergence of positive reference points is plausible. Particularly among transnationalists, the Soviet past is seen as the only just way of life these populations have ever experienced. Their hopes for improvement are connected with an imagined Novorossiyan polity that strongly resembles an idealized Soviet past.

For Ukrainian supporters of the Novorossiyan project, comparisons to Halychyna are quite common; it was mentioned in at least fifteen discussions.

Halychyna is a western Ukrainian region that has its own history of national movements in the Polish and Habsburg Empires. Interestingly, by the end of 2014 and throughout 2015, there were many cases in which discussants compared Novorossiya with Halychyna and today's separatist fighters with Ukrainian Insurgent Army fighters (*povstantsi UPA*). The comparison with Halychyna is based on (1) linguistic, cultural, and historical differences with the rest of the country; (2) the ability to bring civilization to the rest of the country (federalism is seen as a sign of a "higher political urban culture" than the "Ukrainian agricultural oligarchy"); and (3) a specific regional identity based on a colonial and imperial past.

For supporters of Novorossiya living in South Ossetia and Abkhazia, appeals to history are also unique and local. They commonly compare the Novorossiyan project with the idea of the "Caucasian Confederation" project, which, during the Chechen Wars in the 1990s, was seen as a possible way of organizing the populations of Dagestan, Chechnya, Ingushetia, Abkhazia, Cherkessia, and other lands in the North Caucasus. The Caucasian Confederation was imagined as a transnational polity of nationalities living in the Caucasian regions of Russia, Georgia, and even Azerbaijan.

In all cases, the transnationalist group compares their past and present experiences to an imagined Novorossiyan future. In these comparisons, which their imperialist peers rarely understand, the political imagination and vision of the transnationalist group is based on a politically and socially just order.

5. Conclusions

The contemporary Novorossiyan myth is a complex ideological construction shared by two groups that can be identified vis-à-vis their attitudes toward the West as well as towards Russia's imperial and Soviet past. One of the groups can be termed "imperialist" and the other "transnationalist". My analysis suggests that the Novorossiyan myth refers to—and is endorsed by—some communities living in territories that are today ruled by Ukraine, Moldova and Georgia. Supporters of the Novorossiyan myth usually feel excluded from political, social, and cultural life in their respective countries.

In both groups, the Novorossiyan myth lives from elements of conservatism, imperialism, and revanchist neo-Sovietism. Novorossiyan *conservatism* refers to historical justice and a seemingly glorious past as sources of legitimacy for a separate political entity in the northern Black Sea lands. In many ways, this conservatism coincides with the ideology of Vladimir Putin, seeking to provide a "traditionalist alternative" to ideas and policies based on human rights, the rule of law, and the international legal order. Supporters of the Novorossiyan project reject the inclusion of lands between Izmail and Lugansk in Ukraine; of Transnistria in Moldova; and of Abkhazia and South Ossetia in Georgia. In their opinion, historical justice can only be achieved by letting the local populations in these regions create their own legitimate state (or states).

Non-ethnic Russian *imperial* and supra-ethnic Soviet identities create frameworks of collective solidarity that are supported by adherents to the Novorossiya idea. This identity, which is usually not ethnically coded, refers to the experience and memory of these populations under the Russian Empire and the Soviet Union. Although there are clear social similarities among those who call for Novorossiyan solidarity, they rarely refer to any social class or social justice issue. Their calls for solidarity are grounded in historical, collectivist, and conservative terms. Quite often the Soviet social and political experience is portrayed as the ideal order for the future. The current period of Georgian, Moldovan, and Ukrainian independence, in contrast, is seen as highly unjust. *Revanchist* neo-sovietism is thus an important part of the Novorossiyan myth.

Another common feature of the Novorossiyan myth is that all of its supporters share anti-Western and pro-Russian attitudes and have a negative assessment of Ukrainian and Moldovan rule over Russophone populations. However, those supporting strict pro-Russian attitudes make up the group of "imperialists", who claim that Novorossiya can exist only as a part of the Russian Federation. They focus on Soviet and Imperial military glory, and they see the future of Novorossiya connected to the Russian government's foreign and defense policies. The "transnational" group, by contrast, is more focused on social and economic issues of the past. Its members have a negative attitude towards the national majorities of their states, but they see Novorossiya's future as either an independent state or as an autonomous region within Russia. This group is more inclusive in terms of who can be regarded as "Novorossiyan": Russians and Ukrainians in southern Ukraine and Transnistria, as well as Abkhazians and South Ossetians, are seen as legitimate members of a future Novorossiyan polity.

The members of the transnationalist group constitute a transnational community that shares utopian, non-military ideas. They picture themselves as survivors living under the rule of illegitimate national and separatist governments. The political and social change they want is distant and utopian. However, the tensions between their utopian aims and the realities on the ground are not strong enough to make this group try to escape its self-isolation. Their survival is predicated on the increased relevance of conservative values. These are shared by most group members, which in turn increases their ability to associate with other marginalized social groups within Ukraine, Georgia, and Moldova. Furthermore, the orientation towards conservatism and self-isolation diminishes support for left-wing parties that could react to some of this group's preferences.

The transnationalist group may ultimately have an impact on medium-term political outcomes in Georgia, Moldova, Russia, and Ukraine. If these states implement inclusive cultural and socio-economic policies, Novorossiyans could one day be incorporated into national politics. It is important to remember that this group is not eager to take military action, which provides national governments with a limited opportunity to look for common understanding with its members. However, the transnationalist group may also be a source of renewed separatist mobilization; transnationalist Novorossiyans can be seen as objects of contestation, with Chisinau, Kyiv, and Tbilisi on one side and Moscow on the other.

6. Bibliography

Bagalei, Dmitrii. 1889. *Kolonizatsiia Novorossiiskogo kraia I pervyie shagi ego po puti kultury.* Kiev: Tipografiia G.T.Korchak-Novitskogo.

Bottici, Chiara. 2014. *Imaginal politics: images beyond imagination and the imaginary.* New York: Columbia University Press.

Buber, Martin. 1958. *Paths in Utopia.* Boston: Beacon Press.

Evornitskyi, Dmytrii. 1897. *Istoriia zaporozhskikh kazakov: v 3-kh tomakh.* Sankt-Peterburg.

Freeden, Michael. 2008. "Editorial: Thinking politically and thinking ideologically." *Journal of Political Ideologies* 13 (1): 1–10.

Gavriil, Rozanov. 1853. *Otryvok iz povestvovaniia o Novorossiiskom kraie.* Odesa. T.3.

Gavriil, Rozanov. 1857. *Prodolzheniie ocherka istorii o Novorossiiskom kraie. Period s 1787 po 1837 god.* Tver: Tipografiia Gubernskogo Pravleniia.

Kabuzan, Viktor. 1976. *Zaseleniie Novorossii (Iekaterinoslavskoi I Khersonskoi gubernii).* Moskva: Nauka.

Kasianov, Georgiy & Philipp Ther. 2009. *A laboratory of transnational history: Ukraine and recent Ukrainian historiography.* Budapest: CEU Press.

Kasianov, Georgiy. 2009. "'Nationalized' History: Past Continuous, Present Perfect, Future..." In *A laboratory of transnational history: Ukraine and recent Ukrainian historiography*, edited by Georgiy Kasianov and Philipp Ther, 7–24. Budapest: CEU Press.

Kastoryano, Roman. 2000. "Settlement, transnational communities and citizenship." *International Social Science Journal* 165: 307–312.

Lenin, Vladimir (Vladimir Iliin). 1899. *Razvitiie kapitalizma v Rossii.* Sant-Peterburg: Tipo-litografiia Leiferta.

Mannheim, Karl. 1960. *Ideology and Utopia. An Introduction to the Sociology of Knowledge.* London: Routledge & Kegan Paul.

Miller, Dmitrii. 1901. *Zaseleniie Novorossiiskogo kraia I Potemkin.* Kharkov.

Novytskyi, Yakov. 1905. *Istoriia goroda Aleksandrovska.* Iekaterinoslav: Tipografiia Gubernskogo Zemstva.

Portes, Andrew. 1999. "Conclusion: towards a new world—the origins and effects of transnational activities." *Ethnic and Racial Studies* 22 (2): 463–77.

Semenov, Vladimir. 1910. *Rossia. Polnoiie opisaniie nashego otechestva. Novorossiia I Krym.* Sankt-Peterburg: Izdatelstvo A.F.Devriena.

Shebalskii, Petr. 1889. *Potemkin I zaseleniie Novorossiiskogo kraia.* Moskva.

Skalkovskii, Apollon. 1836. *Khronologicheskoie obozreniie istorii Novorossiiskogo kraia.* Odesa. 2 t.

7. Annexes

Annex I

Table 1: VKontakte Sources

Name and hyperlink (in original language)	Type	Number of participants
# Новороссия [https://vk.com/soutukraine]	Miscellaneous (discussions, news, other)	314,192
РЕСПУБЛИКА НОВОРОССИЯ [https://vk.com/the_republic_of_new_russia]	Discussion group	152,205
Новороссия [https://vk.com/novorossia_su]	VK mirror of the Novorossiya website	81,740
НОВОСТИ НОВОРОССИИ [https://vk.com/novnews]	News community	75,347
Сводки ДНР ЛНР Новороссия [https://vk.com/ety_strany]	Discussion group	68,087
Вестник Новороссии [https://vk.com/novoros_news]	News community	34,734
НОВОРОССИЯ	SaveDonbassPeople	Антимайдан [https://vk.com/novorossia_today]	Discussion group	32,930
Сопротивление Новороссии [https://vk.com/revolutioneast]	News community	29,700
ДОБРОВОЛЕЦ.ОРГ	ОБОРОНА НОВОРОССИИ [https://vk.com/dobrovolecorg]	NGO network	25,831
Родное Приднестровье [https://vk.com/rodnoepridnestrovie]	Miscellaneous (discussions, news, other)	23,117
Антимайдан Одесса Новороссия [https://vk.com/novorossiaaa]	Discussion group	22,102

The following criteria were used in the selection of the VKontakte groups: (1) had over 20,000 participants,[1] (2) was active for more than six months during the Donbas War; and (3) covered Novorossiyan issues frequently.

---

1 This quantitative threshold provided me with the ability to analyze discussions in long-living groups (at least six months); the fewer participants the group had, the shorter the debates tended to last. The groups that existed for a longer time also provided interesting data showing how attitudes among pro-Novorossiya activists and their opponents changed over time.

Table 2: Facebook Sources

Name and hyperlink (in original language)	Type	Number of participants
Новороссия [https://www.facebook.com/novorossia/?ref=br_rs]	Media and news	9,396
Новороссия - актуальное [https://www.facebook.com/groups/novorossia.actual/?ref=br_rs]	Discussion group	5,991
Приднестровье [https://www.facebook.com/groups/pridnestrovie/?ref=br_rs]	Miscellaneous	5,002
Novorossia.today [https://www.facebook.com/Novorossiatoday-1452392635033241/?ref=br_rs]	Media and news	4,951
Новороссия = ДНР + ЛНР [https://www.facebook.com/groups/24Novorossiya/?ref=br_rs]	Discussion group	4,009
Novorossia-INFO English [https://www.facebook.com/groups/300259383483318/?ref=br_rs]	Discussion group	2,264
Абхазия 24 [https://www.facebook.com/abkhazia24/?ref=br_rs]	News and discussion	1,894

The following criteria were used in the selection of the Facebook groups: (1) had over 1,000 participants[2]; (2) was active for more than six months during the Donbas War; and (3) covered Novorossiyan issues frequently.

Table 3: Sources from Internet Web-sites[3]

Name and hyperlink (in original language)	Type
Novorossia, [http://novorossia.su/]	Media and discussion
Novorossia Information Agency, [http://www.novorosinform.org/]	News site
Russkaia Vesna – Novorossia, [http://rusvesna.su/tags/novorossiya]	Media and discussion
Novorossiya, [http://novorossiya.name/]	News site

The following criteria were used for the selection of web sites: (1) often cited by VK and FB groups[4]; (2) was active for more than six months during the Donbas War; and (3) covered Novorossiyan issues frequently.

---

[2] This quantitative threshold for Facebook-based communities also provided access to long-lasting discussion groups. VKontakte was much more popular among Russophone populations than Facebook; this is why there is a difference between the thresholds.

[3] Only those materials that had more than 100 comments were analyzed.

Annex II

Table 4: Key Words and Their Use by Pro-Separatist Populations

Key words	Average number of use per month	Frequency in use	Meaning, contested meanings
Novorossiya/ Novorossiyan	Not less than 1,120 times per month	Stable frequency	1. Most frequent use: the name used to refer to the Kharkivska, Luhanska, Donetska, Zaporizka, Dnipropetrovska, Khersonska, Mykolayivska and Odeska oblasts of Ukraine. 2. Less frequent use: all of the above plus Crimea and Transnistria. 3. Least frequent use: two southern oblasts in Russia and Abkhazia. Note 1: This term is used mostly for territories; rarely used to describe a population. "Novorossiyan people" or similar terms were used in 2014 but had almost disappeared by the end of 2015. Note 2: The term had a positive meaning in the first half of 2014; since September 2014, the term has had a more neutral connotation
Ukraine/ Ukrainian	Not less than 1000 times per month	Used more frequently in 2015 (1100) than in 2014 (1000)	1. The state of Ukraine that is now at war with Novorossiya/Russia/the peoples' republics 2. Less used: territories to the north of the Novorossiyan oblasts. Note: The use of the term is predominantly negative. Some "neutralization" of the term arose by end of 2015 (approximately 20% of all uses).
Russia/ Russian	Not less than 950 times per month	Stable frequency	1. The state of that is the only ally of the supporters of Novorossiya. 2. Less used: a state that should accept/defend/introduce its army into Novorossiya. 3. A positive adjective (Russian world, for example), associated with the past and future. Note: in March 2015 and continuously since September 2015, there has been growing concern with the betrayal of pro-Novorossiyan forces. However, this concern is expressed in terms of the betrayal of Moscow, the Kremlin or Putin himself.

---

4   Here I list those web resources that provided groups with material for discussions at least once per month. By doing this I narrowed down the data sources to those that constantly influenced discussions as well as those that shed light on the changes in topics and attitudes of those participating in the discussions.

War	Not less than 940 times per month	Stable frequency	1. War between the people's republics (representing Novorossiya) and Ukraine. 2. Less used: War of Ukrainians against Russians in the "Novorossiyan oblasts." 3. Less used: Humanitarian catastrophe, individual tragedy. Note: Even though many discussants personally experienced war, they predominantly describe it in the terms of a collective experience.
Justice	Not less than 400 times per month	Used more frequently in 2014 (800) than in 2015 (400)	1. Predominantly used either in reference to the past (historical justice leading to the separation of Novorossiya from Ukraine), or the future (joining Russia or creating of some sort of independent republic). 2. Less often: as a characteristic of a future Novorossiyan organization. Note: With several rare exceptions, justice is discussed in collectivist, not individualist terms. It is up to groups to establish justice, not courts.
Enemy	Not less than 400 times per month	Stable frequency (with two peaks in August 2014 and February 2015, when use exceeded 1000 cases per month)	1. Enemies to the populations of the peoples' republics and/or Novorossiya. 2. Ukraine and the West planning to continue exercising control over Russophone populations in the Novorossiyan oblasts. Note: The "West" is constantly used as synonymous with enemy. However, "Europe" is sometimes used in a more neutral way.
Slavs/Slavic	Not less than 200 times per month	Stable frequency	1. A common racial denominator for Russians and Ukrainians, the grounds for some sort of political and "genetic" unity, used as a reason for the unification of a Russian-Ukrainian state and for destruction of the independent Ukrainian state. 2. A term for pan-Slavic unity extending beyond Russia and Novorossiya. An alternative to the West.
West/Europe/U.S.	Not less than 200 times per month	Stable frequency	1. Although these words are used synonymously, in particular the "West" and the "U.S." (as well as visual symbols associated with them, including the American and NATO flags) are seen as existential and historic enemies. 2. Europe has two contrasting meanings: enemy and possible friend. The values associated with Europe vary frequently in the discussions of the future for Novorossiya.

i   Information on the conference can be found at [https://meduza.io/en/feature/2015/09/16/a-congress-of-separatist-rascals] or [https://kauilapele.wordpress.com/2015/09/27/international-expert-conference-9-20-15-dialogue-of-nations-the-right-to-self-determination-part-2-of-3-conference-report/].
ii An articulate example of this type of thinking appeared in Zakhar Prilepin's blogs [http://novorossia.su/] in 2014–15.
iii Kasianov (2009: 11), for example, analyzes the Ukrainian national model in the following terms: "Nationalized history began to fulfill important instrumental functions: legitimize the newly established state and its attendant elite; establish territorial and chronological conceptions of the Ukrainian nation; and confirm the appropriateness of that nation's existence as a legal successor in the consciousness of its citizens and neighbors alike".
iv The official Ukrainian press, for instance, calls the supporters of separatist projects "mercenaries" and "brainwashed" people. See, for example, publications in the most popular Ukrainian media outlets: Censor.net [https://censor.net.ua/] and Ukrainska Pravda [http://pravda.com.ua].
v   This idea of utopian ideological thinking was proposed by Mannheim and Buber (Mannheim 1960: 175–6; Buber 1958: 16ff).
vi The most-cited of their books include: Skalkovskii (1836), Gavriil (1853, 1857), Shebalskii (1869), Bagalei (1889), Miller (1901).
vii Iavornytskyi is the Ukrainian transliteration whereas Evornitskyi refers to the author's book which was written in Russian.
viii In 1910, the most expansive description of Novorossiya was given: a land including governances of Bessarabia, Kherson, Tavria, Yekaterinoslav, Stavropol and the lands of Don Cossacks Regimen (Semenov 1910).
ix A popular name of a major hydroelectric station on the Dnieper River in Zaporizhzhya.
x   Namely 19th century historical books by Brikner, Soloviov, Bagalei, Iavornytskyi and many others.
xi An analysis of these processes can be found in Kasianov & Ther (2009).
xii The case of Abkhazia is especially interesting, as Abkhazia is neither "Slavic" nor a historically Novorossiyan land. Yet, the involvement of Abkhaz mercenaries in the Donbas War was supported by parts of the local population that saw the Novorossiya project as one that might change their own situation for the better.
xiii This number excludes the outright "web discussion bots", participants paid to disseminate special ideas or attitudes in the web-based discussions. I used the criteria outlined at [http://ain.ua/2014/01/23/509984] to identify bots.

Global Symbols and Local Meanings: The "Day of Victory" after Euromaidan

Yuliya Yurchuk

The main focus of this paper is on the transnational framework of remembering. It is analyzed how memory politics concerning the Second World War were transformed in Ukraine after the mass protests of winter 2013/2014 and during the period that followed. By analyzing new trends in memory politics and new features introduced to commemorate the "Day of Victory," it is scrutinized why and how these changes were introduced. The aim of the article is to understand what these new tendencies reveal about Ukrainian society today. What is meant when politicians in Ukraine speak about de-Sovietization? How is it realized and by whom? The main focus is on the transnational framework of remembering, which means, first and foremost, the transnationally established ways of remembering to which memory actors refer when they address historical issues. The paper tries to grasp the complex nexus between the national and transnational within the constellation of memories in a country that is in the midst of its most turbulent period since the Second World War. It is argued that the transnational framework of remembering is used as a resource both for justification of national memory politics and for claiming a re-orientation in geopolitics.

1. Introduction: The Transformation of Memory Politics in Ukraine

Leading Ukrainian writers have characterized Ukraine's development following the Euromaidan as the end of the post-Soviet era. Zabuzhko (2014) and Andrukhovych (2015), for instance, have written that Ukraine is no longer a post-Soviet state. Indeed, discussions about distancing Ukraine from Soviet legacies—generally referred to as "decommunization"—are central to the discussion about the Ukrainian past, present, and future. It should be mentioned, however, that decommunization campaigns are nothing new in Eastern Europe. Suffice it to say that Kaczynski's politics of memory in Poland rendered the Institute of National Memory a tool of domestic politics (Stola 2012). Decommunization politics also affected Hungary, Estonia, and Latvia, where museums of occupation were established to counterbalance the Western European remembrance of Nazi atrocities with the Eastern European memory of Stalinist repression (Kattago 2008; 2009). Decommunization in these countries was vehemently criticized by Russian officials, indicating that memory is an important issue in geopolitics. As Tatiana Zhurzhenko has argued, "no different from energy politics, memory politics is less about the communist past than about the future political and economic hegemony on the European continent—in other words, it is always the geopolitics of memory" (Zhurzhenko 2007).

After the Orange Revolution in 2004, the anti-communist position became a main characteristic of memory politics in Ukraine. As a result, in 2005, during Victor Iushchenko's presidency, the traditional military parade on 9 May was cancelled. This was the most visible change in approach to Victory Day in Ukraine since the country's independence, and it marked a shift from Soviet to European memory. The next shift, also under the agenda of decommunization in memory politics, came ten years later, after another revolutionary event—Euromaidan. This shift was larger in scope and had far more visible consequences.

This paper analyzes this most recent transformation of memory politics in Ukraine. My hypothesis is that by trying to eliminate Soviet legacies, memory actors in Ukraine are re-orienting themselves from one large master narrative (Soviet) toward another large master narrative, which is considered European or global. I argue that the transnational framework of remembering is used as a resource both for justification of national memory politics and for marking a re-orientation in geopolitics. I further claim that transformations of memory politics are framed through references to a transnational culture of memory where war is mainly remembered from the perspective of victims, thus condemning all war in general.[i]

This perspective emphasizes the reconciliatory purpose of memory politics. A re-orientation of memory is not unproblematic, as the military conflict in east Ukraine is contributing to the complexity of approaches to memory. In a country at war, the cherishing of pacifist reconciliatory ideals becomes difficult. Nevertheless, attempts are still made to shape transnational and reconciliatory memories of the Second World War. This article explores the ways in which this is done in practice. Here, I address transnationalism, which can be seen as a "mode of cultural reproduction" (Vertovec 2009: 7). I apply a symbolic approach to transnationalism that tackles the re-figuration of cultural codes and focuses on the dynamics of symbols and their meanings over time and space.

This study is empirically based on speeches of the Ukrainian President Petro Poroshenko and other officials, legislation in the files of memory politics, new symbols and practices introduced during 2014–2016 to commemorate the end of the Second World War, as well as videos produced by two different organizations (the government's Institute of National Remembrance and the non-governmental organization Information Resistance) to celebrate the 70th anniversary of the end of the war. This corpus of material sheds light not only on state-sponsored memory politics but also on civic initiatives. To address such diverse material, an interpretative approach drawing on studies of interpretative anthropology, as proposed by the American anthropologist Clifford Geertz (1971), has been applied. Following Geertz's methodological and theoretical considerations, the social world can be understood as a "web of meanings" which, through thorough reading of texts and videos, enables a presentation of a "thick description" (Geertz 1971: 5) of commemorative practices. Based on this thick description, it is then possible to distinguish the narrative patterns produced by memory actors that shed light not only on recent changes in memory politics but also on the current political and societal situation in Ukraine.

2. Geopolitical Orientation and Memory in post-Maidan Ukraine: New Symbols, New Meanings

Directly after Euromaidan, when Ianukovych fled Ukraine and Crimea was annexed by Russia, the interim government appointed a new director of the Institute of National Remembrance—Volodymyr Viatrovych. In the past, Viatrovych had been the director of the Center of Research on the Liberation Movement, an institution dedicated to the history of the OUN (Organization of Ukrainian Nationalists) and UPA (Ukrainian Insurgent Army).[ii] Under the presidency of Iushchenko, he was also director of the Institute of National Remembrance. Viatrovych's interest in and devotion to the history of the OUN and UPA influenced the ways in which memory politics were shaped. The Institute of National Memory became the main authority on producing, managing and directing commemorative practices at the national level. The memory of the Second World War became the focus of the new politics of memory.

One of the first and most important changes in the representation of the end of the war was the introduction of a new symbol of Victory day in 2014—the red poppy and the slogan "never again". According to Viatrovych, this new symbol of victory shows the ethnic (Ukrainian) dimension of victory and, at the same time, emphasizes the Ukrainian place in European memory culture (Viatrovych 2014). Indeed, the poppy is used symbolically in memory culture in several European countries, but it is questionable whether it can be claimed to have exclusive "European-ness". It was first used as a symbol by the American Legion to remember all those who fell in the First World War. It was inspired by the poem "In Flanders Fields," written by the Canadian physician Lieutenant-Colonel John Macrae in 1915. Later, the symbol was adopted in the United Kingdom, Australia, Canada and New Zealand. It is usually used in celebrations of Remembrance Day, 11 November (Winter 1995; 2006). Thus, the poppy is associated, first and foremost, with the First World War. In Poland, however, the poppy became a symbol of the Battle of Monte Cassino in 1944. The memory of this battle carried a strong anti-Soviet meaning in post-war Poland (Goldfarb 1992). Correspondingly, it seems that just like any symbol, the poppy carries different meanings depending on the contexts in which it is used. In Ukraine in 2014, when the poppy became a symbol of victory in the Second World War, it replaced the old Soviet symbol of Victory Day, another red flower—the carnation (see Picture 1). In a symbolic gesture, the Institute of National Remembrance tried to eliminate Soviet associations with Victory Day and to position Ukraine within European memory culture.

In 2015, in the context of the Ukrainian–Russian war, which had continued for more than a year and had cost the lives of more than five thousand people, the slogan "Never Again" was amended with the new phrase "We win". Thus, the complete slogan became *"We remember. We win."* In this way, emphasis was added to convey the patriotic and victorious feelings of a nation at war and to connect the present to the past with the following logic: "*if we won against the Nazis in the past, we will win the war now"*. The slogan further served to declare the new direction of memory, with an emphasis on reconciliation. Through the wording *"We remember. We win,"* two modes of remembrance were represented: remembrance of the Victory over Nazism (the tradition of commemoration traced from Soviet times) and remembrance of the sacrifice of those who had fallen in the war in east Ukraine.

Picture 1: Symbols of Victory Day and Victory over Nazism

On the left: Symbol used for Victory Day commemoration in 2014. "1939–1945 nikoly znovu" (never again). On the right: "We Remember. We win." This symbol was introduced in 2015 to celebrate the victory over Nazism. Source: Website of Institute of National Remembrance, [http://www.memory.gov.ua].

When Volodymyr Viatrovych commented on this, he emphasized that this new approach to memory would be implemented in order to reconcile all views of history and that this memory would be directed not to grandfathers but to grandsons, who hold different interpretations of the past (Viatrovych 2015). Memory was thus inscribed with some didactic functions: it was supposed to enlighten the younger generations and to provide them with a version of the past that would satisfy everyone. While claiming to reconcile all views of history, the new memory politics presupposed that there is only one version of history to which everyone should adhere.

Arguably, it is very difficult to produce one common interpretation of the history of a war in which one nation's people were fighting in different armies and sometimes on opposite sides. Therefore, some distinctive elements had to be identified that would make it possible to connect the diverse experiences of many people into one common memory framework. This "unifying" element was the narrative of *stateless victimhood,* which conveyed the story of Ukrainians who were fighting for others' interests. As Ukrainians had no country of their own, they were used by other states in pursuit of often-contradictory interests, as argued by Viatrovych.

When the Institute of National Remembrance implements such a "unifying" approach and simultaneously claims that it is thereby introducing a "European" memory, it conveniently ignores the fact that the very term "European" is arbitrary. It means only what the Institute wants it to mean. In fact, it is very difficult to say what European memory actually is. Many scholars have attempted to describe it; at best, perhaps, it can be tentatively outlined as encompassing the following historical episodes, as outlined by Claus Leggewie (2008): the Holocaust, crimes of Soviet communism, expulsions and large transfers of people, crimes against humanity at the edges of Europe (Armenian genocide), the European colonial past, immigration, and European unification after 1945. Of course, there is a remarkable asymmetry of memory between those countries that became part of the Soviet bloc and those that did not (Blacker, Etkind and Fedor 2013). In Western Europe, memory of the war is centered on the memory of the Holocaust as the "negative founding myth of Europe" (ibid.: 219).

In Ukraine, however, as in other Eastern European countries, the memory of communist repression occupies a central place in memory culture. This "competition of victimhood" makes it more difficult for Ukraine to inscribe its own memory into the western European framework of memory. However, officials from the Institute of National Remembrance did not enter into the discussion of what European memory is. Instead, they used the term in a way that served their own interests in the given context. Thus, during the years 2014–2015, "European" meant "non-Russian", and this term served as a powerful vehicle to create distance from Russia, with which Ukrainians shared their past but with which they did not want to share their future. As Viatrovych explained, this presentation distances Ukraine from the Russian mythology of "Great Victory," which is one of the main ideological constructs in the Russian world (Viatrovych 2015). It becomes clear that attempts to "Europeanize" memory are used with "nationalizing" intentions in the local context. As a result, a "glocalization"[iiii] of memory can be observed, wherein the pool of global (or in the present case, more western European) symbols becomes re-contextualized and appropriated locally for local purposes. Even if memory relates to one specific past event that was experienced globally, this memory has many different connotations in each specific locality.

Similarly, Daniel Levy and Natan Sznaider have written about the effects of globalization on collective memory, arguing that the Holocaust became a cosmopolitan memory that did not replace national memories but rather reconfigured them (Levy and Sznaider 2002). Arguably, transnational symbols applied to Ukrainian politics of memory might also one day reconfigure memory, as they bring up topics that are largely neglected in national memory, for instance, the role of witnesses or local collaborators during the Holocaust.

New Dates in the Calendar (1): Day of the Defender of the Motherland
In 2015, a new date for the celebration of the "Day of the Defender of the Motherland" (*Den' Zahysnyka Vitchyzny*) was introduced. In the Soviet Union, this day had been celebrated on 23 February since 1922. However, in 2015 it was shifted to 14 October, a date with a long history in the Orthodox Church as the Day of Intercession of the Theotokos (or the Protection of Our Most Holy Lady Theotokos/Pokrova). This day is also associated with the Cossack period, as the Cossacks considered the Holy Lady as their holy protectoress. In 1999, this day was established as the official day of Cossackdom in Ukraine (Verkhovna Rada of Ukraine 1999). Moreover, 14 October was also celebrated as the Day of the UPA. As Serhiy Hromenko, a historian from the Institute of National Remembrance, remarked, the new date for the celebration of the "Day of the Defender of the Motherland" was selected to distance Ukraine from Soviet legacies that "have nothing to do with Ukrainian history" (Hromenko 2015). In this way, the entire Soviet period of Ukrainian history is refuted and presented as something foreign.

Nevertheless, despite this declaration of distance from Soviet legacies, the content of the celebration of the Day of the Defender remained almost the same as in previous years (at least at the official level), with the celebration being reduced to a masculine equivalent of 8 March (Women's Day). Everyone is now supposed to congratulate men and to celebrate their masculinity and their exclusive role as the "defenders of the Motherland". According to Hromenko's explanation of the importance of the day, women are mentioned only as "mothers and wives of the defenders". He thereby marginalizes the experiences of hundreds of women who are currently directly involved in military actions in the east of the country while officials give their interviews (ibid.). Whereas gender can be used as a significant transnational and transcultural framework of reference (Bennett 2006; Scott 1999), it is neglected and used only in a stereotypical way. Thus, the quest for transnational principles of memory politics remains, to a large extent, at the declarative level only. In his speech about this date in the Ukrainian calendar, President Petro Poroshenko (2015) stated:

> You know that I have taken a decision to announce the Day of the Defender of Motherland is no longer 23 February. We have chosen the Day of Pokrova, 14 October, the old

> Cossack day.... I understand that because of a long-lived tradition the women will greet their men... It is up to each individual to decide what to do, but the day from now on is totally stripped of any political meaning. My wife and I have agreed that she will not greet me on 23 February, she will wait until 14 October. I hope that others will follow our example.

Remarkably, the President did not mention that the same 14 October is also celebrated as the day of the UPA. Perhaps, in his view, the Orthodox tradition is a safer foundation for this shift in the national calendar. He also criticized the "gendered" coloring of the celebration of the Soviet-styled Day of the Defender. At the same time, though, he mentioned the tradition of celebrating this day in his own family in the exact style of the Soviet celebration—a wife greeting her husband. While long-lived traditions appear to be difficult to erase, some changes have been made. In 2016, the Institute of National Remembrance launched the project "War does not make exceptions: Women's stories of WWII". This project was aimed at drawing attention to the problems of gender inequality in representations of war experiences.[iv] Thus, declarations of a movement towards a transnational framework of remembrance do have the potential to influence re-configuration of the national memory or at least arouse some new reflections within state memory politics.

New Days in the Calendar (2): Day of Memory and Reconciliation

In May 2015, the authorities decided to extend to two days the celebrations marking the end of the Second World War. Thus, 8 May was declared the *Day of Memory and Reconciliation,* and 9 May was declared the *Day of Victory over Nazism in the Second World War*. The Ukrainian historian Oleksandr Zinchenko (2015), then also a consultant to the Head of the Ukrainian Institute of National Remembrance, explained these new amendments to memory politics in the following way:

> Last year the Russian media, mostly from a propagandist point of view, started to broadcast information that in Ukraine 9 May will be cancelled. But we wanted to show that we not only commemorate this day but we also want to pay more attention to memory and reconciliation. The day of memory and reconciliation is needed for reconciliation between different versions of the past.

Again, memory politics are transformed as a response to Russia. In addition, the new date is explained through the reconciliatory narrative, indicating that reconciliation has become a buzz-word. On a meta level, reconciliation does link Ukrainian memory politics to a western European framework of remembrance, where reconciliation became the central trope in speaking about reconciling the memories of victims and perpetrators, emblematized by the global practice of establishing truth and reconciliation commissions as a path toward conflict resolution and post-conflict governance (Trouillot 2000).

3. The Transnational Claims of the "Laws on Decommunization"

The director of the Institute of National Remembrance, Volodymyr Viatrovych, claimed that the new approach to memory sought to include the memories of each and every Ukrainian (Viatrovych 2015). However, perhaps the biggest contradiction to his words were the new "laws on decommunization" adopted in May 2015. These laws aroused waves of criticism among scholars not only in Ukraine but also around the world.[v] The "Laws on decommunization" include four separate "laws" that are quite different in the historic themes, motivations and subjects they address. However, in Parliament they were presented as a whole, which made the discussion of their relevance very complicated. The laws include the following: The Law on the Commemoration of the Victory over Nazism in the Second World War 1939–1945 (Verkhovna Rada of Ukraine 2015a); The Law on Condemnation of the Communist and National-Socialist (Nazi) Totalitarian Regimes in Ukraine and Ban on Propaganda of their Symbols (2015b); The Law on the Status and Commemoration of the Memory of the Fighters for the Independence of Ukraine in the 20th century (2015c) and the Law on Granting Access to the Archive of the Repressive Institutions of the Communist Totalitarian Regime 1918–1991 (2015d). As seen from their titles alone, these laws refer to very different issues in the politics of memory.

What is common to these laws is that almost all of them refer to transnational entities, including the United Nations Organization and the European Union, for legitimization and justification. Thus, The Law on the Commemoration of the Victory (…) provides as one of its bases the UN Resolution No. A/RES/59/26 of 22 November 2004, which declares 8 and 9 May as days of memory and reconciliation. This declaration proposes that UN members use these days (or one of them) to commemorate the end of the war. The declaration is further mentioned in the "Explanatory Note" to the Project "Resolution on the Day of Memory and Reconciliation" drafted by the team of deputies of the Ukrainian Parliament. This document states that Ukraine's adherence to the UN General Assembly recommendation concerning 8 and 9 May "would be an important step towards European values and will contribute to the consolidation of the Ukrainian people" (Verkhovna Rada of Ukraine 2015).

This new geopolitical orientation is presented as a way of resolving possible conflicts in the country in the future. These laws are claimed to be able to secure the country's sovereignty and to rebuild historical justice for the crimes of the past. For instance, the Law on Access to the Archives states that it stems from the conviction that "to promote better understanding of recent history can help to avoid conflicts and hostility." Furthermore, it declares that it aims to "promote the establishment of dialogue in society...not to let the crimes of the totalitarian regimes happen... to promote the renewal of historical and social justice, eliminating the threat to the sovereignty, territorial integrity and national security of Ukraine" (ibid.). Correspondingly, through references to transnational entities, the proponents of these laws strengthen their national memory agenda.

While these laws are presented as cures for a society saturated with conflicts, in reality they can serve as strong catalysts for conflicts and tensions in society. The Ukrainian historian Vasyl' Rasevych (2015) has noted that the Law on Access to the Archives is more connected to the revanchist ambitions of the ruling authorities towards the previous regime than to the ambition to allow access to documents which, above all, are interesting to the relatives of repressed people and to professional historians. Indeed, the laws of decommunization represent a case in which the national memory agenda is justified through references to a transnational framework of remembrance. Furthermore, such references legitimize the power of the Institute of Remembrance, which became virtually the only organization responsible for memory politics in Ukraine after 2014. If there is some common European framework of memory, it is characterized by a high degree of self-reflectivity and a belief in the contingency of historical interpretations. What is accomplished by "Europeanization" in the Institute's style is the opposite of such reflexivity, as it is believed that only one version of history is possible. Moreover, the "laws of decommunization" seem to show that people at the Institute believe that it is up to the state to ensure that everyone shares the same view of the past.

4. Visual Representations of the Day of Victory over Nazism

In 2015, to mark the celebration of the 70th anniversary of the end of the Second World War, the Institute of National Remembrance produced a collection of short videos that were intended to educate people on the role of the Second World War in Ukrainian history and on the role of Ukrainians in this history. These videos were created by the Institute at the initiative of the government of Ukraine to show the "role and the place of Ukraine as a country that won in the Second World War (within the context of the project "Ukrainians among the United nations that won over the aggressor"; "*Ukraiinci v lavah Obiednanyh nacii peremohly agresora*").[vi]

In total, the collection included twelve videos lasting up to one minute each. Created by a well-known Ukrainian director, Oleh Sanin, these videos demonstrate the strategies and the content of memory used to produce the official memory politics aimed at the broader public.

First, in these videos Ukraine is placed within a wider European and global history. This inclusion is most vividly presented in the video that shows a field of poppies (see Picture 2). The flower starts to grow from the body of one individual, then more flowers gradually appear on the map of Ukraine, and then they appear on the map of the whole of Europe. This symbolizes that the death on the battlefield of a single individual is put into the broader context of not only of one country but of Europe as well. Besides, it suggests that the war in Ukraine today is also put into the broader European context.

Picture 2: "We remember! We win! Video 8–9 May 2015."

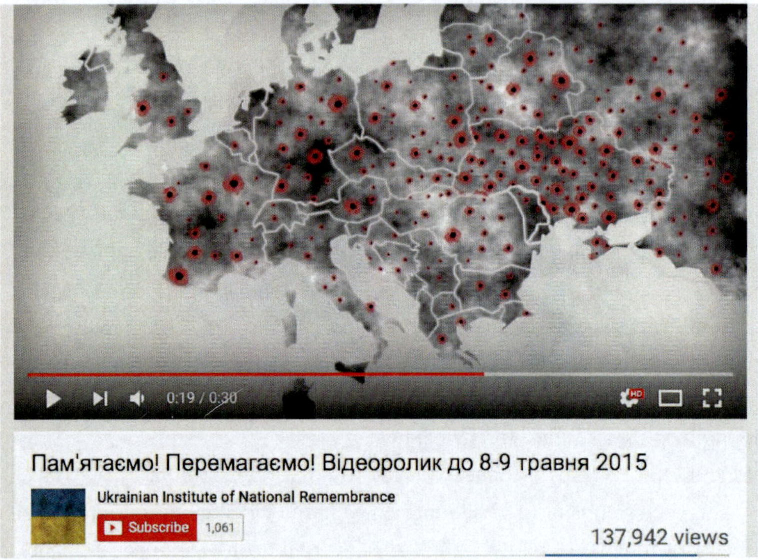

Source: Ukrainian Institute of National Remembrance (2015a).

In the videos, Ukraine is presented as one of the allied countries, together with the USA, France, and the United Kingdom. The US army is the one shown most frequently, while the Soviet Army is almost entirely absent or is only shown implicitly. In the graphical information, though, it is stated explicitly that up to six million Ukrainians fought for the Soviet Army (Ukrainian Institute of National Remembrance 2015b). To highlight Ukraine among the range of nations who won the war, it is emphasized that Ukraine was made a member of the UN in recognition of the Ukrainian sacrifice in the war (ibid. 2015c). As stressed in the video, "a 'united victory' (spil'na peremoha) would be impossible without unbreakable human dignity" (ibid.). The trope "united victory" is coined to emphasize the contribution of all allied forces to the victory. This was the first time that this phrase had been used to describe victory, indicating a shift from the Soviet description of "great victory" to "united victory". This shift is aimed at both creating distance from the Soviet past and inscribing Ukraine as belonging to the allied West, as if there was no Cold War period, and as if Ukraine was a sovereign state that could be an equal member of the Allied countries. The repetition of the importance of "human dignity" without citing any nationality serves to underscore the universal and transnational dimension of the victory.

Picture 3: "Together (we) stopped the aggressor. 7 million Ukrainians fought Nazism with the United nations"

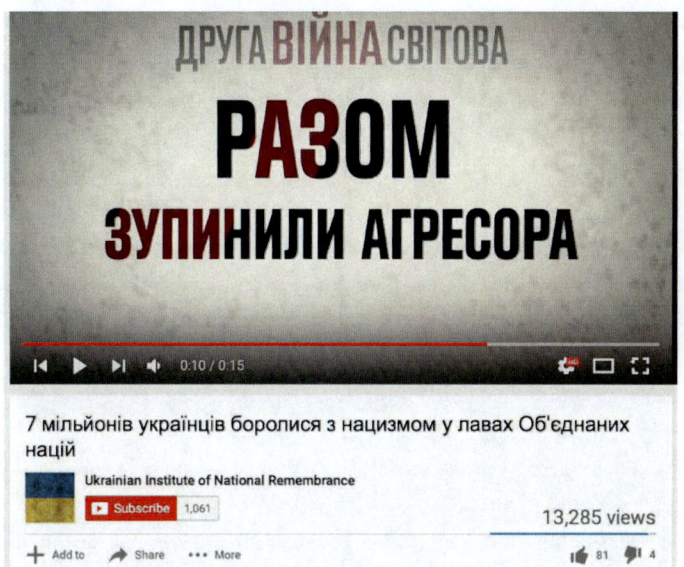

![Picture 3 - YouTube video screenshot showing "ДРУГА ВІЙНА СВІТОВА РАЗОМ ЗУПИНИЛИ АГРЕСОРА" with caption "7 мільйонів українців боролися з нацизмом у лавах Об'єднаних націй" by Ukrainian Institute of National Remembrance, 13,285 views]

Source: Ukrainian Institute of National Remembrance (2015d).

Volodymyr Viatrovych characterized this new approach to remembrance as "Ukrainian, not Soviet, in style" (Viatrovych 2015). He claimed that the main emphasis of such remembrance is not on the triumph but on the tragedy of the Ukrainian people, who had to fight for others' interests. However, this contradicts the way Ukraine is presented in the video, where the country is portrayed as an equal partner with the Allied forces (called "United Nations" in the videos). Yet, the narrative of stateless victimhood seems to be the only way in which the Institute can create a coherent history of Ukraine's role in the war. Viatrovych further mentioned the reconciliatory purpose of this approach to remembrance, saying that such memory politics must reconcile those who were fighting on different sides in the past. This line of reasoning is also repeated in other videos (ibid.). Thus, in videos and in the comments of the officials responsible for their production, the narratives of stateless victimhood and reconciliation are realized and reinforce each other. Decommunization, understood as distancing from the Soviet past, serves as the main driving force behind the creation of these narratives.

Remarkably, Volodymyr Viatrovych mentions that the memory of the war is a characteristic feature of people in the "DNR" and "LNR", whom he considers "bearers of the values and the historical myths propagated by Russia, whereas Russia tries to export these myths to Ukraine through propaganda" (ibid.). Similarly, Serhiy Lysenko, the head of the department of Second World War history of Ukraine at the National Academy of Science, says that 9 May was Soviet propaganda and, consequently, the new memory politics are an act of historical justice (Lysenko 2015). Thus, memory is again framed in response to Russian propaganda, and memory politics are conditioned by the conflict in the east.

Perhaps the most tangible representations of the continuity between the Second World War and the war in Donbas are the videos "Letters" featuring two letters from mothers to their sons (Ukrainian Institute of National Remembrance 2015e) fighting at the front and a letter from a son to his father (ibid. 2015f). While the letters are from the Second World War, the video images are from the war in present-day Ukraine (see Picture 4). Thus, the parallel "We remember. We win" is reflected in the videos very successfully. Undoubtedly, the most emotional video features 97-year-old Ivan Zaluzhnyi, a Soviet Army veteran from Zaporizhzhia, who speaks about the death of his grandson, Ivan Hutnyk-Zaluzhnyj, who was killed in the war in Donbas (18.12.1990–10.08.2014) (ibid. 2015g). Whereas the videos are aimed at refuting Soviet legacies, the past makes itself visible in the story of family members who are fighting and sacrificing their lives in a war on the same land but belonging to different states.

Picture 4: Letter to a father at the front

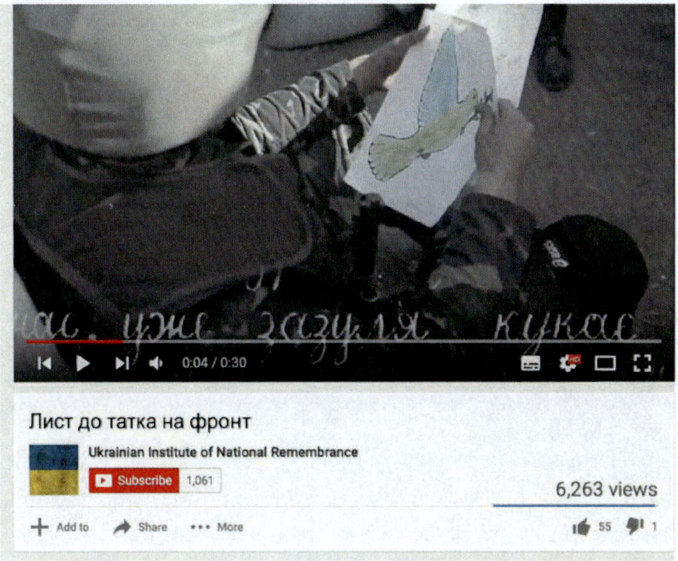

Source: Ukrainian Institute of National Remembrance (2015e).

5. Information Resistance: Saving the "Soviet" in "Post-Soviet"

In April 2015, the non-governmental organization Information Resistance produced two videos: "Ukraine. Day of Victory. Grandfather" and "Ukraine. Day of Victory. Grandmother" which are presented under the common theme "We remember. We are proud. We will win" dedicated to the 70th celebration of the end of the Second World War (Information Resistance 2015a, b). These videos were supported by the National Guard of Ukraine, the National Military History Museum, and sponsored by the company "Tabasco". The videos reflect on the connection between memories of the Second World War and the war in Donbas. They show two generations of grandsons and granddaughters and grandfathers and grandmothers. While the older generation includes veterans of the Red Army, the younger generations serve in the Ukrainian army and fight in the war in Donbas. The videos are the products of a truly transnational team, as they were directed by a talented film director from Israel, Eli Sverdlov. The roles of the members of the older generation are performed by Volodymyr Talashko and Nina Antonova, stars of Soviet cinema. The mere appearance of these legendary actors in the videos provides a strong emotional connection to Soviet films about the war. Notably, these videos are in Russian, which was discussed in the interviews with the producers of the videos.

Dmytro Tymchuk (2015), the coordinator of Information Resistance, and who is also a deputy of the Parliament, said that these videos "are aimed at stopping the wave of propaganda and speculations about the Day of Victory". Tymchuk claimed that people in Ukraine's south and east are neglected by the state. He and his team wanted to reach out to people in these regions so that they do not have to rely exclusively on information produced by Russian propaganda. He explained that these videos "are in Russian as they show the truth; they show people who are speaking Russian, who love Ukraine and have Ukrainian passports" (ibid.). Tymchuk noted that these videos are a direct response to Russian propaganda, arguing that Ukraine was losing the information war and that these videos attempt to counterbalance Russian myths of victory (ibid.). Aleksandr Smirnov (2015), the creative director of the company Tabasco, who financed the production, agreed that these videos are an "ideological response to Moscow, which is trying to monopolize the victory over the Third Reich... we dedicate these videos first of all to those in the east who continue to believe in the Russian world and in the ideologies it proposes".

The videos are presented as an addition to official memory politics, which Information Resistance believes neglect a considerable part of the Ukrainian population. Interestingly, to reach these populations, the producers of such additional, if not alternative, memories refer to the Soviet cultural repertoire to convey new meanings aimed at arousing patriotic feelings about Ukraine. As this study focuses only on the production and content of the videos, it is difficult to speculate about the videos' reception and impact. What can be stated, though, is the fact that both the videos made by the Institute and the videos made by Information Resistance refer to transnational memory—Soviet and European/global—to achieve their purposes at a local level. For the Institute of National Remembrance, the purpose is to create a new narrative of victory that situates Ukraine within European history and refutes its Soviet past. For Information Resistance, the Soviet symbols serve as the basis for conveying the idea that people who speak Russian and who respect Soviet veterans can also be Ukrainian patriots. This idea, in their opinion, can counteract the Russian propaganda.

6. Conclusion

Memory politics in Ukraine after Euromaidan carry a strong anti-Soviet agenda, which is generally known as decommunization. This agenda is realized, in practice, through the formation of a new commemorative narrative with references to larger transnational entities such as Europe and the United Nations. Attempts to Europeanize memory are undertaken in order to create a nationalized memory. As a result, memory becomes somewhat glocalized instead of globalized, as the pool of global (or in the present case more Western European) symbols becomes recontextualized and adapted locally. Thus, a transnational framework of remembering is used as a resource both for justification of national memory politics and for marking a re-orientation in geopolitics. Two main narratives are used to convey the new interpretation of history: a narrative of stateless victimhood and a narrative of reconciliation. They both contribute to the formation of a memory of transnational "united victory" instead of the Soviet style "great victory".

Creating some distance from the Soviet past creates a vacuum in memory culture and pushes memory actors to look for other, non-Soviet, alternatives. Nevertheless, as the forms change, the content very often remains the same, as it proves difficult to eradicate the past that one was once a part of. As demonstrated, while referring to a transnational framework of remembering, the official memory actors often work within the old Soviet tradition from which they strive to distance themselves. Partly, this happens because the new memory is formed as a response to Russian propaganda. To stop Russia from appropriating the memory of victory in the Second World War as its own victory, Ukrainian memory actors have to establish their own positions, even if it would be easier not to take any stance at all. Therefore, these actors must address Victory Day even if it is very difficult to use a symbol that resonates with the hearts of many Ukrainians even today, as many families lost relatives during the war.

Starting with the removal of the statue of Lenin in Kyiv in December 2013, decommunization became fashionable, as it symbolizes an abrupt break with Soviet legacies. However, the decommunization process has its pitfalls. A dramatic change in words and symbols does not bring about the same dramatic change in practices. Ukraine remains one of the most corrupt countries in the world, where reforms are very slow or almost non-existent. Perhaps it is too early to expect a dramatic change in practice, and the future will show to what extent a change in words and symbols will bring results.

7. Bibliography

Andrukhovych, Yurii. 2015. "Konflikt na Donbasi tse naspravdi viina kultur." *Pravda zhyttia*. 2 March 2015. Accessed 3 October 2016. http://life.pravda.com.ua/person/2015/03/2/190102/.

Bennett, Judith. 2006. *History Matters: Patriarchy and the Challenge of Feminism.* Manchester: Manchester University Press.

Berger, Peter and Samuel Huntington. 2003. *Many globalizations. Cultural Diversity in the Contemporary World.* Oxford: Oxford University Press.

Blacker, Uilleam, Alexander Etkind and Julie Fedor. 2013. *Memory and Theory in Eastern Europe. Palgrave Studies in Cultural and Intellectual History.* Hounmills: Palgrave Macmillan.

Geertz, Cliford. 1971. *The interpretation of cultures: selected essays.* New York: Basic Books.

Goldfarb, Jeffrey. 1992. *Beyond Glasnot: The Post-Totalitarian Mind.* Chicago: University of Chicago Press.

Hromenko, Serhii. 2015. "Ukraiinci – narod-viisko i Pokrova – nash den'." *Hromaske.tv*. Published online on 14 October 2015. https://www.youtube.com/watch?v=tbx-QE_zbtU.

Kattago, Siobhan. 2008. "Commemorating Liberation and Occupation: War Memorials along the Road to Narva." *Journal of Baltic Studies* 39 (4): 431–449.

Kattago, Siobhan. 2009. "Agreeing to Disagree on the Legacies of Recent History: Memory, Pluralism and Europe after 1989." *European Journal of Social Theory* 12 (3): 375–395.

Krytyka. 2015. "'Anti-Communist Law' in Ukraine." Accessed 16 June 2016. http://krytyka.com/en/taxonomy/term/5392.

Leggewie, Klaus. 2008. "A Tour of the Battleground: The seven circles of Pan-European Memory." *Social Research* 75 (1): 217–34.

Levy, Daniel and Natan Sznaider. 2002. "Memory Unbound: The Holocaust and the Formation of Cosmopolitan Memory." *European Journal of Social Theory* 5 (1): 87–106.

Lysenko, Sehii. 2015. "Vasha svoboda". 8 travnia. Den pamiati ta prymyrennia – nova data v ukraiinskomu kalendari." *Nasha Svoboda Programme.* Published online 26 March 2015. Radio Freedom. Accessed 3 October 2016. htps://www.youtube.com/watch?v=SMKinmdJD04.

Marples, David R. 2015. "To the President of Ukraine, Petro Oleksiiovich Poroshenko and the Chairman of the Parliament of Ukraine, Volodymyr Borysovych Groysman." *Current Politics in Ukraine* Blog, 20 April 2015. Accessed 16 June 2016 https://ukraineanalysis.wordpress.com/2015/04/20/to-the-president-of-ukraine-petro-oleksiiovich-poroshenko-and-the-chairman-of-the-parliament-of-ukraine-volodymyr-borysovych-groysman/.

Melamed, Vladimir. 2007. "Organized and Unsolicited Collaboration in the Holocaust." *East European Jewish Affairs,* 37 (2): 217–248.

Motyka, Grzegorz and Dariusz Libionka. 2002. *Antypolska Akcja OUN-UPA 1943–1944. Fakty i interpretacje.* Warszawa: Wyd. IPN.

Motyka, Grzegorz. 2011. *Od rzezi wołyńskiej do akcji Wisła.* Kraków: Wyd. Literackie.

Poroshenko, Petro. 2015. Video on the Facebook Page. Published on 21 February 2015. Accessed 3 October 2016. https://www.facebook.com/petroporoshenko/videos/581832311951165/.

Rudling, Per A. 2006. "Historical representations of the wartime accounts of the activities of the OUN-UPA (Organization of Ukrainian Nationalists-Ukrainian Insurgent Army)." *East European Jewish Affairs* 36 (2): 163–189.

Scott, Joan. 1999. *Gender and the Politics of History.* Columbia University Press.

Smirnov, Alexandr. 2015. "Social Advertisement to the Day of Victory at Ukrainian Crisis Media Center Center". Published online 27 April 2015. Accessed 16 June 2016 https://www.youtube.com/watch?v=ZtOeohBrLRw.

Stola, Dariusz. 2012. "Poland's Institute of National Remembrance: A Ministry of Memory?" In *The Convolutions of Historical Politics,* edited by Alexei Miller and Maria Lipman, 45–58. Budapest, New York: CEU Press.

Trouillot, Michel-Rolph. 2000. "Abortive Rituals: Historical Apologies in the Global Era." *Interventions: International Journal of Postcolonial Studies* 2 (2): 171–186.

Tymchuk, Dmytro. 2015. "Social Advertisement to the Day of Victory at Ukrainian Crisis Media Center Center". Published online 27 April 2015. Accessed 16 June 2016. https://www.youtube.com/watch?v=ZtOeohBrLRw.

Ukrainian Institute of National Remembrance, 2015b. "Ukraintsi u Druhii Svitovii viini". Accessed 2 February 2016. http://www.ww2.memory.gov.ua/infog rafika/.

Vertovec, Steven. 2009. *Transnationalism*. London, New York: Routledge.

Viatrovych, Volodymyr. 2014. "Symvoly yaki maiut znachennia: chervoni maky u den' Peremogy." *Uriadovyi Kuryer*, 8 May 2014. Accessed 20 October 2014. http://ukurier.gov.ua/uk/articles/volodimir-vyatrovich-simvoli-yaki-mayut-zna chennya/.

Viatrovych, Volodymyr. 2015. "Vasha svoboda". 8 travnia. Den pamiati ta prymyrennia – nova data v ukraiinskomu kalendari." *Nasha Svoboda Programme*. Published online 26 March 2015. Radio Freedom. Accessed 3 October 2016 https://www.youtube.com/watch?v=SMKinmdJD04.

Winter, Jay. 1995. *Sites of memory. Sites of Mourning: the Great War in European cultural history*. Cambridge: Cambridge University Press.

Winter, Jay. 2006. *Remembering war: The Great War between history and memory in the twentieth century*. New Haven: Yale University Press.

Winter, Jay. 2014. "Commemorating catastrophe: Remembering the Great War 100 years on." *Matériaux pour l'histoire de notre temps* 2014/1 (N° 113–114), 166–174.

Yurchuk, Yuliya. 2014. *Reordering of meaningful worlds: Memory of the Organization of Ukrainian Nationalists and the Ukrainian Insurgent Army in post-Soviet Ukraine*. Acta, Stockholm.

Zabuzhko, Oksana. 2014. "Dvadcat' tri goda my dushu otrashchivali." Colta, 12 March 2014. Accessed 20 June 2016. http://www.colta.ru/articles/literatu re/2396.

Zhurzhenko, Tatiana. 2007. "Geopolitics of memory." *Eurozine*. Accessed 20 June 2016. http://www.eurozine.com/articles/2007-05-10-zhurzhenko-en.html.

Zinchenko, Oleksandr. 2015. "Ukrainski istoryky: potribne prymyrennia adzhe viina ne maie ludskoho lytsia." Published on 7 May 2015. Accessed 20 June 2016. http://www.dw.de/українські-історики-потрібне-примирення-адже-ві йна-не-має-людського-обличчя/a-18435533-4.

Videos cited

Information Resistance. 2015a. "Ukraine. Day of Victory. Grandmother." Published online 27 April 2015. https://www.youtube.com/watch?v=c3EgHMT Dtng.

Information Resistance. 2015b. "Ukraine. Day of Victory. Grandfather." Published online 27 April 2015. https://www.youtube.com/watch?v=eQk6UupEJuA

Ukrainian Institute of National Remembrance. 2015a. "We remember! We win! Video 8–9 May 2015." Published online 27 April 2015. Accessed 3 January 2017. https://www.youtube.com/watch?v=9sI_NuUVSdA.

Ukrainian Institute of National Remembrance. 2015c. "Vichna slava heroiam. Ukraiina v Drihii svitivii viini." Published online 30 April 2015. https://www.youtube.com/watch?v=VAwNHCQhyAg&list=PLitKIb_cEyqfYyrKkiJuPF9M RJDwvQwmY.

Ukrainian Institute of National Remembrance. 2015d. "7 milioniv ukrajintsiv borolysia z nazysmom v lavah objednanyh nacii." Published online 30 April 2015. Accessed 3 January 2017. https://www.youtube.com/watch?v=FPBQQf LgHJM.

Ukrainian Institute of National Remembrance. 2015e. "Lyst do tatka na front." Published online 30 April 2015. Accessed 3 January 2017. https://www.yo utube.com/watch?v=lHfQyR1pm4I.

Ukrainian Institute of National Remembrance. 2015f. "Lyst. Synochku-voiin, bud' shchaslyvym..." Published online 30 April 2015. Accessed 12 June 2016. https://www.youtube.com/watch?v=MqAj9MZZhZM&list=PLitKIb_cEyqfYy rKkiJuPF9 MRJDwvQwmY&index=11.

Ukrainian Institute of National Remembrance. 2015g. "Vichna slava heroiiam. Veteran Ivan Zasluzhnyi vtratyv vnuka u viini na shodi Ukraiiny." Published online 30 April 2015. Accessed 12 June 2016. https://www.youtube.com/w atch?v=kRcsPW4lpx0&list=PLitKIb_cEyqfYyrKkiJuPF9MRJDwvQwmY&in dex=12.

Laws and legal documents cited

Verkhovna Rada of Ukraine. 1999. Decree on the annual celebration of the day of Ukrainian Cossacks on the day of Pokrova of 7 August 1999, № 966/99 (in Ukrainian). Accessed 12 June 2016. http://zakon1.rada.gov.ua/laws/show/966/99.

Verkhovna Rada of Ukraine. 2015. Explanatory note to the project of *"Resolution on the Day of Memory and Reconciliation."* Accessed 12 June 2016. http://w1.c1.rada.gov.ua/pls/zweb2/webproc34?id=&pf3511=50581&pf35401=297269.

Verkhovna Rada of Ukraine. 2015a. Law on the commemoration of the victory over Nazism in the Second World War 1939–1945 (in Ukrainian). Accessed 12 June 2016. http://zakon4.rada.gov.ua/laws/show/315-viii.

Verkhovna Rada of Ukraine. 2015b. Law on condemnation of the Communist and National-Socialist (Nazi) totalitarian regimes in Ukraine and ban on propaganda of their symbols (in Ukrainian). Accessed 12 June 2016. http://zakon4.rada.gov.ua/laws/show/317-viii.

Verkhovna Rada of Ukraine. 2015c. Law on the status and commemoration of the memory of the fighters for the independence of Ukraine in the 20th century (in Ukrainian). Accessed 12 June 2016. http://zakon2.rada.gov.ua/laws/show/314-viii.

Verkhovna Rada of Ukraine. 2015d. Law on granting access to the archive of the repressive institutions of Communist totalitarian regime (in Ukrainian). Accessed 12 June 2016. http://zakon2.rada.gov.ua/laws/show/316-viii.

---

i   On the shift from the memory of heroes to the memory of victims in Western European memory culture, see Winter (2014: 166–174).

ii The history of the OUN and UPA belongs to a difficult body of knowledge, which is knowledge of the past of a group that is difficult to position within the realm of glory, pride or victimhood, e.g. the space of positively laden affects (Yurchuk 2014: 41). The most difficult aspect of the history of the OUN and UPA is the relations of the OUN and UPA with "others" – Jews, Poles, and Germans (Melamed 2002; Motyka and Libionka 2002; Motyka 2011; Rudling 2006). To these difficult aspects we can add the ideology of the OUN and the persecution by the OUN of Ukrainians who did not share the OUN's ideas. Since the 1990s, the history of the OUN and UPA has been the main topic on the anti-communist agenda.

iii For "glocalization" as a form of local appropriation of a global (in practice often American) cultural product, see Berger and Huntington (2003).

iv For the description of this project see the website of the Ukrainian Institute of National Remembrance: [http://www.memory.gov.ua/news/viina-ne-robit-vinyatkiv-zhinochi-istori i-drugoi-svitovoi-informatsiini-materiali-dlya-zmi-do-v].

v The letter to the President of Ukraine, Petro Poroshenko, and to the Chairman of Ukraine's Verkhovna Rada, Volodymyr B. Hroysman, was signed by many scholars in Ukraine and abroad (Marples 2015). See also the discussion of the laws by the Ukrainian and international community of intellectuals in Krytyka (2015).

vi Ukraiinci proty natsyzmu. Instutute of National Remembrance, available at [http://www.memory.gov.ua/news/ukraintsi-proti-natsizmu-10-istorii-pro-spivvitchiznikiv-geroiv-7-armii].

Part III:
Practice-related Transnationalism

Coming to Terms with Odessa Ukraine: The Impact of the Maidan Uprising on the Ukrainian Diaspora

Alexander Clarkson

This article will examine how evolving narratives of national identity have fundamentally influenced the Ukrainian diaspora's interactions with political conflict in Ukraine. In describing the wider social context that helped form the political structures of Ukrainian communities in North America and Europe, the factors shaping the specific identity narratives of different sections of the diaspora will be explored. In the process, this article will set out how these established identity narratives helped determine how Ukrainian communities in Europe and North America interacted with the Maidan Revolution. By examining the statements and responses of key members of these transnational immigrant networks to the political debates surrounding the Maidan Revolution and the war with Russia that followed it, this article will go on to provide new perspectives on how these events have transformed the relationship between the global Ukrainian diaspora and Ukrainian society.

1. Introduction: From Halychyna Ukraine to Odessa Ukraine

For over a century Ukrainians facing economic deprivation and political instability have left their homeland to find work in distant countries. As successive waves of mass migration gained momentum, Ukrainian communities emerged in Europe, North America and even farther afield. From its very beginning, Ukrainian emigration to Europe and North America in the nineteenth century took place in parallel with the first attempts by Ukrainian intellectuals to construct a shared sense of nationhood. A Ukrainian nation-building project that hoped to unite divided territories through a shared linguistic and cultural heritage became intertwined with processes of transnational migration and community-building. This expanding Ukrainian diaspora played a key role in debates over Ukrainian identity as the boundaries of what constituted a possible territorial space for Ukrainian statehood remained contested.

This article will therefore explore the ways in which evolving narratives of national identity have shaped the Ukrainian diaspora's political relationship with developments in Ukraine itself. By setting out the particular social factors shaping the creation of Ukrainian communities in North America and Europe in the late nineteenth and early twentieth centuries, the emergence of particular identity narratives in various parts of the diaspora will be explored. The article will then go on to analyze how this historical context shaped the political responses of Ukrainian communities in Europe and North America towards the Orange and Maidan Revolutions. By examining the statements and responses of key representatives of diaspora communities to the political debates surrounding the Maidan protests and the conflicts in Ukraine that followed it, this analysis aims to provide new insights into how these events have significantly reshaped identity narratives within the global Ukrainian diaspora.

Of particular importance to this analysis is how until the build up to the Maidan Revolution, Ukrainians in Canada and the United States remained largely insulated from cultural shifts in Ukraine that led to the emergence of what could be called a Russophone Odessa Ukraine nationalism. Coming to the fore in the decade between the Orange and Maidan Revolutions, this form of civic nationalist identity in Odessa as well as less cosmopolitan cities such as Kharkiv or Mariupol now complements what Andrew Wilson once defined as Ukrainophone Halychyna Ukraine nationalism and linguistically mixed Dnieper Ukraine nationalism (Wilson 2002: 107–109). This article will contrast this particular North American Ukrainian response to national identity narratives with that of diaspora communities in the EU that had much greater regular contact to their regions of origin (Wallace 2002: 612–613). Yet, while Ukrainian communities in EU states were shaped more by frustration with highly corrupt state institutions in their homeland, they equally embraced forms of civic Ukrainian nationalism that used elements of what Serhii Plokhii has called the "Cossack Myth" to construct a national identity narrative in which linguistic factors play at most a secondary role (Plokhii 2012: 91–93).

As a transnational network linked by a shared country of origin, Ukrainian communities have created one of the most well-established global diasporas. As Saskia Sassen has pointed out, such communities in themselves develop transnational cultural and social spaces that can transmit ideas, literatures and cultural artefacts from countries of origin to countries of settlement and back again (Sassen 2002: 226). In exploring the Turkish diaspora, Ruth Mandel has shown how such transnational networks are more than just a bridge between societies. They can develop their own social infrastructure and ideological framework that combines aspects of the historical legacies of their country of origin with the socio-political context of their countries of settlement (Mandel 2008: 9). Based on theoretical models of transnational migration pioneered by scholars such as Thomas Faist, these approaches set out how diasporas can in themselves become distinct social actors that can help reshape the social framework of both their countries of settlement and countries of origin (Faist 2010: 30).

Such theoretical perspectives have influenced the research of historians and political scientists who have explored the evolution of the Ukrainian diaspora. Historians such as Lubomyr Luciuk have set out how diaspora communities, partially cut off as they were from their country of origin between 1945 and 1990, expanded cultural and religious institutions that had already existed from the first waves of Ukrainian migration in the late nineteenth century into a wider social and political infrastructure designed to protect and promote the interests of the Ukrainian community (Luciuk 1989: 14–46). Halyna Mokrushyna has described how the adversarial relationship between diaspora communities and the Soviet authorities governing Ukraine also accentuated a distance between both sides that forced diaspora institutions to largely rely on their own resources (Mokrushyna 2013: 808). Much of this historiography of the diaspora has pointed to the lack of an independent state. As a consequence, the development of Ukrainian diaspora communities was largely hostile to the political order that a Ukrainian Soviet Socialist Republic subordinated to Moscow represented.

With a long-established history and a high degree of institutionalization, organizations such as the Ukrainian Canadian Congress or the Ukrainian Free University in Munich have extensive archives that can provide historians with detailed outlines of the political evolution of diaspora communities. Since the early twentieth century activists from these diaspora organizations have commented extensively on the political development of their own communities in the press of their countries of origin as well as countries of settlement and generated a plethora of diaspora publications. More recently, social media and the Ukrainian press have also become spaces in which diaspora functionaries and activists have played a vocal role in trying to shape the development of their communities as well as Ukrainian society. By analyzing these sources while reflecting on their particular social context, it is possible to set out how key developments in twentieth century Ukrainian history have affected the evolution of political discourse and ideological belief systems within these diaspora communities in Europe and North America.

To understand the significant shifts in the national identity narratives of the global Ukrainian diaspora after Maidan, it is therefore essential to understand how the social structures of these communities have evolved since the first migrants and refugees from Ukraine arrived in Western Europe and North America.

2. Ukrainian Migration before 1945: Emerging Narratives of National Identity

Emigration from what is now modern Ukraine began with clusters of so-called Ruthenians from Halychyna and Bukovyna who settled in Austria and Germany. By 1900, it had gained such momentum that hundreds of thousands of self-identified Ukrainians were taking the long and perilous journey to Canada and the United States (Satzewich 2000: 283). During the subsequent twenty years, war and revolution displaced Ukrainians from the former Austrian-Hungarian lands as well as from a fragmenting Russian empire, with the reach of Ukrainian diaspora networks spreading to Brazil, Argentina and Australia. These transnational communities became increasingly politicized, as political exiles such as the followers of the neo-Cossack movement of Hetman Skoropads'kyi, the anarchist bands of Nestor Makhno or the revolutionary socialism of Symon Petliura set up rival political structures in diaspora communities to gain recruits for the political comeback in Ukraine they pined for (Grimsted 1998: 184–185).

The regular circulation of intellectuals and clergymen between diaspora communities and Ukrainian regions in the Austro-Hungarian and Russian empires gave them an active role in the formation of a distinct national identity narrative. As a consequence, political movements and church groups founded in the formative period of modern Ukrainian nationalism spread to diaspora communities very quickly after their formation in Ukraine itself. The speed with which youth organizations such as *Plast* or CYM (*Спілка Української Молоді/Ukrainian Youth Organization*) spread from Ukrainian territories to the diaspora in the interwar years was the culmination of the construction of a diaspora infrastructure that directly linked Ukrainian immigrants across North America with the social life of cities like Lviv or Chernivtsi. In a similar fashion, the ability of Ukrainian Orthodox and Ukrainian Greek Catholic churches to develop their own distinct infrastructure in the diaspora helped them to sustain their distinctiveness from rival Russian, Romanian or Polish religious institutions (Subtelny 2009: 561- 563).

As a consequence, church, social and entrepreneurial networks as well as social and political organizations became the founding structures of community life. Ukrainian political émigrés also came into contact with other key political movements in imperial capitals of the states ruling Ukrainian territories. They shared ideas with ideological movements as varied as Zionists, Kadets or Mensheviks in Moscow or Social Democrats and Christian Socialists in Vienna. This complex interaction between local social conditions in Ukrainian heartlands, the political environment in which diaspora communities were settling and ideological shifts in the capitals of the empires that ruled Ukraine was key to the development of crucial figures such as Mykhailo Hrushevs'kyi or Ivan Franko in the emergence of Ukrainian identity as a political project (Szporluk 2001: 75–76).

Such politicization of diaspora milieus was reinforced by particular patterns of migration experienced by Ukrainians from Halychyna and other parts of Ukraine controlled by Romania or Poland. In Canada in particular, the mass internment of citizens from Austro-Hungarian territories, including Ukrainians, helped to reinforce the importance of community organizations working to protect members of the diaspora from the state (Kordan & Farney 2005: 75–76). While most Ukrainians from these Western regions settled permanently in their new places of residence, a significant number engaged in circulatory migration to non-Soviet Ukraine until 1939. Individuals or even whole families would spend a few years in North America before returning to Halychyna or Bukovyna. In Europe, intellectuals and laborers would regularly move back and forth between German, Austrian or French cities and their home regions. As various radical Organization of Ukrainian Nationalist (OUN) factions rose to prominence in the 1920s, the ideas of influential figures aligned with the movement such as Stepan Bandera and Dmytro Dontsov began to spread to diaspora milieus (Kelebay 1980: 82–83). By 1939, the political life of the Ukrainian diaspora mirrored religious and political trends reshaping non-Soviet Ukraine. This dynamic helped to anchor a set of linguistic and ethnonationalist assumptions about Ukrainian identity that shape the stance of most diaspora organizations to this day.

3. Ukrainian Diasporas after 1945: Reshaping National Identity Narratives in Exile

The strong cultural cohesion of Ukrainian communities in North America meant that their institutions were in a position to integrate a large influx of refugees that fled Ukraine after the Second World War. The arrival of many supporters of the OUN and the Ukrainian Patriotic Army (UPA) who had fought Germans, Soviets and Poles in turn helped to reinforce a romanticized ethno-nationalist historical narrative in churches, Sunday schools and youth movements (Himka 2006: 21). Stepan Bandera's presence in Munich until his assassination in 1958 and Dmytro Dontsov's exile in Montreal until his death in 1973 meant that diaspora milieus came into direct contact with the dominant figures of interwar Ukrainian nationalist thought (Subtelny 2009: 561–563).

By the late 1950s, the growing role of émigrés shaped by Soviet rule, or responses to Soviet conquest in the case of Galicia and Bukovyna, led to an enthusiastic adoption of the wider anti-Communist consensus of Cold War North America and Western Europe. In Europe, the high proportion of political émigrés and former UPA fighters ensured that diaspora communities remained implacably opposed to even the slightest official contact with Soviet institutions (Clarkson 2013: 31–32). In Canada as well, Socialist and even Communist organizations that had once played a prominent role in community life were swiftly marginalized by arriving émigrés and Displaced Persons who tended to associate Left wing ideologies with the Soviet regime. Yet, the much greater proportion of pre-war immigrants and their descendants within North American diaspora milieus meant that there were pre-existing leaders within the community whose control of community organizations gave them the power to limit the influence of more radical nationalist elements among émigrés and Displaced Persons arriving after 1945 (Weinfeld/ Troper: 1990: 130). While diaspora organizations became increasingly powerful powerbrokers in US or Canadian urban politics, émigré leaders who dominated the ideological development of key organizations were often based in Europe. Due to the need to retain the loyalty of a diverse and less politicized community, diaspora networks in North America became enmeshed in local domestic politics. At times, this involvement drew the networks away from the focus on Ukraine demanded of them by émigré activists whose entire working life rested on resistance against the USSR.

The shifting attitudes of Soviet political institutions towards what was delicately called the "Ukrainian Question" also had an impact on the political dynamic of diaspora communities. A limited revival of cultural traditions in Ukrainian regions under First Secretary of the Communist Party of Ukraine Petro Shelest created new opportunities in the 1960s for Ukrainian-Canadians and Ukrainian-Americans to visit their country of origin. Thus, less politically active members of diaspora communities came into contact with the Soviet realities of Cold War Ukraine; a process that could alienate those brought up with a nationalist ideal of Ukrainian society as it fostered a sense of connection with a putative homeland (Tillett 1975: 753–754). Though this limited access survived Moscow's decision to purge Shelest and other members of his so-called National Communist faction and replace him with the more docile Volodymyr Shcherbyts'kyi, the barriers to regular interaction between Ukraine and its diaspora continued to foster significant cultural divergences between diasporas and their towns and regions of origin. By contrast, contacts with Soviet Ukraine remained more limited for émigré communities in Germany that contained many former OUN or UPA members. Strong community ties with West European conservative movements and security services reinforced deep hostility to any aspect of Soviet society right up until the collapse of the USSR.

4. Ukrainian Diasporas after 1991: Interaction and Disillusion

With such significant divergences in political outlook and social structure, the collapse of the Soviet Union affected the émigré-dominated diaspora in Germany and the socially much broader Ukrainian communities in North America in very different ways. Though both Canada and the United States saw renewed growth in immigrant numbers from Ukraine, this further expansion did not fundamentally reshape community institutions. In Germany, a numerically smaller community was overwhelmed by new immigrants that continued to circulate back and forth between Ukraine and the cities they had moved to in a way that would have been impossible before 1990 (Wallace 2002: 620–621). While North American diasporas only had a limited degree of contact with the cultural and political context of post-Soviet Ukraine, many of the tensions over language, identity and national myth that were a crucial feature of 1990s Ukrainian politics had a strong impact on the internal development of Ukrainian communities in the European Union (EU).

The manner in which community institutions interacted with a Ukrainian state struggling to establish itself reflected these internal shifts within Ukraine's diaspora. With a considerable range of political and corporate contacts and an extensive fundraising network, organizations such as the *Ukrainian Canadian Congress* or the *World Ukrainian Congress* provided funding for political and cultural initiatives that reflected the ideological outlook of their members. For a Ukrainian political elite strapped for cash, the influx of diaspora organizations offering assistance proved a tempting prospect (Satzewich 2003: 191). Yet, clashing economic worldviews coupled with conflicts over key cultural issues between diaspora groups and post-Soviet institutions in Ukraine meant that the role of the diaspora became enmeshed in wider domestic political conflicts of the 1990s and early 2000s. For nationalist groups with a particularly strong base in Western and Central Ukraine, support from diaspora organizations in North America provided access to financial aid that could help major education as well as cultural or political initiatives (ibid.: 195).

Yet, among political milieus still strongly influenced by the Soviet legacy the role of the diaspora was profoundly controversial. With Soviet propaganda against Ukrainians abroad still fresh in peoples' memories, those in Ukrainian politics who wanted to maintain stronger links with Russia painted diaspora organizations as foreign extremists working to force the Ukrainian language on largely Russophone regions. Even in largely Ukrainian-speaking regions more strident diaspora groups did themselves no favors in trying to influence debates over language and history curricula in schools in ways that local elites often felt did not reflect local concerns (Wilson 2002: 210). As a consequence, while willing to work with diaspora organizations in parts of the country, senior politicians during the Kuchma presidencies between 1994–2004 were very cautious about associating themselves too closely with the diaspora, in order to avoid alienating key voter groups less willing to challenge aspects of Soviet history and culture.

Diaspora groups that attempted to influence Ukraine's political and cultural development contained activists based both in Europe and North America. However, the financial strength of Canadian or American diasporic networks helped to ensure their dominance of such engagement in Ukraine. By contrast, the fact that the Ukrainian diaspora in Germany and other parts of the EU contained an equal if not greater number of new arrivals who had been shaped by the Soviet era meant that church and diaspora organizations had less widespread support in their efforts to influence the broader politics of a newly independent Ukraine. With the exception of a small network of ageing émigrés, mostly based around the Ukrainian Free University in Munich that had been a haven for political exiles since 1945, diaspora organizations engaged in fundraising for charitable efforts focused on apolitical causes such as helping victims of the Chernobyl disaster or providing aid to civil society projects in the towns and villages from which community members originated.

5. Diaspora Responses to the Orange and Maidan Revolutions: From Linguistic Nationalism to Civic Nationalism

These structural differences between Ukrainian communities in North America and Europe need to be kept in mind when approaching diaspora responses to the Orange and Maidan Revolutions. The Ukrainian diaspora in Canada and the United States was often either unaware or suspicious of the cultural shifts that led to the emergence of Russophone Odessa Ukraine nationalism as opposed to the national identity narratives Andrew Wilson conceptualized as Ukrainophone Halychyna Ukraine nationalism and linguistically mixed Dnieper Ukraine nationalism (Wilson 2002: 107–109). By contrast, diaspora communities in the EU that sustained regular contact with their regions of origin remained deeply frustrated with corrupt state institutions in a way that defined attitudes towards developments in their homeland (Wallace 2002: 612–613).

In the winter of 2004/05 these differing perspectives shaped attitudes towards the protests in Kyiv. In a crisis that escalated dangerously after Viktor Ianukovych's challenger Viktor Iushchenko nearly died from poisoning, North American diaspora groups swung behind a protest movement backed by key oligarchs, while many Ukrainian communities in Germany remained more ambivalent about events. Whereas diaspora networks in Europe remained largely focused on small scale projects in aid of local institutions such as schools and hospitals, the support lent by North American diaspora organizations to the ensuing Iushchenko presidency made their role a bone of contention for many voters ambivalent about his focus on language and culture issues rather than economic reform (Wilson 2006: 23–24). Such frustration helped to make the diaspora a convenient target for a resurgent oligarchic milieu backing Viktor Ianukovych. With Ianukovych's success in the 2010 presidential and 2012 parliamentary elections cementing his hold over the political system, North American diaspora initiatives were sidelined. Meanwhile, the low key civil society projects supported by groups in Germany came under growing pressure from regional allies of Ianukovych who considered any projects outside of their control as a threat to their position.

With such a complex pattern of engagement with developments in their country of origin, these differences in social structure and identity narratives between the diaspora in the EU and in North America led to distinct patterns of engagement with the politics of post-Maidan Ukraine. In contrast to a focus on the promotion of forms of historical memory connected to specific and nationalist traditions in the aftermath of the Orange Revolution, a collective reframing of identity narratives among diaspora communities as well as in Ukraine became increasingly apparent at key moments of escalation during the Maidan protests.[i] The adoption of the symbols of the Bandera OUN by both Ukrainophone and Russophone demonstrators who had not previously been associated with nationalist ideologies led to ambivalent responses among diaspora organizations and international support groups for the protest movement. Undoubtedly, the revival of aspects of Stepan Bandera and Dmytro Dontsov's radical ideology among nationalists and their adoption by many Russophone Ukrainians after Maidan was enthusiastically endorsed by certain diaspora milieus. Yet in 2014, key stakeholders within the social mainstream of diaspora communities such as the Ukrainian Canadian Congress were perfectly aware of how controversial a revival of OUN symbols would be within Ukraine as well as with EU partners (Freeland 2014).[ii]

Attempts by senior members of diaspora organizations to distance themselves and the Maidan demonstrations from the more toxic legacies of Second World War Ukrainian nationalism are reflected in comments by Paul Grod, the head of the Ukrainian Canadian Congress, in August 2014:

> He believes that the Ukrainian language issue, which has been dividing Ukrainians in Canada for a long time, should not serve as a barrier for Russian speakers to enter the community anymore. Grod stated that "We have to foster the Ukrainian language, we can't allow it to isolate others." This should help pull Russian- and English-speaking Ukrainians alike into the Ukrainian Canadian community...a message for Russian-speaking Ukrainian Canadians: "We welcome you with open arms" (Zariczniak 2014).

Once armed conflict gained momentum in the Donbas region, an exclusive focus on the Ukrainian language, another pillar of diaspora identity discourse, also became a problematic basis for mobilizing support to halt Russian infiltration. Contrary to deep suspicion over the loyalty of Russophone Ukrainians harbored by much of the diaspora in North America, many volunteer fighters and regular soldiers came from communities in which Russian was the predominant language (Gressel 2015). As a consequence, Ukrainian-Canadian and Ukrainian-American organizations, pledged to defend the dominance of the Ukrainian language, found themselves fundraising for nationalist volunteer battalions dominated by Russian-speakers. This dynamic was reinforced by a shaky interim Ukrainian government doing its best to shore up the support of Russian-speakers after self-inflicted propaganda disasters over the language issue. In this context, while the preservation of Ukrainian as a language of state was still seen as a crucial means of differentiation from neighboring societies, Russian-speakers were also recognized as fully Ukrainian if they adopted a set of shared symbols and cultural norms defining the relationship between the individual and the nation (Onuch & Sasse 2016: 27).

One remarkable sign of this shift within the North American diaspora is the increasingly inclusive rhetoric of diaspora organizations that see themselves as defenders of the purity of the Ukrainian language. While in the 1990s such groups as the Ukrainian National Association or CYM (which was particularly strong in North America) had actively condemned the use of Russian in Ukrainian public life, in the aftermath of Maidan the rhetoric of diaspora organizations was decidedly more inclusive. Rather than automatically condemning Russian speakers, these organizations offered Ukrainian language courses while remaining willing to accept that bad Ukrainian grammar was not automatically a sign of lack of patriotism. Prominent American political scientist and once noted backer of linguistic Ukrainianization Professor Alexander Motyl (2015) summarized this position in stating:

> Compared to regular army conscripts, the volunteers (who number just over 10,000 altogether) are far more motivated, idealistic, and willing to place their lives on the line. Many are close to or above middle age, have families and professions, and served in the Soviet army. The commander of the Donbas battalion, for instance, is an ethnic-Russian ex-businessman from Donetsk. Although all the volunteers would characterize themselves as Ukrainian patriots, many are ethnic Russians or Russian speakers. Although all the volunteers would characterize themselves as Ukrainian patriots, many are ethnic Russians or Russian speakers.

In a situation in which their country of origin faced a mortal threat, North American diaspora activists therefore found themselves advocating language policies that starkly contradicted the agenda they held a few years before. Such a dramatic shift could often be disorienting for many within the diaspora in North America, leading newly engaged diaspora activists to focus on other issues in mobilizing support. As Ed Skibicki, a key figure in organizing pro-Maidan social media campaigns in the diaspora, pointed out:

> I believe that the story of Ukraine is a righteous one and needs to be told to the entire world, not just to our people. So far I think my theory is being proved correct, although we have just begun to scratch the surface of the group's potential. For example, there are approximately a million people each in both Canada and the USA with Ukrainian heritage. This does not even take into account Ukrainian diaspora in the rest of the world. We have had members join from almost every nation you can imagine so I have been pleased with that (Dunnett 2014).

While Ukrainian communities in Europe had already struggled with the integration of Russian-speakers since the early 1990s, the notion of Russian-speakers willing to fight and die for Ukraine represented a fundamental challenge to ethno-nationalist assumptions underpinning diaspora identity in North America. With a profound threat to Ukrainian independence forcing swift action by civil society to compensate for state paralysis, diaspora organizations aiding mobilization had little space to oppose an emphasis within Ukraine on the civic components of Ukrainian national identity (Minakov & Kolodiy 2015: 205–206). As a consequence, diaspora networks acquiesced to the priorities of Ukrainian military, political and civil society leaders rather than trying to actively reshape the debate to reflect their own priorities. The depth of the crisis of 2014 and the way in which Russian-speakers became a key component of a rapidly expanding Ukrainian security sector forced diaspora activists to accept a redefinition of Ukrainian identity that until 2014 had been resisted in North America and evaded in Europe.

6. Ukrainian Diasporas after Maidan: Unity, Identity and the Cossack Myth

Despite this shift towards a stronger civic basis for Ukrainian national identity, there were several key cultural factors that helped diaspora communities to retain a sense of cultural continuity that integrated Maidan, the struggles for Odessa and Kharkiv as well as the Donbas War into a familiar historical narrative. In searching for explanations why civil society, business milieus and established political factions had been willing to engage in tenacious acts of protest, many diaspora activists emphasized a long standing national foundation myth that located the basis of modern Ukrainian nationhood in the sixteenth century Cossack polities that had once fiercely defied external authority.

This emphasis on a Cossack myth familiar to anyone with experience of diaspora church and educational structures helped to link a brutal and confusing war with a recognizable narrative of betrayal, survival and liberation. By providing shared symbols that linked diverse milieus in Ukraine with European and North American diaspora communities, the Cossack myth provided a means through which more problematic aspects of Ukrainian identity discourse could be put aside. Building on a tradition going back to Hrushevs'kyi's initial historical works of the late nineteenth century, deeply problematic aspects of early modern Cossack history such as Hetman Khmel'nyts'kyi's pact with the tsars of Muscovy or anti-Jewish pogroms were glossed over (Plokhii 2012: 91–93). Instead, it was the image of a Cossack republic made up of self-organized bands who decided over the fate of their Hetman that helped diverse milieus in Ukraine and the wider diaspora to build a shared identity narrative during the Maidan uprising and the military campaigns that followed. As the crisis following Russian intervention escalated, this shared Cossack myth was also appropriated by volunteer battalions attempting to bind an often diverse range of recruits into an emerging post-Maidan military ethos (Bolotnikova 2014).

The potency of the Cossack myth in shaping diaspora perceptions can be seen in social media and community commentary that accompanied the rapidly shifting events unfolding in Ukraine in the winter and spring of 2014. From *Plast* scouts collecting money for Ukrainian soldiers to diaspora functionaries visiting the Maidan protest camp, events were regularly described through Cossack symbols and analogies. Allusions to Cossack resistance suffused the commentary of diaspora activists on events in Ukraine in reports such as this post on the visit of a Ukrainian Canadian Congress delegation to Mariupol in May 2015:

> The journey was long as we drove deep into the ATO (Anti-Terrorist Operation) zone to this famous city situated in southeastern Ukraine on the Sea of Azov, founded on the site of a former Cossack encampment named Kalmius and known throughout the years for its industrial might. Today, Mariupol has become a symbol of Ukrainian resistance against Russian aggression...its people defiantly declaring their unity within Ukraine and building trenches to protect their families and beloved city while Ukrainian forces liberated the city from terrorists last May, halted numerous offensives and continue heroically defending Mariupol to this day (Kaszarny 2015).

When witnessing the mass protests first hand or through social media, diaspora activists recognized the allusions to the Cossack myth that permeated Maidan from its very beginnings. It was this shared imagery of the Cossack warrior defending his or her freedom from a tyrannical ruler that enabled diaspora communities to reconcile their own traditionally ethno-nationalist narrative of Ukrainian identity with the social heterogeneity of early twenty first century Ukraine. Key moments such as clashes between Maidan protesters and Berkut police units for control of Hrushevs'kyi Street or the final street battles of late February 2014 were interpreted with familiar frames of reference. The latter were based on the Cossack myth and enabled diaspora observers and supporters to revise their assumptions about Ukrainian society while still retaining a sense of cultural continuity. The appearance of protesters in Cossack dress, the ritual warning drumming on Hrushevs'kyi Street, the creation of relatively disciplined paramilitary units within Maidan self-defense that consciously modelled their structure of military organization on the Cossack bands—all these factors were key to enabling this enormous conceptual leap from one model of identity to another in a very compressed period of time (e.g. Sviatnenko 2013).[iii]

This use of the Cossack narrative to reinforce shared narratives of identity despite linguistic and religious diversity gained redoubled importance in the military mobilization efforts that followed the fall of Ianukovych. With the Ukrainian Army in a near terminal crisis in April and May 2014, the use of Cossack titles, symbols and language provided a unifying element that could anchor a chaotic war effort with a familiar warrior ethos. This shared symbolic resource became a key feature of volunteer battalions, in terms of dress, rhetoric and symbols to the extent of even shaping responses to combat on the battlefield. Despite the often underrated ideological differences between various nationalist battalions as well as within the Ukrainian military and intelligence services, the language of the Cossack myth helped to instill a particular warrior codex that could be presented as uniquely Ukrainian.[iv]

The re-enactments by military personnel of the legendary nineteenth century painting *Reply of the Zaporozhian Cossacks to Sultan Mehmed IV* by Ilya Repin became a common theme during the height of the battles for the control of Donbas. Reframed to mock the current President of Russia instead of a historically distant Turkish Sultan, pictures of Ukrainian soldiers playing out the poses of Repin's masterpiece went viral throughout 2014 across Ukrainian and diaspora social media

(Babylon'13 2014). From the perspective of transnational diaspora networks not particularly familiar with the specific ideological concerns shaping volunteer battalions or the neo-Soviet traditions of regular military units, the Cossack myth provided a point of identifiable connection with the war effort.

7. The Diaspora and the Post-Maidan Ukrainian State: Cossack Dreams, Post-Revolutionary Realities

While the Cossack myth was a crucial symbolic resource that strengthened the commitment of Ukrainian diaspora communities to the Maidan uprising and the subsequent war effort, it was the survival of the modern Ukrainian state that proved crucial in shaping the form this engagement took. The movements that came together on the Maidan were driven by a profound distrust of state institutions that were seen as corrupt and oppressive. Both popular defiance of police intimidation and the seizure of administrative buildings after the Verkhovna Rada (Ukrainian parliament) enacted the so-called Dictatorship Laws of 16 January 2014 represented the culmination of deep popular resentment over the extent to which the state was failing its citizens at home and abroad (Maksym 2014).

Many members of Ukrainian communities in North America who worked or lived in Ukraine since independence shared this sense of profound disillusionment as the realities of an oligarch-dominated society clashed with the myths of their own identity narrative. For large swathes of the Canadian and American diaspora Kuchma's equivocation about the role of the Russian language and Ianukovych's comeback in 2010 were taken as profoundly frustrating signs that the state was dominated by Russified elites unwilling to protect Ukrainian culture. By contrast, for Ukrainian communities in EU member states the disillusion was often more the result of regular contact with corrupt state institutions that obstructed business projects, property purchases and other forms of engagement with day to day life in Ukraine (Wallace 2002: 620–621). In this context, the Maidan movement's demand for state reform resonated strongly with diaspora communities disappointed in the fact that the post-Soviet state had not built the Cossack utopia that nationalists had yearned for when dreaming of an independent Ukraine.

Despite such profound disappointments, diaspora organizations engaged with civil society initiatives focused on reform of existing state institutions instead of a utopian vision of dismantling them and starting anew. Though more radical milieus within diaspora communities actively supported nationalist groups such as the Svoboda Party or the Pravyi Sector, the main community organizations in Canada, the United States and Germany worked with non-governmental organizations and state institutions that had a reformist rather than a revolutionary emphasis. Similarly, in the rush to rebuild Ukraine's security infrastructure after March 2014, diaspora communities provided far more aid to volunteer regiments that cooperated with the state such as Donbas, Dnipro-1 and even the radical nationalist Azov rather than units such as Pravyi Sektor or Sich (MacKinnon 2015). As was the case within Ukrainian society itself, diaspora organizations preferred partners willing to restore political stability rather than those groups that openly threatened to use violence against institutions that did not fulfil their demands.

Having become part of the domestic political establishment in their countries of settlement, the main diaspora organizations in North America were reluctant to challenge those established political and military elites that demonstrated their loyalty to the Ukrainian state. Though younger activists based in Germany or Canada built strong connections to reformers or radical nationalists through social media and then directly during the Maidan protests, functionaries in the largest diaspora organizations had cooperated with friendly factions within Ukrainian state institutions since the late 1980s. The fact that such senior political leaders and civil servants that shared a patriotic Ukrainian cultural agenda with compatriots in Germany or Canada could still be profoundly corrupt was often seen as a nuisance to be overcome through dialogue by high-ranking diaspora functionaries. This emphasis on co-operation with established elites in the hope of reform rather than confrontation to bring about a socio-political rupture was summed up in this exchange between the head of the Ukrainian World Congress Eugene Czolij and President Poroshenko in June 2014:

> "Attitude towards Ukrainians abroad will make them feel that the state considers them as partners in achieving common goals and needs their attention. Today, we count on a fruitful and constructive cooperation," Petro Poroshenko claimed. In his turn, Eugene Czolij noted that the Ukrainian World Congress is also willing to have a fruitful cooperation with current authorities. "We are coming to you with a question—how can the Ukrainian World Congress and the Ukrainian expat community help Ukraine in these times," he said. The Head of State highly evaluated the support from the Ukrainian community for the native state in trying times. "In the past few months, we have felt the support of foreign Ukrainians. Euromaidan has united not only Ukraine, but also Ukrainians all over the world," he noted...He also stressed the importance of accelerating measures aimed at the struggle against corruption. "But the main thing now is peace and preservation of territori-

al integrity of the state," Petro Poroshenko claimed (Ministry of Foreign Affairs of Ukraine 2014).

Indications of how the diaspora could have responded, had Maidan protests or Russian military operations led to a complete collapse of the Ukrainian state, can be seen in the traumatic experience of other immigrant milieus. From Turkish guest workers in 1980s Germany to transnational networks from societies in the Arab world over the last two decades, a crisis resulting in a collapse of trust in the state has often had a radicalizing effect on diaspora communities (Østergaard-Nielsen 2003: 78–82). Such knock-on effects of destabilization in a country of origin have often drawn immigrant communities to the side of political movements whose actions accelerated a conflict spiral. Other diasporas faced with armed conflict in their countries of origin have often become a major source of funding and personnel for movements that operated outside state control (Realuyo 2014: 120–123). With considerable levels of population circulation between EU member states and Ukraine as well as a rose-tinted view of the ethno-nationalist legacy of Stepan Bandera in North America, in the hyper-charged atmosphere of 2014 the risks were high of a similar radicalizing effect on diaspora milieus feeding back into events in Ukraine.

While the Maidan protests were driven by mass defiance of state authority, the speed of President Ianukovych's fall ensured that hostility within diaspora communities towards Ukrainian state institutions dissipated quickly. Though such diaspora support efforts were initially linked to civil society and volunteer paramilitaries resisting Russian aggression, these groups gradually connected mobilization calls with a wider effort to restore state power in a framework based on the rule of law. This shift was also reflected in a level of engagement with state institutions in countries of settlement not seen since the Cold War. Particularly, as diaspora organizations in the EU and North America worked hard to lobby their governments to provide high-tech weaponry and financial support to a Ukrainian state struggling for survival. For many diaspora activists and organizations, support for an uprising against the misuse of state power swiftly shifted to support for a national mobilization effort to save Ukrainian statehood.

8. Conclusion: Shared Myths, New Narratives

The past two years have not just seen remarkable turmoil in Ukraine; they have also fostered a shift in attitudes among large parts of the Ukrainian diaspora that would have been considered unimaginable for previous generations. Even a decade ago, many diaspora organizations in North America pushed Ukrainian governments to adopt a more clearly defined ethno-nationalist agenda and looked at what they considered to be the neo-Soviet tendencies of the Ukrainian state with great skepticism. For Ukrainian communities in the EU, disillusion with the deep-seated corruption that had created the conditions necessitating emigration also fostered skepticism over national identity debates that dominated Ukrainian politics and state institutions impervious to change.

The Maidan protests helped to accelerate a cultural and political process of reassessment among diaspora communities in both the EU and North America. The intensity with which supporters of civic models of Ukrainian identity as well as nationalist groups for which language debates only played a secondary role helped drive the Maidan protests forward had a profound impact on identity discourses within diaspora milieus. Intellectual debates within Ukraine are coming to reshape diaspora attitudes as well, fostering acceptance that a Russophone Odessa Ukraine could be as loyal and worth defending as more established forms of Dnieper Ukraine or Halychyna Ukraine identity that Andrew Wilson considered to be the cultural foundations of Ukrainian statehood in the 1990s (Wilson 2002: 107–109). The manner in which a diaspora mobilization effort became linked with the defense of Ukrainian statehood also revived a focus on institutional engagement and reform that had largely gone into abeyance after profound disappointment set in over the stagnation of the 1990s and the failures of the Orange Revolution.

Crucially, by reaching back to the Cossack myth to build a shared framework for debate and defiance, the movements on the Maidan and the military units struggling to defend Ukraine against Russian aggression used a symbolic resource that was immediately recognizable to diaspora communities less familiar with the nuances of contemporary Ukrainian society. By building their Cossack fortress, Maidan protesters not only used a shared ideological language that could mobilize resistance within Ukraine, they created a dynamic that is transforming identity discourses across the diaspora in ways that will continue to resonate over the coming decades.

9. Bibliography

Babylon'13. 2014. "Letter to the Tsar." 29 August 2014. Accessed 14 May 2016. https://www.youtube.com/watch?v=bVm-yFrmoAo.

Bolotnikova, Svetlana. 2014. "Cossack against Cossack." *OpenDemocracy*, 30 July 2014. Accessed 22 April 2016. https://www.opendemocracy.net/od-russia/svetlana-bolotnikova/cossack-against-cossack.

Clarkson, Alexander. 2013. *Fragmented Fatherland: Immigration and Cold War Conflict in the Federal Republic of Germany*. Berghahn Books.

Dachverband der Ukrainer in Deutschland. 2011. Accessed 29 April 2016. http://www.dach-ukraine.de/de/.

Dunnett, Chris. 2014. "Foreign Supporters of Ukraine: Interview with Ukrainian Activist Abroad." *WNU*, 29 July 2014. Accessed 11 May 2016. http://news.ukraine-in.ua/en/culture/647364.

Faist, Thomas. 2010. "Diaspora and Transnationalism: What Kind of Dance Partners?" In *Diaspora and transnationalism: Concepts, theories and methods*, edited by Rainer Bauböck and Thomas Faist, 9–34. Amsterdam: Amsterdam University Press.

Freeland, Chrystia. 2014. "My Ukraine: A Personal Reflection on a Nation's Dream of Independence." *Brookings Institution*. Accessed 12 May 2016. http://aa61a0da3a709a1480b1-9c0895f07c3474f6636f95b6bf3db172.r70.cf1.rackcdn.com/content/research/essays/2015/myukraine.html

Gressel, Gustav. 2015. "The Ukraine-Russia War." *European Council on Foreign Relations*, 26 January 2015. Accessed 14 April 2016. http://www.ecfr.eu/article/commentary_the_ukraine_russia_war411.

Grimsted, Patricia K. 1998. "The Odyssey of the Petliura Library and the Records of the Ukrainian National Republic during World War II." *Harvard Ukrainian Studies* 22: 181–208.

Himka, John-Paul. 2006. "A Central European Diaspora under the Shadow of World War II: The Galician Ukrainians in North America." *Austrian History Yearbook* 37: 17–31.

Kelebay, Yarema G. 1980. "Three fragments of the Ukrainian Community in Montreal, 1899-1970: A Hartzian Approach." *Canadian Ethnic Studie/Etudes Ethniques au Canada* 12 (2): 74–87.

Kordan, Bohdan S. and James Farney. 2005. "The predicament of belonging: The status of enemy aliens in Canada, 1914." *Journal of Canadian Studies* 39 (1): 74–89.

Koszarny, Lenna. 2015. "A report by Chair of the UCC Advisory Council in Ukraine Lenna Koczanry on visit she and UCC National President Paul Grod made to the front lines near Mariupol in the Donbass." *Ukrainian Canadian Congress (Facebook Page)*, 1 May 2015. Accessed 14 April 2016. https://www.facebook.com/lenna.koszarny.9/posts/10204275452037479.

Luciuk, Lubomyr .1989. "Trouble All Around: Ukrainian Canadians and Their Encounter with the Ukrainian Refugees of Europe 1943–1951." *Canadian Ethnic Studies-Etudes Ethniques au Canada* 21 (3): 37–54.

MacKinnon, Mark. 2015. "Bypassing official channels, Canada's Ukrainian diaspora finances and fights a war against Russia." *The Globe and Mail*, 28 February 2015.

Maksym, Kateryna. 2014. "Euromaidan Newsletter #4." *Euromaidan Newsletter*, 13–20 January 2014.

Mandel, Ruth. 2008. *Cosmopolitan Anxieties: Turkish Challenges to Citizenship and Belonging in Germany.* Duke University Press.

Minakov, Mykhaylo and Ivan Kolodiy. 2015. "Ukrainian Sovereignty between Civic Activism and Oligarchic Renaissance." *Krytyka Magazine,* March 2015: 205–206.

Ministry of Foreign Affairs of Ukraine. 2014. "President of Ukraine Petro Poroshenko met President of the Ukrainian World Congress Eugene Czolij and President of the Ukrainian Canadian Congress Paul Grod." Press Release, 11 June 2014. Accessed 27 April 2016. http://mfa.gov.ua/en/news-feeds/foreign-offices-news/24099-prezident-ukrajini-zustrivsya-iz-prezidentom-svitovogo-kongresu-ukrajinciv-jevgenom-cholijem-ta-prezidentom-kongresu-ukrajinciv-kanadi-pavlom-grodom.

Mokrushyna, Halyna. 2013. "Is the classic diaspora transnational and hybrid? The case of the Ukrainian Canadian Congress." *Nations and Nationalism* 19 (4): 799–818.

Motyl, Alexander. 2015. "Ukraine Doesn't Have a Warlord Problem." *Foreign Policy*, 26 March 2015.

Onuch, Olga and Gwendolyn Sasse. 2016. "The Maidan in Movement: Diversity and the Cycles of Protest." *Europe-Asia Studies*: 1–32.

Østergaard-Nielsen, Eva. 2003. *Transnational Politics: The Case of Turks and Kurds in Germany.* London and New York: Routledge.

Pétiniaud, Louis. 2015. "The Cossacks and their legacy as National Symbols in post-Maidan Ukraine: The Renewal of a Shifting National Myth." Paper presented at the ASN World Convention, Columbia University, 23–25 April 2015.

Plokhii, Serhii. 2012. *The Cossack Myth: History and Nationhood in the Age of Empires*. Cambridge: Cambridge University Press.

Realuyo, Celina B. 2014. "The Terror-Crime Nexus: Hezbollah's Global Facilitators." *Prism: A Journal of the Center for Complex Operations* 5 (1): 116–131.

Sassen, Saskia. 2002. "Global cities and diasporic networks: Microsites in global civil society." *Global civil society* 2002: 217–40.

Satzewich, Vic. 2000. "Whiteness Limited: Racialization and the Social Construction of 'Peripheral Europeans'." *Histoire Sociale/Social History* 33 (66): 271–289.

Subtelny, Orest. 2009. *Ukraine: A History*. University of Toronto Press.

Sviatnenko, Sviatoslav. 2013. "Euromaidan as a descedent of Zaporizhian Sich." *beyondtheEU*, 9 December 2013. Accessed 12 April 2016. http://beyondthe.eu/euromaidan-as-a-descedent-of-zaporizhian-sich/.

Szporluk, Roman. 2001. "The Making of Modern Ukraine: The Western Dimension." *Harvard Ukrainian Studies* 25 (1/2): 57–90.

Tillett, Lowell. 1975. "Ukrainian Nationalism and the Fall of Shelest." *Slavic Review* 34 (4): 752–768.

Wallace, Claire. 2002. "Opening and Closing Borders: Migration and Mobility in East-Central Europe." *Journal of Ethnic and Migration Studies* 28 (4): 603–625.

Weinfeld, Morton and Harold Troper. 1990. "Jews and Ukrainians in Canada: A Comparative Study of Diaspora-Homeland Relations." *Jewish Political Studies Review*: 121–136.

Wilson, Andrew. 2002. *The Ukrainians: Unexpected Nation*. Yale Nota Bene.

Wilson, Andrew. 2006. "Ukraine's Orange Revolution, NGOs and the Role of the West." *Cambridge Review of International Affairs* 19 (1): 21–32.

Zariczniak, Larysa. 2014. "Paul Grod: Community Should Stay United." *New Pathway*, 28 August 2014.

---

i   A good example of this process is the evolving coverage of the Euromaidan protests on the Euromaidan Canada Committee's website. This fundraising committee for supporters of the Maidan protests in Canada barely mentions language issues. "Euromaidan Committee Canada", Accessed 10 May 2015, [http://euromaidancanada.ca/].

ii   Typical of such distancing from the legacy of Banderite nationalism are key passages in Chrystia Freeland (2014). Freeland is a prominent journalist with a Ukrainian diaspora background who went on to become a cabinet minister in the Trudeau government.

iii   Both diaspora and Maidan activists were already making these allusions at the very start of the Euromaidan protests. Sviatnenko (2013) is only one of many similar articles in December 2013.

iv   Covered well in a preliminary paper by Louis Pétiniaud (2015).

The Influence of Protest Movements on the Development of Diasporic Engagement: The Case of Euromaidan and its Impact for the Ukrainian Diaspora in Poland and Germany

Andriy Korniychuk, Magdalena Patalong and Richard Steinberg

The Euromaidan protest movement did not only lead to the mobilization of the Ukrainian society, but also of the Ukrainian diaspora. Since the protests, many Ukrainians living abroad are involved in a broad range of activities, both formally and informally. Based on the findings of eighty-eight semi-structured interviews conducted in Poland and Germany, the Institut für Europäische Politik (Berlin) and the Institute of Public Affairs (Warsaw) examined various forms of engagement of Ukrainians residing abroad, their self-organization, co-operation and motivation to act. Based on theoretical considerations on the term 'diaspora' and with a focus on its transnational character, this paper will present certain aspects of this research and compare similarities and differences of Ukrainian engagement in Poland and Germany. Similarities include both the role of Euromaidan in uniting a heterogeneous community and strengthening a common identity as well as the crucial role of religious institutions and social media for connecting the engaged. Differences, on the other hand, relate to the degree of institutionalization of engagement and the level of support by the Polish and German societies.

1. Introduction

Since the first Euromaidan protest events unfolded on Independence Square in Kyiv in November 2013, academic research has focused predominantly on the sociology of the protests with a nation-level approach (Kyiv International Institute of Sociology and Ilko Kucheriv Democratic Initiatives Foundation 2013, Onuch 2014, Tucker et al. 2014: 8–19). However, the organization and structure of the external support of the subsequent transformation process that was provided by the Ukrainian diaspora is an increasingly important dimension of Ukraine's development that has not yet been systematically investigated. Therefore, a transnational approach can be acknowledged as a promising strategy for further research.

It appears highly relevant to study the future of nation-building in Ukraine through the prism of transnationalism. In this regard, Euromaidan serves as an illustrative example of the mass mobilization of Ukrainian society that has transcended social cleavages and physical borders. From the perspective of diasporic studies, it is valuable to analyze to what extent the noticeable shift in social interactions due to the proliferation of modern technologies and globalization change the nature of human interactions across borders and existing cleavages. Finally, the potential of a virtual civil society to mitigate the negative effects of the decline of traditional social group engagement has already been part of scholars' attention (Kittilson & Dalton 2011). However, the analysis of the importance of its manifestation through the phenomenon of a digital diaspora has yet to be properly understood.

This paper addresses this research gap through a comparative case study of the Ukrainian diaspora's contribution to the political processes in Ukraine. This study has been conducted in Germany and Poland, two countries that have constituted preferable destinations for Ukrainian migrants prior to and post Euromaidan. The primary goals of the study were to portray the variety of civic engagement practices among Ukrainians in both countries, analyze their strategies of cooperation and elaborate on the barriers that different groups of engaged individuals encounter in their daily activities. Although researchers frequently analyze the Ukrainians who move abroad in terms of lost human capital, i.e., with respect to brain drain effects (Friesenhahn et al. 2013, Twigg 2014: 33), this paper chose another framework. The conducted research addressed the existing transnational ties, the instruments that facilitate the communication among Ukrainians and the role of diaspora in the democratic awakening of Ukrainian society. Thus, it is argued that the process of Ukrainian transformation can be understood in a more comprehensive manner through the proper analysis of its transnational characteristics.

2. Project Description

This research occurred within the framework of the project "Ukrainians in Poland and Germany—Civic and Political Engagement, Expectations, and Courses of Action" of the Institute of Public Affairs, Warsaw, and the Institut für Europäische Politik, Berlin. Accordingly, this study encompassed the following steps:

1. Mapping the fields, intensity and structure of the diaspora of Ukrainians' engagement and its potential contribution to the process of democratization in Ukraine;
2. Exploring how the Ukrainian diaspora was influenced by the developments in Ukraine since November 2013; and
3. Providing recommendations on how public and private actors at the EU level and in Poland, Germany and Ukraine can support Ukrainians' civic engagement in both countries to indirectly support the process of democratization in Ukraine.

Within this comparative case study, forty-four guided interviews were conducted in each country. These included interviews with persons who are "actively engaged"[i] and with "experts"[ii], although in particular cases, the respondents could be regarded as individuals who embrace both roles. Concerning the selection of samples, the goal was to reach a maximum of heterogeneity of interviewees to encompass the entire range of civic engagement in both countries. The first interview partners were selected on the basis of a desktop research of formal organizations and informal initiatives. A snowball sampling complemented this methodology, where the interviewees were asked for recommendations of additional interview partners. The interviews were conducted in waves to control for heterogeneity and to ensure the adequate regional representation of the studied initiatives/activities.

Considering the large amount of collected data[iii,] this paper presents selected aspects of the study and focuses on the similarities and differences of Ukrainian engagement in Poland and Germany. The complete results were published in Polish[iv] and in German[v] in both countries in May 2016.

3. Diaspora—a Blurry Term

The Ukrainian diaspora has played a considerable role in Euromaidan and in civil society thereafter. During Euromaidan and its aftermath, many new diasporic organizations, initiatives and projects emerged that supported Ukraine's struggle for democratization. Different actors of the Ukrainian diaspora have supported the stabilization of Ukraine not only monetarily through money transfers but also ideologically and politically. Digital media has deepened the constant international and transnational communication and exchange of views between activists in Ukraine and the Ukrainian diaspora (cf. Krasynska 2015: 177–198).

The use of the term diaspora has proliferated in the last thirty years, and it is a rather "blurry term", as can be observed in the interdisciplinary debate on the nature of a "diaspora" (e.g., Safran 1991, Cohen 1997, Brubaker 2005, Faist 2010). In addition, researchers with different scientific backgrounds have been emphasizing the important role of a "diaspora" for national democratic transformations (cf. Mayer 2005: 18). Originally, "diaspora", which derives from the Greek word for "dispersion", has been used to describe the spread of Jewish, Armenian and Greek people throughout the world. Starting in the late 1980s, the term was also used to characterize in some way dispersed people. The transnational turn in the early 1990s has brought a change of perspective that focuses on migrants not merely as victims or objects of integrational approaches but also as social agents. In a sense, this perspective can be regarded as an "empowerment of migrants" (Faist 2010: 11).

Although in the beginning, diaspora was mostly used as a term with a negative connotation, it became a source to describe collective identities that focused on the transnational aspects of forced and voluntary migration, as can be seen in Paul Gilroy's "The Black Atlantic" (Gilroy 1993). In the 1990s, Kchachig Tölölyan (1991) identified diasporas as "the exemplary communities of the transnational moment". Accordingly, diasporas are not simply explained by a model of linear migration from one country to another. Instead, the ties and networks that migrants develop towards their homeland and other people who live in dispersal are at the center of attention. Through modern technology that offers new possibilities of communication, members of diasporas build transnational connections to one another (Krasynska 2015, Vertovec 2004). In this context, as Faist indicates, the focus lies on transnational processes that open up new transnational spaces. Simultaneously, the category of nations remains important through "intense connections to national or local territories" (Faist 2010: 14) in diasporic activities. This connection leads to the assumption that diasporas form a new phenomenon between national and transnational categories.

The approach of focusing on processes instead of specific groups has since been used by different scholars. In his article "The 'diaspora' diaspora", Rogers Brubaker (2005: 4) argues that the problem of the "diasporization" of every somewhat dispersed population has led to a large amount of applications and definitions that make it almost impossible to use "diaspora" as an analytic category. Notwithstanding the broadened use of "diaspora", Brubaker identifies three elements that are widely accepted to be constitutive of diasporas (ibid.: 5–8).

The first criterion, which is the most widely accepted, focuses on the dispersion in space. This dispersion can be interpreted broadly including dispersion across or within national borders. The second criterion is the "orientation to a real or imagined homeland as an authoritative source of value, identity and loyalty" (ibid.: 5). This orientation often includes a mystification of the homeland. However, the criterion of homeland orientation has been de-emphasized by several scientists. The third criterion as stated by Brubaker is a certain type of boundary-maintenance. This criterion follows the argument that a distinctive solidarity forms a distinctive community (ibid.: 6). However, this argument has been contradicted by the emergence of a transnational perspective on diaspora that emphasizes boundary-erosion rather than boundary-maintenance.

In his paper, Rogers Brubaker identifies the problems of using these criteria to depict a diaspora as an entity. Understanding diaspora as an ethno-national entity by using these criteria enables the statistical measurement of the number of people who live in a diaspora in a defined area. Simultaneously, Brubaker makes it clear that "not all those who are claimed members of putative diasporas themselves adopt diasporic stance" (ibid.: 12). To counteract the problem of groupism, he proposes the following:

> to speak of diasporic stances, projects, claims, idioms, practices, and so on. We can then study empirically the degree and form of support for a diasporic project among members of its putative constituency [...]. And we can explore to what extent, and in what circumstances, those claimed as members of putative diasporas actively adopt or at least passively sympathize with the diasporic stance (ibid.: 13).

In this context, Brubaker argues for using diaspora as a category of practice. Related to the research project on the civic engagement of the Ukrainian diaspora in Germany and in Poland, this definition enables a broad concept of diaspora that includes all the people who engage in diasporic projects. This concept leads to the assumption that diaspora is constituted as an "imagined community" based on active social practices and communication (Anderson 1991). Nevertheless, this assumption does not necessarily mean that the people who are actively engaged define themselves as a diaspora or as part of a diaspora. Understanding a diaspora merely as a category of practice helps the researcher to describe the diversity and cleavages within the Ukrainian diaspora that actively engages in civil society. Focusing on stances rather than on a diaspora as an entity broadens the scientific approach.

4. Similarities of Ukrainian Engagement in Poland and Germany

The findings of the research have been divided into two blocks, namely, the similarities and the differences of civic activity in Poland and Germany. This section addresses the similarities that were identified, and the differences will be presented in the next chapter. The similarities include (1) the formation of cleavages in the diaspora and the role of Euromaidan in uniting a heterogeneous community and contributing to the strengthening of a common identity. Furthermore (2), in terms of interconnectedness, in both countries, religious institutions and social media played a crucial role in connecting civic engagement during Euromaidan and its aftermath.

Euromaidan as a Unifying Factor
During the research activity in Poland, four main realms of Ukrainian engagement were identified, specifically migrant organizations and initiatives, ethnic minorities (Union of Ukrainians in Poland), the church (predominantly Greek-Catholic) and the Ukrainian embassy, including consulates. In discussing the nature of Ukrainian activity in Poland, it is important to elaborate on the cleavages that were observed among Ukrainians before the first protests started in Poland and whether they persisted after the movement had ended. Arguably, the most noticeable cleavage that can be identified prior to Euromaidan, which still had an impact on civic activity after the protest movement had ended, is the division between the Ukrainian minority and migrants.

Before Euromaidan began, these differences were mostly a result of the objectives that both groups attempted to meet during their activities. Migrant-led initiatives primarily assisted with legal counselling and on-going support with residence in Poland (integration assistance). The Ukrainian minority (The Union of Ukrainians in Poland) predominantly addressed the preservation of the Ukrainian language and culture in Poland, while the embassy embraced the functions traditionally associated with such institutions. The role of the church as a mediator/coordinator of civic activity in Poland will be discussed in a separate chapter.

These differences in practice resulted in a lack of consent on which terms the inner-diasporic cooperation could be established. The representative of the Ukrainian minority summarized that *"For Ukrainian migrants, it was incomprehensible that despite having Polish citizenship, we [the minority, A.K] might feel Ukrainian."* Based on the answers of the respondents, one could argue that in Poland prior to Euromaidan, the Ukrainian minority and migrants from Ukraine, with minor exceptions, did not see great potential or possibilities for joint activities. Moreover, misunderstandings that pertain to the goals, which both groups attempted to meet in their activities, were a common occurrence.

Furthermore, the findings suggest that different factors impacted cleavage formation in the Ukrainian diaspora in Poland. These factors are age[vi] and the stability of residence in Poland[vii] to a larger extent and the level of education or type of employment in Poland (low skilled compared with high skilled jobs) to a smaller extent. The picture that emerged out of the conducted interviews in principle reflects the social stratification of the Ukrainians who reside in the country (i.e., minority, students, low-skilled migrants, highly skilled migrants) who, in the aggregate, constitute a heterogeneous group.

During the interviews, the respondents emphasized that the Euromaidan protest movement, despite the identified cleavages in the Ukrainian diaspora, could fully unite the divided community under common values.[viii] With reference to Putnam's (1993) research, our findings confirm that Euromaidan in Poland had an impact on the development of bonding and bridging social capital in the Ukrainian community. A young activist confirms this observation: *"I didn't know any of these people, we all met at the embassy [of Ukraine during anti-government demonstrations, A.K.]."*

The protest events contributed to a greater visibility[ix] of Ukrainians both internally (networking that led to the development of bonding and bridging social capital among the members of the diaspora) and externally (to the Polish society). Correspondingly, considering the respondents' answers, this visibility may help to address the existing cleavages. The visibility aspect showed a positive influence on protest activity, support for Ukraine (e.g., financial support, medical treatment, exchange programs for children) and the emergence of new Ukrainian initiatives in Poland (e.g., Foundation Euromaidan Warsaw, Ukrainian World and Ukrainian House in Warsaw). The research findings, however, suggest that after the high point of mobilization had passed, most of the cleavages persisted, which often created barriers for further successful cooperation among different groups of Ukrainians and the later institutionalization of civic activity (which predominantly relies on voluntary, non-formal activity). Despite the experiences of cooperation during Euromaidan, the lack of regular dialogue within the community was identified as a major impediment to the further success of the civic engagement of the Ukrainians in Poland. *"The biggest issue is the lack of dialogue. We need to talk to each other. That is the basic requirement."*

Similar to Poland, the interviews with actively engaged persons revealed the heterogeneity of the Ukrainian community in Germany. The community differs regarding socio-structural factors such as the level of education (intellectuals and students compared with workers), place of origin (Western Ukraine compared with Central and Eastern Ukraine) and religion (Ukrainian Orthodox, Greek Catholic, and Jewish) or forms of particular groups such as the wives of German spouses. However, unlike in Poland, these differences were hardly perceived as cleavages by the interviewees.

Furthermore, the research revealed that the Ukrainian community in Germany is divided into two distinct groups, namely, the "old diaspora" and the "diasporic community".[x] The old diaspora, on the one hand, encompasses the Ukrainians who have lived in Germany for several generations and are sometimes organized in large and significant communities such as in the south of the country. The diasporic community, on the other hand, includes a considerable number of Ukrainians that only migrated to Germany several years ago, e.g., for studying or working purposes. These Ukrainians do not regard themselves as part of the old diaspora, as the interviews made clear. Instead, they consider themselves as Ukrainians who live in Germany only temporarily or for an infinite time. As one activist from Berlin indicated, *"I'm a Ukrainian permanently living here, who will live eventually somewhere else or perhaps not, it doesn't matter, but I consider Berlin as my home and Ukraine as my home country."* Simultaneously, these Ukrainians acknowledge a stronger perception of their Ukrainian identity and an enhanced sense of belonging to a loose Ukrainian community in Germany—a profound change compared with the situation before November 2013. In fact, the interviewees described the significant impact that the Euromaidan protests and its aftermath had on their sense of belonging to the diaspora. *"Since the beginning of the demonstrations on Euromaidan, [I] became also part of the diaspora [...]."* This change can be explained by the increased linkage among Ukrainians, which contributed to the awareness that a Ukrainian community exists. In addition, consistent with the theoretical reflections in this paper, the intensified active engagement was a relevant factor and supported the assumption of a diaspora as an "imagined community" (Anderson 1991) that is constituted through active engagement.

The events since November 2013 not only strengthened the Ukrainian identity of active engagement and their sense of belonging but also further enabled the Ukrainian community to jointly express their support for Ukraine and organize common activities and initiatives, regardless of the differences among the socio-structural groups and the cleavage between the old diaspora and the diasporic community. Nevertheless, although the joint engagement during the Euromaidan protests weakened the perception and the role of the socio-structural differences, the cleavage between the old and new diaspora arguably has continued to exist in the long term. Some interviewees feel that this continuation is connected to the very traditional and religious way of life of the members of the old diaspora. *"For me [it is] a bit difficult to communicate with the people of the old diaspora. [...] [They are...] also very religious."* This observation identifies the generation gap between the old diaspora and the diasporic community, which occasionally makes cooperation and joint engagement difficult.

Interconnectedness: The Role of the Church and Social Media
During this research, religious institutions emerged as important actors that facilitate the process of civic engagement in Poland, and they are predominantly neutral platforms for the cooperation and networking among individuals.[xi] One Ukrainian activist indicated that *"All our activities were starting after the Sunday mass in church."* The importance of the church can be explained by several factors. From a practical standpoint, the representatives of clergy state that sacral architecture is highly visible on the map of the town. Therefore, for Ukrainian newcomers in Poland, it is much easier to locate churches in the city center than the offices of non-governmental organizations (NGOs) or embassies. Historically, Greek-Catholic churches were a valuable ally to the Ukrainian minority in their attempts to protect the Ukrainian cultural heritage in Poland. Furthermore, it is important to note that in many cases, the assistance from churches has been organized in a much more efficient manner (decentralized structures of cooperation, no need for consent to hold a fundraiser on the premises of churches, etc.) compared with the regular activity of NGOs and individuals, which is relevant for a mass movement such as the Euromaidan.

The impact of the church on interconnectedness also resulted from the low levels of trust of Ukrainians in public institutions. This absence of trust can be considered a remnant of the Soviet legacy (*homo [post] sovieticus* mentality) and subsequent lack of well-developed social capital that would enable them to become actively involved in relations with Polish and Ukrainian authorities.[xii] Therefore, churches, which are viewed as institutions that can still be trusted, continue to play a significant role as information (sometimes counseling) and integration centers for Ukrainians. This role is particularly the case for migrants who work in low-skilled jobs and often face concrete problems with finding professional assistance outside the migrant community (especially if they reside far from large cities, where non-governmental activity is low, see Grzymała-Kazłowska 2008). An engaged Ukrainian recalled that *"Church is the place that unites, it is not just a religious place, but a meeting platform, which assembles all of us."* Representatives of the clergy confirmed the observation. *"We tried to help these people, explain how to live in Poland, explain that here laws are different than in Ukraine. We held meetings with authorities, police representatives, different foundations."*

In addition, religious institutions serve as a legitimizing factor for various initiatives in Poland because activity that is conducted under the consent of a parish/church is deemed more trustworthy by the majority of Ukrainians than initiatives connected to the Ukrainian authorities. Moreover, the permanent availability of space (free of charge) to hold meetings and to network emerged in the interviews as a major factor that contributed to the development of the civic engagement of Ukrainians.

However, the positive feedback regarding the role of religious institutions from the respondents in Poland must be qualified to a certain extent. The position that religion potentially has a divisive effect was equally encountered in the interviews. For instance, being part of Greek-Catholic or [Russian] Orthodox churches may condition an individual's approach to different initiatives within the Ukrainian community. Consequently, the case described represents an example of the dual influence of certain factors, which emerged as both unifying and disintegrating simultaneously, and paints a very complex picture of the relationships among Ukrainians who reside abroad.

Before the Euromaidan protests, the Ukrainian community in Germany was characterized by a low level of interconnectedness among its members, except for the old diaspora, which was already highly institutionalized. According to several interviewees, a plausible explanation of this phenomenon lies in the high motivation of many Ukrainians to integrate into the society of emigration and their low interest in involvement with their compatriots. *"I had no special interest [in the life of Ukrainians in Germany – M.P.]. My goal was to be integrated here into the country, into the Germany society."* Euromaidan, then, was the initial trigger for increased networking among the members of the Ukrainian community. The church, particularly the Greek-Catholic church, played an important role in this process because, independently from their denominational allegiance, it often provided a platform for Ukrainians to meet and discuss current issues: *"When I, for example, meet the Ukrainians somewhere, then it is this [church – M.P.] community. [...] And there we held so many talks it was done regularly in the service and the regulars, in the church, and there, people mostly talk about politics."* This platform was further important for Ukrainian engagement because ideas for activities and initiatives emerged also within the church, as the interviewees stated. Nevertheless, the role of the church as an instrument for self-organization is less important compared with Poland because the organizational structures of Ukrainian churches are considerably less developed and therefore cannot provide the same resources as Ukrainian churches in Poland. A stronger institutionalization of Ukrainian churches in Germany could provide great potential for the networking and further engagement of Ukrainians.

An additional factor that was encountered during the research relates to the phenomenon of the digitalization of the diaspora. This digitalization refers to the increasing usage of digital media within the diasporic community as an alternative communicational space in addition to actual physical communication. As confirmed by empirical research (Onuch 2014, Tucker et al. 2014, Kyiv International Institute of Sociology and Ilko Kucheriv Democratic Initiatives Foundation 2013), Euromaidan is an example of the penetration of innovative technologies into a mass protest movement, civic activities and the development of civil society in general. Certainly, this was not the first time that social media has played a major role in a protest movement as the examples of the Arab Spring and the Gezi Park protests in Turkey show. However, researchers indicate that the variety of online tools that are being used is what distinguishes the Ukrainian case from other cases (Bohdanova 2014: 133–142). Our analysis confirms that the Ukrainian diaspora also actively used various online tools to support the protest movement.

Both during and after the protests, social media has played an important role in uniting migrants.[xiii] The digitalization of traditional channels of interest representation arguably constitutes a new type of democratic forum, an e-Agora of postmodernity, which serves as a platform for a diaspora to meet and discuss the issues of utmost importance to the community. For a diaspora, social media constitutes a source of more reliable information. *"Even I started using Facebook [older representative of minority – A.K.]. Previously I thought this was some kind of a toy for kids, but now I can follow the events second by second."* Moreover, platforms such as Facebook create a useful forum for networking. *"Via Facebook, e-mails, phone we co-operate with many people without even personally knowing them."* Finally, for many active Ukrainians, social media is an indispensable tool for work and co-operation that transcends the borders of a single state. *"Facebook is my work tool. I need it for communication with my acquaintances all over Europe."*

In Germany, the emergence of a digital diaspora can also be observed. Social media such as Facebook functioned not only as an instrument for connecting the diaspora with its homeland, particularly during Euromaidan and its aftermath, but also for networking within the Ukrainian community in Germany. The level of interconnectedness has considerably increased since November 2013 because the use of social media facilitated establishing new contacts and extending personal networks. Furthermore, the interviews revealed that the digitalization of the diaspora and the increased linkage among members also triggered the impulse for an increase of active engagement, which has contributed to the development of a broader and more diverse landscape of initiatives and organizations in Germany over the last two years. First, social media was used to call for joint activities, which according to the interviewees, often developed into concrete and regular engagement. *"It started with Facebook activities and also a friend of ours. [...] She was, so to say, the first that called us to organize the first protest in Berlin. And I think that was the trigger for establishing the 'Euromaidan Wache'."* Second, the presence of initiatives and organizations on social media made it possible to acquire new activists. As the interviewees emphasized, this acquisition was performed, for example, when Ukrainians actively searched online for other Ukrainians and active engagement in their region. An activist described the important role that social media plays in the Ukrainian community in Germany as follows. *"Facebook is just a medium that by now plays a role in all spheres because through Facebook it is easy to communicate, keep in contact, and exchange news. It is a bit like glue in-between [people]."*

In addition to connecting Ukrainians in Germany, social media is also an important tool for networking with the homeland. Thus, social media allowed Ukrainians to follow the events on Euromaidan in real time and has enabled the constant exchange of information on current events and developments in Ukraine. Furthermore, social media is crucial for active engagement, particularly in the field of humanitarian aid where the people who are engaged are in regular contact with local partners.

5. Differences in Ukrainian Engagement in Poland and Germany

Although Ukrainian engagement in Poland and Germany exhibited many similarities, the interviews revealed several differences between the two cases. These differences are partly accounted for by the different histories of the Ukrainians who live in these countries. Consequently, a different structure and perception of the Ukrainian diaspora between the representatives of the Ukrainian community and the representatives of the host country emerged. The Ukrainians in Poland comprise the largest group of foreigners (see Annex 1)[xiv] and are actively represented in the public discourse, whereas the Ukrainians in Germany only constitute a small number (see Annex 2)[xv], which preconditions their low visibility.

As a result of these different histories, Ukrainian engagement in Poland before Euromaidan was organized and institutionalized to a much higher degree than in Germany. Because of the Ukrainian minority that has lived in Poland since the Second World War and their internal location and territorial displacement (including Operation Vistula), the Ukrainian community in Poland was able to use the experience and knowledge of already implemented projects and existing organizations and networks for their civic engagement during Euromaidan. Although minority representatives do not always work on the same initiatives and in the same organizations as Ukrainian migrants, their knowledge of Polish society is highly valuable. Their practical experience in the transformation process in Poland is an advantage for the civic engagement of Ukrainians both in Poland and in their homeland through the sharing of best practices.

The organization and institutionalization of the "old Ukrainian diaspora" in Germany is not comparable to the Ukrainian minority in Poland. The cooperation between the "old diaspora" and the "diasporic community" is much more sporadic.

In addition, as the interviews revealed, joint projects with German citizens are relatively scarce compared with the common Ukrainian-Polish initiatives that became an everyday practice. Therefore, Ukrainian engagement in Germany in most cases only began to emerge and to formalize after the Euromaidan protest movement, which turned out to be a valuable learning exercise for the diaspora.

Through the interviews, it became clear that Ukrainians are experiencing different levels of support and recognition in Poland and Germany. The interviewees in Germany described a much more skeptical attitude towards their engagement and the Ukrainian conflict in general. In Poland, Ukrainians play a significant role in the debate regarding Crimea and the war in Eastern Ukraine, but in Germany, this was not the case, and Ukrainian voices were not often heard in the media. Instead, the interviewees complained about a Russia-focused perspective in the German media. Quite often, Ukraine has been regarded as a "post-soviet state" that is still part of the Russian sphere of influence.[xvi] Consequently and in contrast to Poland, there is only little interconnectedness between the Ukrainian diasporic community and German actors such as civil society or political institutions. However, networks are slowly evolving. Thus, many Ukrainian activists not only focus on political or humanitarian engagement but also attempt to promote Ukrainian matters, culture and history through different events that are aimed at the German public.

Finally, for the Ukrainians in Germany, public visibility and countering Russian propaganda were treated as the utmost priority, whereas the Ukrainians in Poland faced a struggle to maintain an interest in Ukraine among civil society activists, decision-makers and the wider public. After two revolutions and continuous political turmoil in the country, many Poles lost interest in the events and the reform process that unfolded in Ukraine. Moreover, the exhaustion from the uncertain situation in Ukraine left many Ukrainian activists discouraged to continue their work for the good of the country. Based on the described situation, in both countries, close cooperation among different groups of engaged Ukrainians and the professionalization of their activities is arguably a prerequisite for more successful future initiatives.

6. Concluding Remarks

Euromaidan was able to bring together scattered groups of Ukrainians who actively engaged in civil society in Germany and Poland for a limited period of time. The protest movement can be viewed as an initial spark to create a sense of community in a "new Ukrainian diaspora". It has become clear that Euromaidan has led to the emergence of a diasporic community in terms of diasporic civic activities and, in many cases, has created a sense of belonging in both countries. This observation is consistent with the theoretical thoughts on diaspora by Rogers Brubaker that were described in chapter 3. The diasporic community is often constituted through diasporic stances, projects, initiatives and organizations, which are no longer confined by social or physical borders. Although Euromaidan was able to break the existing cleavages—minorities compared with migrants and the classification based on the stability of residence, age and level of education—for a short period of time, they remained intact from the long-term perspective. This cohesion can be observed in a wide range of initiatives and organizations that exist and emerged, which has created a broad landscape of active engagement however frequently divided.

Another important observation in Poland and in Germany is the particular roles of religious institutions and social media as further constituting factors. In the case of Ukraine and its diaspora, it could be observed that in a situation where the ties in the community were initially weak, social media, the usage of innovative technologies and the available alternative meeting platforms such as the church constituted important elements for building social capital, i.e., regular daily activities. Therefore, the digitalization of civil society had the potential to impact the formation of social capital among the Ukrainian communities in both countries.

The emergence of a digital diaspora has further implications on the diaspora. Cigdem Bozdag (2013: 51) identifies the importance of digital communication for the constitution of diasporic communities. Analyzing communication processes helps to understand "diaspora" as a transnational phenomenon without neglecting its diversity and hybridity. The diasporic community may not be viewed as the "emblem of transnationalism" (Tölölyan 1991: 5) because of the focus on national territories. However, the diasporic community includes several transnational elements through its transnational ties and networks particularly through social media. Although the category of nations remains important for the self-positioning and identity-building of the interviewees, transnational processes and communication add a new dimension to the constitution of the diasporic community. This finding validates the decision to analyze diaspora as a category of process. Furthermore, the chosen approach appears to be more valuable when considering that the notion of diaspora as an entity has been highly contradicted by the internally heterogeneous Ukrainian diaspora that has been examined in both countries.

Although the presented findings suggest that the democratization of Ukraine was not necessarily considered as the primary goal of civic engagement, the work of actively engaged persons in Ukraine and the constant exchange of information between the diaspora and their homeland may also have long-term implications on the development of local civil society. A question that remains to be answered in further research is whether the nature of the civic activity among the members of the diaspora has contributed to the emergence of a new common identity of Ukrainians.

7. Bibliography

Anderson, Benedict. 1991. *Imagined communities: reflections on the origin and spread of nationalism*. London: Verso.

Badescu, Gabriel, and Eric Uslaner. 2003. *Social Capital and the Transition to Democracy*. London and New York: Routledge.

Bohdanova, Tetyana. 2014. "Unexpected revolution: the role of social media in Ukraine's Euromaidan uprising." *European View* 13 (1): 133–142.

Bozdag, Cigdem. 2013. *Aneignung von Diasporawebsites. Eine medienethnografische Untersuchung in der marokkanischen und türkischen Diaspora*. Wiesbaden: VS Verlag für Sozialwissenschaften.

Brubaker, Rogers. 2005. "The 'diaspora' diaspora." *Ethnic and Racial Studies* 28 (1): 1v19.

Brubaker, Rogers. 2011. "Nationalizing states revisited: Projects and processes of nationalization in post-Soviet states." *Ethnic and Racial Studies* 34 (11): 1785–1814.

Cohen, Robin. 1997. *Global Diasporas. An Introduction*. London: UCL Press.

Faist, Thomas. 2010. "Diaspora and Transnationalism: What Kind of Dance Partners?" In *Diaspora and transnationalism: Concepts, theories and methods*, edited by Rainer Bauböck and Thomas Faist, 9–34. Amsterdam: Amsterdam University Press.

Federal Office for Migration and Refugees Germany. "Migrationsbericht 2014." Accessed 2 October 2016. http://www.bamf.de/SharedDocs/Anlagen/DE/Publikationen/Migrationsberichte/migrationsbericht-2014.html?nn=1663558.

Federal Office for Migration and Refugees Germany. "Migrationsberichte 2011–2014." Accessed 30 June 2016. http://www.bamf.de/DE/DasBAMF/Forschung/Ergebnisse/Migrationsberichte/migrationsberichte-node.html.

Frane, Adam. 2007. *Social Capital and Governance. Old and New Members of the EU in Comparison.* Berlin: Lit Verlag.

Friesenhahn, Günter J.; Hanjo Schild; Hans-Georg Wicke and Judit Balogh. 2013. *Learning mobility and non-formal learning in European contexts: Policies, approaches and examples.* Strasbourg Cedex: Council of Europe Publishing.

Gilroy, Paul. 1993. *The Black Atlantic. Modernity and Double-Consciousness.* London: Verso.

Grzymała-Kazłowska, Aleksandra. 2008. *Między jednością a wielością. Integracja odmiennych grup i kategorii migrantów w Polsce* [Between unity and quantity. The integration of different groups and categories of migrants in Poland]. Ośrodek Badań nad Migracjami WNE UW, Warsaw.

Kenny, Kevin. 2013. *Diaspora: A very short introduction.* New York NY: Oxford University Press.

Kittilson, Miki Caul, and Russel J Dalton. 2011. "Virtual Civil Society: The New Frontier of Social Capital?" *Political Behavior* 33 (4): 625–644.

Krasynska, Svitlana. 2015. "Digital Civil Society: Euromaidan, the Ukrainian Diaspora, and Social Media." In *Ukraine's Euromaidan. Analyses of a Civil Revolution,* edited by David R. Marples and Frederich V. Mills. Stuttgart: Ibidem-Verlag.

Kucharczyk, Jacek; Agnieszka Łada; Gabriele Schöler and Łukasz Wenerski. 2015. *Close together or far apart? Poles, Germans and Russians on the Russia-Ukraine crisis.* Warsaw: Instytut Spraw Publicznych.

Kyiv International Institute of Sociology and Ilko Kucheriv Democratic Initiatives Foundation. 2016. Survey "Maidan 2013: who is standing for what and why?" Accessed 28 June 2016. http://maidan.org.ua/2013/12/majdan-2013-hto-stojit-chomu-i-za-scho/.

Mayer, Ruth. 2005. *Diaspora. Eine kritische Begriffsbestimmung.* Bielefeld: Transcript Verlag.

Mayring, Philipp. 2010. *Qualitative Inhaltsanalyse: Grundlagen und Techniken.* Basel/Wiesbaden: Beltz.

Ministry of Foreign Affairs of Poland. "Consular report 2015." Accessed 30 October 2016. https://www.msz.gov.pl/pl/informacje_konsularne/raporty_konsularne/raport_konsularny_2015.

Onuch, Olga. 2014. "Social networks and social media in Ukrainian 'Euromaidan' protests." Washington Post (last modified 2 January 2014). Accessed 30 September 2016. https://www.washingtonpost.com/news/monkey-cage/wp/2014/01/02/social-networks-and-social-media-in-ukrainian-euromaidan-protests-2/.

Putnam, Robert. 1993. *Making Democracy Work. Civic Traditions in Modern Italy.* Princeton: Princeton University Press.

Safran, William. 1991. "Diasporas in Modern Societies: Myths of Homeland and Return." *Diaspora: A Journal of Transnational Studies* 1 (1): 83–99.

The Office for Foreigners in Poland. "Annual Reports." Accessed 28 June 2016. http://udsc.gov.pl/statystyki/raporty-okresowe/zestawienia-roczne/.

The Office for Foreigners in Poland. "Ongoing analysis of the situation in Ukraine." Accessed 28 June 2016. http://udsc.gov.pl/statystyki/raporty-specjalne/biezaca-sytuacja-dotyczaca-ukrainy/.

The Office of Foreigners in Poland. "Data-pertaining to the-proceedings in regard to the foreigners in Poland in first half of 2016." Accessed 30 September 2016. http://udsc.gov.pl/wp-content/uploads/2014/12/Dane-liczbowe-dotyczace-postepowan-prowadzonych-wobec-cudzoziemcow-w-pierwszej-polowie-2016-roku.xls.

Tölölyan, Khachig. 1991. "The nation-state and its others: in lieu of a preface." *Diaspora: A Journal of Transnational Studies* 1 (1): 3–7.

Tucker, Joshua; Megan Metzger; Duncan Penfold-Brown; Richard Bonneau; John Jost and Jonathan Nagler. 2014. "Protest in the Age of Social Media." *Carnegie Reporter* 7 (4): 8–19.

Twigg, Judyth. 2014. "Ukraine: Trends and Regional Dynamics in Population, Health, and Migration." *PONARS Eurasia Policy Memo* 344.

Vertovec, Steven. 2004. "Cheap Calls: The Social Glue of Migrant Transnationalism." *Global Networks* 4 (2): 219–224.

8. Annexes
Annex I – Ukrainians in Poland
Table 1: Status of Ukrainians in Poland

STATUS OF UKRAINIANS IN POLAND	
Permanent Residence	20,252
Long-term EU Residence	2,796
Temporary Stay	42,451
Asylum	-
Refugee Status	2
Subsidiary	35
Humanitarian Reasons	202
Tolerated Stay	3
IN TOTAL	**65,866**

Source: The Office for Foreigners in Poland, data on the total number of Ukrainian migrants holding valid residence permits, as of 1st January 2016 (The Office for Foreigners in Poland, "Annual Reports").

Table 2: Reasons for stay

REASONS FOR STAY	2013	2014	2015	2016 (as of 4/30/16)
Family	2,450	2,726	3,888	3,236
Education	2,351	3,798	7,054	2,668
Work	3,863	8,307	23,925	11,327
Other	931	2,277	2,997	-
IN TOTAL	**9,595**	**17,108**	**37,883**	**17,231**

Source: The Office for Foreigners in Poland, data on Ukrainian migrants who were granted temporary residence permits in Poland, issued decisions from 2013 to 2016 (The Office for Foreigners in Poland, "Ongoing analysis of the situation in Ukraine").

Annex II – Ukrainians in Germany
Table 3: Duration of stay

DURATION OF STAY IN YEARS (as of 2014)	Less than 4	4–8	8–10	10–15	15–20	20–30	30 and more	IN TOTAL
Ukrainian citizens	24,140	13,889	9,060	48,455	25,555	6,760	83	127,942

Source: Federal Office for Migration and Refugees ("Migrationsbericht 2014"), data on the duration of stay of Ukrainian migrants in Germany.

Table 4: Permits of residence—reasons for stay

PERMIT OF RESIDENCE – REASONS FOR STAY	2011	2012	2013	2014
Family	1,772	1,937	2,141	2,642
Education	1,014	1,137	1,071	1,385
Work	1,441	1,495	1,304	1,759
Other	267	215	228	439

Source: Federal Office for Migration and Refugees ("Migrationsbericht 2011–2014"), data on Ukrainian migrants who were granted permanent and non-permanent residence permits in Germany (issued decisions from 2011 to 2014).

---

i Possible forms of active engagement include formal engagement within organizations, informal engagement with initiatives or individual engagement (including new forms of engagement, e.g., social media).

ii The experts are either experienced in cooperating with Ukrainian organizations or have an overview of the landscape of civic engagement of the Ukrainian diaspora, both through either their profession or personal interests.

iii For the transcription and the codification of the interviews, the program "f4analyse" was used. Based on the theoretical foundation of qualitative content analysis by Mayring (2003), the interviews were codified and analyzed.

iv Agnieszka Łada and Katrin Böttger, eds., #EngagEUkraine. Zaangażowanie społeczne Ukraińców w Polsce i w Niemczech (Warsaw: Institute of Public Affairs, 2016).

v Katrin Böttger and Agnieszka Lada, eds., #EngageEUkraine – Engagement der Ukrainer in Polen und Deutschland" (Warsaw: Institute of Public Affairs, 2016).

vi The "generation gap" is a particularly acute issue for the Ukrainian minority, whose young representatives have tended to assimilate in Polish society in recent years.

vii Short term compared with long-term residence is especially relevant for migrants, who tend to invest more resources in civic activity if their stay is more stable.

viii Examples include dignity, freedom, independence of the country, better well-being, etc.

ix Several respondents saw the "visibility aspect" as the most important achievement of Euromaidan. *"For me, the happiest moment was when I realized that we are no longer anonymous."*

x These groups are comparable to the Ukrainian minority and the Ukrainian migrants in Poland because they share some characteristics. However, they should not be equated, because, unlike in Poland, the diaspora in Germany does not have an official status as a minority. Furthermore, there are also significant differences between these groups, which will be discussed in chapter 5.

xi The initiatives of diaspora, as documented during the research, are very often organized around the churches of two confessions (predominantly Greek-Catholic and sometimes Orthodox). Particularly for the Ukrainians who come from the Western part of the country, the Greek-Catholic church has traditionally played a very significant role (during World War II and under the communist regime, it helped to protect in a way Ukrainian values and language).

xii Researchers have analyzed the relatively low public trust in politics among the citizens of post-communist countries, who overall tend to perceive civil servants/ politicians as corrupt and untrustworthy (Frane 2007, Badescu & Uslaner 2003).

xiii The majority of migrants were very active and remain active on Facebook. As far as we have observed, Twitter is used to a much lesser extent in distributing information on the internet that is related to Ukrainians in Poland.

xiv According to the data from the Office of Foreigners and the Ministry of Foreign Affairs, it is estimated that approximately one million citizens of Ukraine may reside in Poland (by far the largest group of migrants). However, the majority of migrants are involved in circular migration (approximately 900,000 were holders of visas, and around 70,000 were holders of residence permits). For a more detailed overview, see the following sources (available in Polish): The Office of Foreigners "Data-pertaining to the-proceedings in regard to the foreigners in Poland in the first half of 2016"; and the Ministry of Foreign Affairs of Poland "Consular report 2015".

xv According to the Migration Report 2014 of the Federal Office for Migration and Refugees in Germany, Ukrainians constitute 1.6% of the foreign population in Germany. In comparison, Turkish migrants constitute 17.4%, Polish migrants comprise 9.9% and Russian migrants represent 7.3% of the foreign population (Federal Office for Migration and Refugees Germany, "Migrationsbericht 2014").

xvi This evaluation of the current situation by the interviewees is further confirmed by a survey conducted by IPA and Bertelsmann-Stiftung in 2015 (Kucharczyk et al. 2015: 12). According to this study, 61% of the Polish population name Russia as the aggressor in the ongoing conflict, whereas in Germany, only 39% take this position. Another 43% regard both Ukraine and Russia as perpetrators. Although the media coverage of the events on Euromaidan, the annexation of Crimea and the war in Eastern Ukraine have led to greater support for Ukraine, the interviewees describe that most of the German population remains indifferent or hostile towards their activities.

Part IV:
Socio-structural Transnationalism

The International Links of Ukrainian Oligarchs. Business Expansion and Transnational Offshore Networks

Heiko Pleines

In order to analyze which practices Ukrainian oligarchs deploy to embed their businesses into different transnational contexts, their export activities, foreign direct investments and offshore links are examined. It is demonstrated that the business model of Ukrainian oligarchs is primarily based on a competitive advantage in the home market resulting from well-developed political connections. Accordingly, oligarchic business in Ukraine is not a matter of international expansion but instead concerns the prevention of competition in the domestic market and a strong reliance on non-transparent transnational offshore networks to conceal ownership and profits. As a result, Ukraine's oligarchic business now faces two transnational challenges. First, economic integration with the EU endangers rent-seeking opportunities in the Ukrainian market. Second, the transnational drive for transparency and against offshore centers increases the risk of criminal prosecution.

1. Introduction

Based on the classical definition of oligarchy, i.e., the rule of a few self-interested elites, the term "oligarch" denotes entrepreneurs who use their wealth to exert political influence. In this context, the concept of an oligarch is closely associated with political corruption, and the term is primarily used in the analysis of formally democratic systems with authoritarian tendencies, such as those found in Latin America, South-East Asia and, since the 1990s, in Eastern Europe. In a narrower sense, which is how the term will be used here, the concept does not include politicians or civil servants who use their political influence to obtain control over (both state-run and private) economic activities.

In post-Soviet Ukraine, the influence of the oligarchs has increasingly come to be seen as a central feature of the political regime. The literature has focused on their influence on political decision-making, examining informal networks with political actors and affiliation with parliamentary factions in Ukraine's national parliament,[i] as well as on their impact on election campaigns and power shifts, with some attention devoted to oligarchic media ownership[ii].

There is consensus in the literature that oligarchs have formed a symbiotic relationship with Ukrainian politicians. In return for preferential treatment of their businesses, in areas ranging from privatization (e.g. Pleines 2008) over state aid (e.g. Dimitrova & Dragneva 2013) to energy trade (e.g. Balmaceda 2013) and state procurement (e.g. Stewart 2013), oligarchs offer politicians financial and media support, particularly during election campaigns, as well as bribe payments. Thereby, oligarchs distort democratic decision-making processes through informal and corrupt deals with political decision-makers and, as a result of related media reporting, discredit Ukraine's political system in the eyes of a large part of the population.

Accordingly, controversies in the academic debate concern not the nature of the political role of the oligarchs, but merely the degree of their impact. As political scientists dominate the academic debate, the business interests of the oligarchs have received less attention. The implicit assumption seems to be that oligarchs engage in all businesses in which political support promises considerable profits.

However, there are a small number of studies contending that changes in the business interests of the oligarchs also lead to changes in their political role. These studies examine primarily international business interests, as they are assumed to provide new perspectives to Ukrainian businesspeople. More specifically, as one of the major long-term political issues in Ukraine is the country's foreign policy orientation between Russia and the EU, the international business links of the oligarchs have been treated as a determining factor in this important question. The respective studies all restrict their analysis to a narrow aspect of the broader question and often also to a limited number of oligarchs (Dimitrova & Dragneva 2013; Gorodnichenko & Grygorenko 2008; Puglisi 2003b, 2008).

The broader picture of oligarchs' increasing international links would suggest—in what Vertovec calls the first take on transnationalism—a social formation that spans borders, in this case as part of a transnational capitalist class, referring to the economic dimension of transnationalism as described by the same author (Vertovec 2009).

In this contribution, I therefore analyze which practices Ukrainian oligarchs deploy to embed their businesses into different transnational contexts, and based on this I arrive at a first assessment of the effects they have on Ukraine's international relations.

This analysis starts from the mainstream approach of business and management studies, which treats internationalization and transnationalization as an attempt to remain competitive in a globalizing economy through the creation of more efficient (international) production chains and access to additional (foreign) markets. While this approach assumes that companies compete in free and fair global markets, in recent years increasing attention has been devoted to attempts by transnational companies to increase their profits through manipulations of legal regulations. In this context, companies can use transnational links to reduce taxation and conceal illegal gains. Such manipulations range from the registration of profits in low-tax countries to secret offshore accounts and outright money laundering. They will be covered in a separate part of this chapter.

The present analysis is restricted to business links. It does not cover the transnationalization of oligarchs as private individuals, e.g., through their holiday resorts, places of residence or children's education abroad. Although these aspects may have an important impact not just on the lifestyle of oligarchs but also on their integration into what Vertovec calls the transnational capitalist class, it would require a completely separate (and hardly feasible) research endeavor.

The period covered in this analysis ranges from the late 1990s, when oligarchs emerged as important actors on Ukraine's political scene, to the present (i.e., 2016). It does not cover all large Ukrainian companies but only those that are, for at least a part of the period under investigation, part of a (formal or informal) business group controlled by an oligarch. In the project on which this contribution is based, an oligarch is defined as a politically active entrepreneur for at least one year within the period from 2000 to 2016, wherein the relevant selection criteria are[iii] (1) business interests as core activity[iv], (2) political activity at the national level[v], (3) estimated wealth of at least $200 million in at least one year since 2000[vi] and (4) no affiliated position in a business empire, as the focus of the analysis is on business and not on oligarchs as individuals.[vii]

Based on these selection criteria, a total of twenty-nine oligarchs have been identified for the period from 2000 to 2016. A separate table, which could not be included here due to space limitations but is available online, provides an overview of the major features of these oligarchs and their businesses.[viii]

2. Business Internationalization

Business internationalization in the classical sense is primarily pursued through the acquisition or foundation of companies abroad. According to standard business theory, the main motives for foreign direct investments (FDI) by companies are resource seeking (i.e., access to natural resources and technology), cost-reduction seeking (e.g., cheap labor) and market seeking (i.e., access to new customers) (Buckley 1988; Dunning 1994; Hymer 1976).

However, as FDI requires knowledge of and contacts in foreign countries, the stage model assumes that internationalization takes place in three (in the ideal type, consecutive) steps: (1) exports via independent representatives or agents; (2) the establishment of an overseas sales subsidiary; and (3) the foundation of overseas production units (Johanson & Vahlne 1977). Becoming a transnational enterprise would require a further step, whereby overseas units become so important that the company is no longer focused on any single domestic market as the home market.

At the lower stages of internationalization, private agricultural and food companies from Ukraine have made the most dynamic progress through the rapid expansion of exports (Belaya 2015; Melnik 2013). The share of agriculture and the food industry in Ukraine's total exports rose from 12% in 2005 to 31% in 2014 (State Statistics Service of Ukraine 2015). The other major exporting industry in Ukraine is the ferrous metals industry, which still accounts for one-quarter of Ukraine's exports. Ukraine's heavy industry (mining, metals and heavy machine building) traditionally accounts for close to half of Ukraine's exports. The only further major exporting industry in Ukraine is the chemical industry.

Of the twenty-nine oligarchs identified in this study, twenty are primarily active in these export-oriented industries, namely eleven in heavy industry, seven in agriculture/food and two in chemicals. The remaining oligarchs focus on the domestic service sector (banks, retail, media, real estate) or on the domestic energy sector.[ix]

Although it has been argued that after an initial phase of consolidation, Ukraine's oligarchs have begun efforts to restructure their businesses to improve profitability through vertical integration (Gorodnichenko & Grygorenko 2008), FDI is not a major part of related strategies. Overall, outward FDI from Ukraine has remained very small. The country's total stock of outward FDI stood at a mere $10 billion in 2014 (for comparison: Russia's outward FDI stock was nearly fifty times larger).[x]

According to a compilation by the Ukrainian business journal Invest Gazeta, very few Ukrainian companies have engaged in FDI. A large part of the small overall number of FDI projects from Ukraine has been conducted by six holdings of oligarchs, namely Ferrexpo (Zhevago), Group DF (Firtash), ISD (until 2009, Haiduk), Privat Group (Kolomois'kyi and Boholiubov) and SKM (Akhmetov) (Invest Gazeta 2012). Roshen (Poroshenko) has to be added given its investments in Lithuania and Russia. As many oligarchs operate their businesses through offshore holdings, as will be described below, exact figures on their FDI are not available. However, for none of the holdings does FDI form a vital part of the production chain, nor do foreign investments contribute a major share to turnover or profits.

Instead of going global, Ukraine's oligarchs, primarily, attempt to prevent the access of international competitors to their domestic market. Through the example of the steel industry, Troschke and Wittmann (2014) have argued that the lack of competition in the Ukrainian domestic market, which is ensured by oligarchs through their political connections, causes companies to restrain from investments in the modernization of production facilities. To a large degree, the business models of the oligarchs are not based on profit-seeking, i.e. the production of competitive goods, but on rent-seeking, i.e. on legal and illegal state support. The Economist (2014) has estimated that in 2006 and again in 2013, only approximately 10% of the wealth of Ukraine's billionaires came from sectors of the economy that were not dominated by rent-seeking.

The most prominent case in which rent-seeking by Ukrainian oligarchs had a transnational dimension is the natural gas trade, i.e., the import from and transit through Russia, which is organized by the Russian company Gazprom. In the 1990s, Ukrainian companies only engaged in deliveries on the domestic market. This changed when Gazprom decided to transfer responsibility for the gas trade with Ukraine to intermediary companies, officially to get rid of a debt-ridden and conflict-prone market, but obviously also to create a non-transparent environment that allowed the company's management to siphon off profits. The first intermediaries in the Ukrainian Russian gas trade were dominated by Russian businesses. However, after the Orange Revolution in Ukraine, the new intermediary company was 50% owned by Ukrainian partners. On the Ukrainian side, oligarch Dmytro

Firtash was in control and able to build a business holding on the basis of his international cooperation in the gas trade, which comprises large parts of Ukraine's gas industry and chemical industry (Balmaceda 2013; Kusznir 2006).

The gas sector reform that Ukraine is currently preparing in order to comply with the rules of liberalized EU energy markets—as foreseen in the Association agreement between Ukraine and the EU—will, if properly implemented, put an end to rent-seeking in natural gas exports (Kończuk 2015). The gas trade thus points to another important area of Ukrainian oligarchs' transnational links.

3. Integration Into Transnational Offshore Networks

While the degree of Ukraine's visible business internationalization is low, the country seems to be much better integrated into non-transparent transnational offshore networks. As Heathershaw and Cooley (2015: 1) argue in the case of Central Asia:

> Re-orienting our focus away from formal trade flows to the more hidden offshore world and institutions of contemporary finance, we see, in fact, multiple connections between the Central Asian region and the global economy, often via post-Soviet business networks and global legal institutions. Whilst this interconnectedness may begin in the financial realm, it has economic and political, domestic and international ramifications. Over the past two decades, Central Asian elites have learned to use global financial institutions and offshore vehicles to split the legal personality of nominally state-controlled assets. They have also laundered money through shell companies and structured side payments from their dealings with external actors, including telecommunications companies, energy multinationals and even foreign militaries.

This overall picture is also true for Ukraine. A telling example concerning bribe payments is the holding of oligarch Dmytro Firtash, Group DF, which was organized under the laws of the British Virgin Islands. According to US investigators, Group DF and its partners paid millions of dollars in bribes to Indian state officials to secure licenses for a mining project. According to the accusations, Firtash "authorised payment of at least $18.5 million in bribes to officials of both the State Government of Andhra Pradesh and the Central Government of India to secure the approval of licenses for the project."[xi] To obtain information on the on-going investigations, Firtash paid bribes of approximately $0.5 million to German police officers, who contacted the US authorities (Zeit online 2016).

Offshore links can also be used for theft and money laundering on a large scale. A prominent American investigative journalist, Andrew Cockburn (2015), has described an alleged offshore scheme run by Kolomois'kyi's Privatbank, which has been used to siphon off $1.8 billion in IMF support for the banking sector:

> The scheme, as revealed in a series of court judgments of the Economic Court of the Dnipropetrovsk region monitored and reported by Nashi Groshi, worked like this: Forty-two Ukrainian firms owned by fifty-four offshore entities registered in Caribbean, American, and Cypriot jurisdictions and linked to or affiliated with the Privat group of companies, took out loans from PrivatBank in Ukraine to the value of $1.8 billion. The firms then ordered goods from six foreign "supplier" companies, three of which were incorporated in the United Kingdom, two in the British Virgin Islands, one in the Caribbean statelet of St. Kitts & Nevis. Payment for the orders—$1.8 billion—was shortly afterwards prepaid into the vendors' accounts, which were, coincidentally, in the Cyprus branch of PrivatBank. Once the money was sent, the Ukrainian importing companies arranged with PrivatBank Ukraine that their loans be guaranteed by the goods on order.
> But the foreign suppliers invariably reported that they could not fulfill the order after all, thus breaking the contracts, but without any effort to return the money. Finally, the Ukrainian companies filed suit, always in the Dnipropetrovsk Economic Court, demanding that that foreign supplier return the prepayment and also that the guarantee to PrivatBank be cancelled. In forty-two out of forty-two such cases the court issued the identical judgment: the advance payment should be returned to the Ukrainian company, but the loan agreement should remain in force.
> As a result, the loan of the Ukrainian company remained guaranteed by the undelivered goods, while the chances of returning the advance payments from foreign companies remain remote. "Basically this transaction of $1.8 bill[ion] abroad with the help of fake contracts was simply an asset siphoning [operation] and a violation of currency legislation in general," explained Lesya Ivanovna, an investigator with Nashi Groshi in an email to me. "The whole lawsuit story was only needed to make it look like the bank itself is not involved in the scheme . . . officially it looks like PrivatBank now owns the products, though in reality [they] will never be delivered.

In a separate case, in December 2015, the Latvian Financial and Capital Markets Commission imposed a fine of $2 million on the Latvian subsidiary of Privatbank and ordered the dismissal of its CEO and managing board in reaction to an investigation of the bank's role in the theft and laundering of money from Moldovan banks (The Baltic Times 2015). In Moldova, the theft of approximately $1 billion had caused a political crisis (Demytrie 2015).

Moreover, many offshore networks are used to avoid taxation and insecure property rights in the home country. The significance of offshore relations for Ukraine's business can be estimated from the fact that the by far largest destination of FDI from Ukraine is Cyprus, which accounted for more than $6 billion out of a total outward FDI stock of about $10 billion. Furthermore, one-fifth of inward FDI in Ukraine, equal to $9.9 billion, comes from Cyprus (UNCTAD 2012). This suggests that Ukrainian FDI going to Cyprus in large part returns to Ukraine and stands behind many of the more than 2000 Ukrainian companies that are owned by offshore holdings (Samsonova & Yurchenko 2013). Following a similar logic, the list of the largest affiliates of foreign transnational companies in Ukraine, compiled by UNCTAD as of 2010, starts with the Metinvest Holding of Ukrainian oligarch Akhmetov, which is registered in the Netherlands (UNCTAD 2012).

According to a report by investigative journalists in 2013, Ukrainian businesspeople stood behind a total of approximately 15,000 offshore structures. Of the oligarchs examined here, they identify Poroshenko and Tihipko as owners of offshore holdings (Samsonova & Yurchenko 2013). The so-called Panama papers, based exclusively on leaked documents from the law firm Mossack Fonseca, featured Poroshenko as the most prominent Ukrainian client for offshore services (e.g. Konończuk 2016). The Panama papers include 469 offshore entities linked to Ukraine. This suggests the integration of a broader group of Ukraine's elites into transnational offshore networks, as compared to, e.g., Azerbaijan and Kazakhstan (with just 8 offshore entities managed by Mossack Fonseca), Belarus (35 entities) or Poland (161) and Germany (197). Nevertheless, Ukraine remains a small player in transnational offshore networks, as the Panama Papers alone identify a total of 11,516 offshore entities with links to Russia.[xii] As the transnational networks are non-transparent by their very nature and as the Panama papers reveal only limited information on a very limited number of cases, it is impossible to analyze patterns of the oligarch's offshore networks.

At the same time it has to be noted that in the case of most oligarchs the transnational engagement in offshore networks is not an innovative practice, but rather the use of professional financial services provided by offshore specialists. It seems that, for example, Poroshenko simply asked the offshore law firm Mossack Fonseca to transfer the ownership claims to his assets into offshore legislation. The law firm then created the link to the transnational offshore network.[xiii] The cases of Firtash and Akhmetov described above could fit into a similar pattern. Professional offshore financial service providers are asked to create offshore networks in order to arrange investments and bribe payments. As Privatbank is itself a financial service provider, it seems to be more directly involved in the creation of transnational offshore networks, as the two cases outlined above illustrate.

4. The Impact on Ukraine

Although the specific international and transnational links of individual oligarchs may be rather weak, their total engagement with foreign economies may be more than the sum of its parts, particularly in its impact on foreign policy making. Seen from the state- and power-centered perspective of a geopolitical or geo-economics approach, Ukraine is the object of a power struggle between the EU and Russia. Both are attempting to integrate Ukraine into their sphere of (economic) influence through a combination of incentives and threats. Obviously, the decision of Ukraine's government concerning its foreign policy is of vital importance in this context. As it has been argued that Ukraine's oligarchs have a strong influence on the government, their foreign policy preferences are clearly relevant for Ukraine's integration stance vis-a-vis Russia and the EU (Dimitrova & Dragneva 2013).

In a different take, interdependence theory focuses on the emergence of new actors, e.g., transnational companies, and argues that growing ties between countries in the wake of modernization, which are not exclusively but largely economic, reduce the risk of conflicts between countries, as they increase dependence and, thereby, cooperation and integration. In the case of Ukraine, the relevant question would then be whether the country's interdependence links it more strongly to Russia or to the EU.[xiv]

Analyzing the situation in Ukraine after the Orange Revolution of 2004, Puglisi (2008: 55) has claimed that

> in their effort to acquire social legitimization, to consolidate their ownership rights and to expand control over business assets across Ukraine's border, a number of prominent Ukrainian businessmen became active supporters of Ukraine's engagement in the international community, thus playing a potentially important role in the setting of their country's foreign policy preferences.

However, she also cautions,

> not only mistrust and apprehension of the world market, but the specific preferences of big businessmen who are close to or form part of the country's political leadership [...] might derail western-oriented efforts to the advantage of tighter bonds with Russia. [...] The murky deals concluded around energy issues with Russia are a clear illustration of this risk (ibid.: 81).[xv]

Dimitrova and Dragneva (2013: 672) also highlight the ambivalent position of oligarchs in this respect:

> Our interpretation of the mixed picture of convergence with EU demands within foreign and security policy highlights two important factors [...]. The first one is the existence of specific incentives for some informal veto players, such as gas and coal oligarchs, to accommodate Russia's position, and Russia's tendency to create issue linkages between gas and geopolitics. The second is that convergence with most of the EU's measures and actions in CFSP and ESDP is not very costly for the Ukrainian leadership in terms of electoral support or resources.

To make sense of this ambivalent picture, the different interests of oligarchs, depending on their type of internationalization, need to be taken into account. Ukraine's oligarchic business is marked by a plurality of transnational links with different impacts. The classical business internationalization in the form of FDI is of only limited relevance. As a result, the official business of oligarchs is linked to the outside world primarily through exports, while approximately one-third of the oligarchs (mainly smaller ones) do not have any relevant international business activities. As the oligarchs do not have a real international business, their foreign policy preferences are not guided by an investment agenda. Foreign trade, i.e. dependence on raw material imports from Russia and access to Russian or EU markets for exports, is clearly higher on the agenda of many oligarchs.

The other major international link of Ukraine's oligarchs is created through transnational offshore networks. The concealment of ownership structures and profits is of core relevance for many oligarchic holdings. Offshore activities thus create a link to a dubious and in some instances outright illegal part of the transnational economy outside major production and sales activities. Accordingly, oligarchs have an obvious interest in avoiding international pressure on offshore networks and in defending their rent-seeking opportunities in the domestic Ukrainian market.

As a result, for the oligarchs, Ukraine's integration with the EU is not so much a matter of foreign policy or foreign markets but of EU rules for free competition (as opposed to rent-seeking). As Dimitrova and Dragneva (2013: 678) state, "We find that their position is driven not so much by attitudes to EU integration in general, but by the potential losses from policy change. Most of all, we find that their position is critically linked to control over the political system of rent distribution (or protection from rent losses)."

Moreover, the control over rent distribution is not only challenged by EU competition rules but would, in the event of closer integration of Ukraine with Russia or the Eurasian Economic Union, also be challenged by Russian oligarchs (who are more powerful in both economic and political terms). Langbein (2016: 19) thus concludes in her case study of the Ukrainian car industry, which features Vasadze as one of the oligarchs covered in this chapter, that

> the strategies of both the EU and Russia even provided opportunities for Ukrainian oligarchs with stakes in the domestic car industry, who were not interested in transparent forms of economic interaction in the first place, to pursue rent-seeking strategies that undermined any chance for sustainable development of the industry.

Concerning the integration into transnational networks, this leads to the conclusion that, firstly, Ukraine's oligarchs are primarily involved in offshore networks, which they employ not only for profit hiding and insuring ownership rights but also in the case of foreign direct investments. Secondly, the actual involvement of Ukraine's oligarchs in transnational practices is in most cases very limited as they simply hire specialized service providers. Accordingly, the major impact of transnational networks on Ukraine's oligarchs does not stem directly from active involvement, but from interests caused by the allegiance to offshore networks of dubious legality.

5. Conclusion

The business model of Ukrainian oligarchs is primarily based on a competitive advantage in the home market due to well-developed political connections in an environment marked by limited rule of law and insecure property rights. Accordingly, oligarchic business in Ukraine is not a matter of international expansion but instead concerns the prevention of competition in the domestic market and a strong reliance on non-transparent transnational offshore networks to conceal ownership and profits.

As a result, Ukraine's oligarchic business now faces two transnational challenges. First, economic integration with the EU endangers rent-seeking opportunities in the Ukrainian market. Second, the transnational drive for transparency and against offshore centers increases the risk of criminal prosecution.

The reaction to these challenges is likely to differ across the oligarchs. The smaller oligarchic holdings with no international links will suffer most from the domestic economic crisis, and many may not survive it. Of the larger oligarchic holdings those active in heavy industry and the energy sector are much more dependent on rent-seeking and offshore activities than are those in agriculture and the food industry. This is precisely why oligarchs from heavy industry and the energy sector are currently striving to block reform measures that threaten their rent-seeking activities. Furthermore, the omnipresence of rent-seeking has prevented the emergence of any strong pro-market business group, which the government could recruit to counterbalance oligarchic opposition to the implementation of the reform agenda foreseen in the Association Agreement with the EU.

Overall, Ukraine's oligarchs are neither fully integrated into the transnational economy nor are they a force for increasing transnational business ties. However, their fate is in many cases directly linked to the future of transnational offshore networks.

6. Bibliography

Aslund, Anders. 2014. "Oligarchs, Corruption and European Integration." *Journal of Democracy* 25 (3): 64–73.

Balmaceda, Margarita. 2013. *Politics of Energy Dependency: Ukraine, Belarus, and Lithuania between Domestic Oligarchs and Russian Pressure.* Toronto: University of Toronto Press.

Belaya, Vera. 2015. "Agrarwirtschaft in der Ukraine." *Ukraine-Analysen* 145: 2–10.

Buckley, Peter J. 1988. "Foreign Investment: The Motives." In *Handbook of International Trade*, edited by Michael Z. Brooke and Peter J. Buckley, 203–212. London: Macmillan.

Cockburn, Andrew. 2015. "Undelivered Goods. How $1.8 billion in aid to Ukraine was funneled to the outposts of the international finance galaxy." The Harper's Blog, 13 August 2015. http://harpers.org/blog/2015/08/undelivered-goods/.

Darden, Keith. 2008. "The Integrity of Corrupt States: Graft as an Informal State Institution." *Politics & Society* 36 (1): 35–60.

Demytrie, Rayhan. 2015. "Moldova anger grows over banking scandal." BBC News, Chisinau, 14 September 2015. http://www.bbc.com/news/world-europe-34244341.

Dimitrova, Antoneta and Rilka Dragneva. 2009. "Constraining external governance. Interdependence with Russia and the CIS as limits to the EU's rule transfer in Ukraine." *Journal of European Public Policy* 16 (6): 853–872.

Dimitrova, Antoneta and Rilka Dragneva. 2013. "Shaping convergence with the EU in foreign policy and state aid in post-Orange Ukraine. Weak external incentives, powerful veto players." *Europe-Asia Studies* 65 (4): 658–681.

Dunning, John H. 1994. "Re-evaluating the Benefits of Foreign Direct Investment." *Transnational Corporations* 3 (1): 23–51.

Dyczok, Marta. 2005. "Breaking Through the Information Blockade. Election and Revolution in Ukraine 2004." *Canadian Slavonic Papers* 47 (3-4): 241–264.

Fisun, Oleksandr. 2012. "Electoral Laws and Patronage Politics in Ukraine." *PONARS Eurasia Policy Memo No. 229*.

Gorodnichenko, Yuriy and Yegor Grygorenko. 2008. "Are oligarchs productive? Theory and evidence." *Journal of Comparative Economics* 36 (1): 17–42.

Heathershaw, John and Alexander Cooley. 2015. "Offshore Central Asia. An Introduction." *Central Asian Survey* 34 (1): 1–10.

Hellman Joel S., Geraint Jones and Daniel Kaufmann. 2003. "Seize the State, Seize the Day: State Capture and Influence in Transition Economies." *Journal of Comparative Economics* 31 (4): 751–773.

Herron, Erik S. 2002. "Causes and consequences of fluid faction membership in Ukraine." *Europe-Asia Studies* 54 (4): 625–639.

Hymer, Stephen H. 1976. *The International Operations of National Firms, a Study of Foreign Direct Investment*. Cambridge, MA: MIT Press.

Invest Gazeta. 2012. "Na kakikh kontinentakh ukrainskie predprinimateli imeyut aktivy i biznes interesy." Top-100 rejting 2: 32–33.

Johanson, Jan and Jan-Erik Vahlne. 1977. "The Internationalization Process of the Firm – A Model of Knowledge Development and Increasing Foreign Market Commitment." *Journal of International Business Studies* 8 (1): 23–32.

Konończuk, Wojciech. 2015. "Reform #1. Why Ukraine has to reform its gas sector." *OSW Commentary* 181.

Konończuk, Wojciech. 2016. "President Poroshenko and the 'Panama papers'." *OSW Analyses*. 06 April 2016. http://www.osw.waw.pl/print/24255.

Kowall, Tina. 2006. "Leonid Kutschma und die Oligarchen. Vom Gewinnen und Verlieren der Macht." In *Zwischen Diktatur und Demokratie. Staatspräsidenten als Kapitäne des Systemwechsels in Osteuropa*, edited by Ellen Bos and Antje Helmerich, 117–133. Münster: LIT.

Kubicek, Paul. 2001. "The limits of electoral democracy in Ukraine." *Democratization* 7 (2): 117–139.

Kudelia, Serhyi. 2012. "The sources of continuity and change of Ukraine's incomplete state." *Communist and Post-Communist Studies* 45 (3-4): 417–428.

Kusznir, Julia. 2006. "RosUkrEnergo." *Ukraine-Analysen* 2: 10–11. http://www.laender-analysen.de/ukraine/pdf/UkraineAnalysen02.pdf

Kuzio, Taras. 2007. "Oligarchs, Tapes and Oranges: 'Kuchmagate' to the Orange Revolution." *Journal of Communist Studies and Transition Politics* 23 (1): 30–56.

Langbein, Julia. 2016. "(Dis-)integrating Ukraine? Domestic oligarchs, Russia, the EU, and the politics of economic integration." *Eurasian Geography and Economics* 57 (1): 19–42.

Leshchenko, Serhiy. 2015. "Sunset and/or Sunrise of the Ukrainian Oligarchs after the Maidan?" In *What does Ukraine think?*, edited by Andrew Wilson, 99–107. London: European Council on Foreign Relations.

Levitsky, Steven and Lucan A. Way. 2010. *Competitive authoritarianism. Hybrid regimes after the cold war*. Cambridge: Cambridge University Press.

Matuszak, Sławomir. 2012. "The oligarchic democracy. The influence of business groups on Ukrainian politics." *OSW Studies* 42.

Melnik, Kateryna. 2013. "The peculiarities of formation and development of agricultural holdings in Ukraine." *Problems of World Agriculture* 13 (4): 122–130.

Orlova, Daria. 2010. "Standards of Media Coverage of Elections in Ukraine." In *Public Service Broadcasting: A German-Ukrainian Exchange of Opinions*, edited by Olexiy Khabyuk and Manfred Kops, 95–104. Working Paper No. 277. Cologne: Institute for Broadcasting Economics at the University of Cologne.

Pleines, Heiko. 2008. "Manipulating politics. Domestic investors in Ukrainian privatisation auctions 2000–2004." *Europe-Asia Studies* 60 (7): 1177–1197.

Pleines, Heiko. 2009. "The political role of the oligarchs." In *Ukraine on its way to Europe, Interim results of the Orange Revolution*, edited by Juliane Besters-Dilger, 103–120. Frankfurt/M.: Peter Lang.

Pleines, Heiko. 2016. "Oligarchs and Politics in Ukraine." *Demokratizatsiya* 24 (1): 105–127.

Protsyk, Oleh and Andrew Wilson. 2003. "Centre politics in Russia and Ukraine. Patronage, power and virtuality." *Party Politics* 9 (6): 703–727.

Puglisi, Rosaria. 2003a. "The rise of the Ukrainian oligarchs." *Democratization* 9 (3): 99–123.

Puglisi, Rosaria. 2003b. "Clashing Agendas? Economic Interests, Elite Coalitions and Perspectives of Cooperation between Russia and Ukraine." *Europe-Asia Studies* 55 (6): 827–845.

Puglisi, Rosaria. 2008. "A window to the world? Oligarchs and foreign policy in Ukraine." In *Ukraine. Quo vadis?*, edited by Sabine Fischer, 55–86. Chaillot Paper 108. Paris: EU Institute for Security Studies.

Samsonova, Yuliya and Alisa Yurchenko. 2013. "Maskarad." *Vlast Deneg* 29 (30): 8–12.

State Statistics Service of Ukraine. 2015. Commodity Pattern of Foreign Trade of Ukraine, January-July 2015. Available online http://ukrstat.gov.ua/operativ/operativ2015/zd/tsztt/tsztt_e/tsztt0715_e.htm

Stewart, Susan. 2013. "Public Procurement Reform in Ukraine: The Implications of Neopatrimonialism for External Actors." *Demokratizatsiya* 21 (2): 197–214.

Szostek, Joanna. 2014. "The media battles of Ukraine's EuroMaidan." *Digital Icons* 11: 1–19.

The Baltic Times. 2015. "Latvian regulator hits Privatbank with record fine for Moldova bank fund laundering." 16 December 2015. http://www.baltictimes.com/latvian_regulator_hits_privatbank_with_record_fine_for_moldova_bank_fund_laundering/.

The Economist. 2014. "The countries where politically connected businessmen are most likely to prosper." 15 March 2014.

Troschke, Manuela and Florian Wittmann. 2014. "Inside oligarchs versus outside India. Technical (non)progress and environmental effects in Post-Soviet Steel." *IOS Policy Issues* 1. http://www.ios-regensburg.de/iospublikationen/diskussio nspapiere/policy-issues/1-2014.html.

UNCTAD. 2012. "Investment Country Profile: Ukraine 2012." United Nations Conference on Trade and Development. Available online http://unct ad.org/en/PublicationsLibrary/webdiaeia2012d2Ukraine_en.pdf

Vertovec, Steven. 2009. *Transnationalism*. London, New York: Routledge.

Way, Lucan. 2005. "Rapacious individualism and political competition in Ukraine 1992–2004." *Communist and Post-Communist Studies* 38 (2): 191–205.

Winters, Jeffrey A. 2011. *Oligarchy*. Cambridge: Cambridge University Press.

Zeit online. 2016. "LKA-Beamte sollen jahrelang Schmiergeld angenommen haben." 22 April 2016. http://www.zeit.de/gesellschaft/zeitgeschehen/2016-04/me cklenburg-vorpommern-lka-schmiergelder-verdacht.

---

i   Relevant studies include (in alphabetical order by author): Aslund (2014), Darden (2008), Kowall (2006), Kudelia (2012), Kuzio (2007), Leshchenko (2015), Matuszak (2012), Pleines (2009), Puglisi (2003a), and Way (2005).
On the role of oligarchs in the creation of parliamentary factions and the balance of power in Ukraine's national parliament, see Herron (2002), Kubicek (2001), Protsyk & Wilson (2003), Fisun (2012).
For broader conceptualizations of the political role of oligarchs see: Hellman, Jones & Kaufmann (2003), Levitsky & Way (2010), Winters (2011).

ii   On media ownership see e.g. Dyczok (2005), Orlova (2010), Szostek (2014).

iii For an elaboration on the selection criteria see: Pleines (2016).

iv   Politicians or civil servants who use their political influence to obtain control over economic activities but continue to focus on politics are not included. For this analysis it is, therefore, not relevant how much wealth President Viktor Ianukovych had amassed, as this did not transform him into an entrepreneur.

v   Political activity can be informal or formal, but it should be clear that the entrepreneur seeks to influence political decision-making processes at the national level on a regular basis. This excludes oligarchs who are active in local or regional politics only.

vi   The only exception is Serhii Kurchenko, who has been included, although no estimates of his wealth are available in the lists of millionaires used in this study. He began his major business only in 2013, when it was assumed that he owned more than $200 million, but his companies had already been confiscated by the state in the wake of criminal proceedings before new wealth estimates were published in 2014.

vii The most prominent example of this is Hennadii Boholiubov, who is a partner of Ihor Kolomois'kyi in the Privatbank holding group. In this analysis, Privatbank is treated as one unit of analysis (represented in this study by Kolomois'kyi).

viii The table is available online as an Excel file at [http://www.forschungsstelle.uni-bremen.de/UserFiles/file/table-oligarchs-overview.xls]

ix Author's own compilation. For details, see the table with data for individual oligarchs, which is available online as an Excel file at [http://www.forschungsstelle.uni-bremen.de/UserFiles/file/table-oligarchs-overview.xls]

x Figures for outward FDI stock (1990–2014), according to the UNCTAD World Investment Report 2015, are online available at [http://unctad.org/en/Pages/DIAE/World%20Investment%20Report/Annex-Tables.aspx]. The figures for the overall wealth of oligarchs are based on own compilation. Data and sources are available online as an Excel file at [http://www.forschungsstelle.uni-bremen.de/UserFiles/file/table-oligarchs-overview.xls]

xi The original charges have been published online at [http://www.pravda.com.ua/cdn/graphics/2015/09/sprut_dmitrija_firtasha/index.html?attempt=1] as an embedded pdf file.

xii All figures are from the database built on the leaked Panama Papers, which is available online at [https://offshoreleaks.icij.org/]

xiii The related documents are available at: [https://panamapapers.icij.org/the_power_players/]. For an interpretation see Kanończuk (2016).

xiv On the case of Ukraine the only academic study making an explicit reference to this is: Dimitrova & Dragneva (2009).

xv For an analysis of an earlier period by the same author see: Puglisi (2003b).

Ukraine in the Russian Mass Media: Germany as an Example of Russian Information Policy

Susanne Spahn

Against the backdrop of the Ukraine conflict, Russia has intensified its influence on the spread of information on Russian politics in Germany. In the last few years, the Russian government has massively extended its state media and created an expansive network of partners around the globe to spread its view of Ukraine. In Germany, the Russian media's network of German and Russian experts and supporters circulates official Russian views in the media. By analyzing more than fifty actors of the network and roughly five hundred German and Russian media sources, this study offers insights on the spread of misinformation through the network and its influence on the German public.

1. Introduction: Mass Communication as an Instrument of Russia's Transnational Soft Power

This article aims to analyze the image of Ukraine as presented by state-owned Russian mass media in programs that are specifically designed for Germany. With regard to the war in Ukraine, Russia has intensified its information policy in Germany. Russian state media have greatly expanded in recent years. Furthermore, they have created a network of German cooperation partners, Russian and German experts and supporters, who spread official Russian positions in German mass media and influence the public image of Ukraine. In this context, a relevant question is how efficient Russia is at influencing public opinion in Germany. This article examines which actors, institutions and factors play the most important roles in Russian transnational information policy, particularly in Germany.

Only a few publications have examined the activities of Russian foreign mass media so far. In 2014, Peter Pomerantsev and Michael Weiss (2014) analyzed the development of a Russian information war from a global perspective in their report "The Menace of Unreality: How the Kremlin Weaponizes Information, Culture and Money". However, overall comprehensive analyses of the Russian foreign media are still missing. This text tries to fill that gap.

This analysis is based on a case study of Russian information policy in Germany (Spahn 2016). In this study, 50 actors in the Russian state media network in Germany were identified, and more than 500 sources showing their activities and positions were examined. The analysis was conducted on two levels and is presented accordingly: First, how the Russian mass media network functions on an operational level in Germany will be examined. Second, the content of Russian information policy will be analyzed. The goal of this second section is to scrutinize the image of Ukraine as spread by Russian media and the contradictions that occur between perceptions of Ukraine in Germany-based Russian and genuinely German mass media.

The empirical analysis will show that Russian state media do not have as wide a range in Germany as is sometimes assumed. This narrow range, on the one hand, limits their potential to influence public opinion in Germany. On the other hand, influential German politicians and journalists who are frequently present in Germany-based Russian mass media openly support official Russian positions in domestic nation-wide media. In this context, the image of Ukraine spread by Russian media is only loosely linked to reality. The function of the image seems to be to justify Russia's intervention in Ukraine and to establish a concept of the enemy with the aim of mobilizing people in Russia and abroad.

On a conceptual level, the article aims to evaluate Russian soft power in Germany. It intends to examine how successful Russia is at influencing the German public. In Joseph Nye's theory of international policy, soft power is defined as the "ability to change the behavior of states" (Nye 1990: 155). In contrast to hard power, which uses, for example, coercion by military means, soft power is a co-optive power, that is "the ability of a country to structure a situation so that other countries develop preferences or define their interests in ways consistent with its own" (ibid.: 168). Soft power resources include cultural attractions, ideologies, and international institutions. Nye mentions the capacity for effective communication as well (ibid.: 164, 167–168).

The theoretical section of this study addresses the Russian perception of Western soft power as well as the Russian counter concept. Since the regime changes in Georgia (2003), Ukraine (2004) and Kyrgyzstan (2010), Russia has increasingly invested in its soft power. In that process, Russia has aimed at strengthening authoritarian regimes in neighboring countries, presumably with the intention of preventing democratic regime changes that could spill-over into Russia (Makarychev 2012; Vanderhill 2013).

Russian soft power is quite different from the European Union's (EU) and the United States' understanding of soft power. The West supports civil society and independent media in post-Soviet countries with the intention of weakening authoritarian regimes. The Russian leadership, in contrast, regards the Western promotion of democracy as a threat to its own power and as an intervention into its sphere of influence. Russian soft power can therefore be understood as an instrument of defense against the tools of Western soft power with the aim of not being weakened by the West (Meister & Puglierin 2015: 1–4).

Russian soft power activities have intensified considerably with regard to the Ukraine conflict. Russia claims Ukraine as part of its sphere of influence and sees its power as threatened by the regime change in Kiev in February 2014 and the association agreement between Ukraine and the EU (ibid.). One important aspect of these activities is the Russian international media campaign.

The background of Russian information policy is rooted in the perception of an information war as a component of modern warfare. The corresponding concept was developed by the Russian Military chief of staff Valerij Gerasimov, the military theorist Anatolij Streltsov, and others (Franke 2015: 27–31). Colonel Streltsov serves as an advisor to the Russian National Security Council and has written several influential books about strategies of information security. On the basis of Nye's concept of soft power, Streltsov developed a Russian version of "miakhkaia sila". This term can be translated as "soft power" as well as "soft force", but the latter fits the Russian perception better.

Streltsov differentiates between a political information war and a technical information war. On a political level, he tries to prevent Russia from being "slandered" abroad; this aim is supposedly achieved in cooperation with the media. On a technical level, cyber weapons are supposed to destroy the information infrastructure of the enemy (ibid.: 29–30). This perception broadens the definition of soft power by Nye because it includes the use of cyber weapons. It also contradicts Nye, who excludes force and pressure in his understanding of soft power (Sergunin & Karabeshkin 2015: 252–254). The Russian perception of soft power thus has a broader meaning and, while generally applied to non-military means, can include coercive methods.

Russian information policy also bears a transnationalist element. Here I refer to Steven Vertovec, who refers to transnationalism as a site of political engagement (Vertovec 2009: 10–11). According to Vertovec, actors have political aims and pursue them by operating beyond borders. Russian transnational actors are presented by international media companies, which cooperate in Germany with different actors (politicians, journalists and organizations) and are not linked with the German government.

2. The Transnational Context of the Russian Media Campaign: Methods and Data

I now turn to my analysis, which is based on a dataset of fifty media actors and five hundred sources. In the first step, the actors of Russia's transnational network were identified. Second, a text corpus was created by compiling media outlets of Russian foreign media in Germany as well as German publications about the Ukraine conflict. Russian media reports published in Russia were included as well. Third, an analysis of the text corpus was conducted to obtain results about the role the actors play within the network of the Russian state media in Germany. For this purpose, the method of qualitative text analysis was applied (Gläser & Laudel 1999, 2004: 191–200). The actors were associated with different variables, such as "Russia" or "Ukraine-conflict", and in this way, the relevant contributions were extracted. Each actor's role in the debate, as well as the personal and institutional intertwining of the actors, was evaluated (Gläser & Laudel 1999: 10–11, 21–22; Gläser & Laudel 2004: 197–202).

Russian foreign media, their cooperation partners and their German supporters were examined using methods of content analysis. The part of the analysis that focused on argumentation patterns found in media reports was conducted within the framework of the linguistic media discourse approach developed by Ekkehard Felder (2012: 115–174). Its basis was a text corpus composed of Russian and German media reports. In the next step, controversial issues, so-called 'agonal centers', were defined. These are discourse elements involving controversial interpretations of events or different claims of validity (ibid.: 132–144). Agonal centers as analytical figures of media discourse analyses help in identifying central sub-issues of discourses that represent discursive competition. With regard to the question of the promoted image of Ukraine in Russian and German media, agonal centers highlight the differences in conflict perception.

3. Political and Historical Background: The Functioning of the Media in Russia and the International Media Campaign

A look at history reveals that journalism in Russia has been linked to the state since the establishment of the first newspaper by Peter the Great in 1702 (Albrecht 2008: 33). In the Soviet Union, media also served the state. Journalists held a "special place of honor in the great struggle of building communism" (ibid.), as the first secretary of the Communist Party Nikita Chrushchev once noted. Only before the collapse of the Soviet Union was there a short period of time during which the media regarded themselves as the fourth power in the state. However, the Russian media were never fully democratized. One of the main obstacles was the elite's traditional understanding of the media as an instrument of power. In addition, the emergence of private property was a new phenomenon and oligarchs took control of the media, particularly national TV channels. In practice, journalists have mostly served as a voice for the powerful. Apart from a small independent minority, most media have represented the interests of the government or oligarchs and thus have been a tool of their donors (Albrecht 2008: 41–59; Trautmann 2002: 475–481).

After Vladimir Putin was elected president in the year 2000, one of his first deeds was to establish state control of information. In subsequent years, the media system changed significantly. Opposition oligarchs such as Boris Berezovskii and Vladimir Gusinskii were forced to leave the country. Today, the most important TV channels are controlled by the state (*Pervyi kanal, Rossiya*) and by state-affiliated companies such as Gazprom Media (*NTV*) or by loyal oligarchs (Albrecht 2008: 108; Trautmann 2002: 489–498; Blum 2014: 128–135; Amelina 2006: 273–285). The Russian media system can be classified as state-dominated and commercial (Blum 2014: 135). 91% of the population stay informed via TV. Only 1% of Russians read independent Newspapers such as *Novaia Gazeta*, and 4.5% listen to the radio program *Echo Moskvy* or watch the channel *Ren TV* (ibid.: 132–133). In addition, laws have been tightened to make independent media reporting more difficult. Critically minded journalists are prosecuted and sometimes even murdered (Albrecht 2008: 71–74; Blum 2014: 129–131).

Television has played a central role in stabilizing the authoritarian regime of president Putin. Putin and his government dominate the news and present themselves as successful leaders (Amelina 2006: 293). Patriotism dominates TV programming, particularly following the annexation of Crimea, helping to foster an approval rating of 80 to 90% in the opinion polls for Putin. Arguably, TV programs follow a nation-building mission. According to studies, the majority of Russians expect the news to show patriotism and evoke nostalgia for the Soviet Union (Hutchings & Rulyova 2009: 51–56, 213–214).

The Russian Media's Transnational Campaign on Ukraine
The Russian leadership started an international media campaign regarding the Ukraine conflict. President Putin himself took charge of information policy in foreign countries. The news agency *RIA Novosti*—the largest and most modern agency in Russia—merged with the radio station *Golos Rossii* (Voice of Russia) to become the International Information Agency *Rossiya Segodnia* (Russia today) in accordance with Putin's decree (Lenta.Ru 2013). In November 2014, *Rossiya Segodnia* launched an international media project called "Sputnik International". By the year 2015, *Rossiya Segodnia* planned to broadcast in 130 cities in 34 countries in 30 languages (Sputnik News 2014). Russia has relied on its established foreign media, which is the news agency *RIA Novosti*, the radio station *Voice of Russia* and the TV channel *RT* (Dornblüth 2014a). Currently, *RT* runs 22 offices in 19 countries (Reporter ohne Grenzen 2013). *Rossiya Segodnia* maintains a network of 40 branches all over the world (MIA n.d.).

The TV channel *RT* plays the most important role in foreign countries, as the extensive financial resources of the company indicate (Chasov-Kassia & Silverman 2014). *RT* has planned a French and German program. Regarding the German context, *RT Deutsch* started a German website on 5 November 2014. A TV channel was supposed to follow in 2015 but has not been launched yet (Brunner 2014). In fact, there are doubts that the international media campaign will be fully realized. Due to the currency losses of the ruble, the budget of *RT* and *Rossiya Segodnia* for 2015 shrunk to €301m by August 2015. At the time of budgeting, in September 2014, it comprised €444m—a loss of value of approximately one third (Chasov-Kassia & Silverman 2014). Still, Russia significantly increased its spending on *RT* and *Rossiya Segodnia* in 2015. Central government funding rose by a third in terms of rubles; €340m will be spent on foreign media. This increase in spending underlines the growing importance the Kremlin has attached to its international media operations. They accounted for 34% of total central government media spending in 2016, compared to 25% the year before (Ennis 2015).

The most remarkable aspect of this targeted setup of a broad transnational Russian media network is that these efforts are accompanied by the open avowal that the Russian information policy is an integral part of hybrid or non-linear warfare. This policy is confirmed by statements of leading Russian media managers. Editor-in-chief of *RT*, Margarita Simonian, called the broadcaster *RT* a "ministry of defense" of the Kremlin, as much "a weapon as every weapon" (Reporter ohne Grenzen 2013: 35). The USA is a major focus of the information war because it is regarded as an enemy in a continuing Cold War and as a mastermind behind the regime change in Ukraine in February 2014. The USA's main allies, primarily Germany, also serve as major targets in Russia's purposeful (dis-)information campaign.

Russia's Media Network in Germany
In Germany, Russian information policy aims at creating understanding for Russian positions and establishing a counter public to the German media, which is manipulated from the point of view of Russian media. A striking example of this counter-campaign is *RT Deutsch*'s main political show named "The missing part". The Russian TV show promises to present 'the truth', which the German mainstream media are accused of hiding (RT Deutsch n.d.). The German government has been heavily criticized for its policy towards Russia, for example in terms of the sanctions in reaction to the annexation of Crimea. The Russian foreign media support German opposition to this policy against Russia and thus put pressure on the German government.[i]

The transnational network of the Russian information policy in Germany includes organizations as well as individual actors. The most important corporate actors are the Russian state media (*Rossiya Segodnia*) with their integrated radio and news website *Sputniknews*, TV channel *RT Deutsch*, and video agency *Ruptly*. Whereas all of these are based in Berlin, the *Agency for Internet Research* is located in St. Petersburg, Russia. The Russian state media in Germany cooperate with left and rightwing populists, such as the editor in chief of the magazine *Compact*, Jürgen Elsässer, and the director of the internet TV program *Ken FM*, Ken Jebsen. These individual media actors are often present in the Russian state media, where they are introduced as 'German experts' or 'expert interview partners'. They advertise Russian media and spread official Russian foreign policy positions while attending various events. They also organize events themselves, such as the discussions "Compact live" in Berlin, as well as other conferences and web-petitions. In their own media, Elsässer and Jebsen also publish content favorable to Russian politics. The Russian media *RT* and *Rossiya Segodnia* report regularly about the events attended or organized by these cooperation partners. In sum, this cooperation can be classified as a media partnership (Spahn 2016: 23).

German actors also arise within the network. Several German journalists, politicians and organizations publicly express their sympathy and even strike an uncritical attitude towards Russian positions in the Ukraine conflict. Journalists such as Udo Ulfkotte, Eva Herman, Mathias Bröckers, Paul Schreyer, Gabriele Krone-Schmalz and Jakob Augstein publish books and media outlets that show a very lopsided understanding and defense of Russian policy (Augstein 2014; Bröckers & Schreyer 2014; Herman 2014; Ulfkotte 2014).[ii] In addition, Krone-Schmalz and Augstein also take part in talk shows on German national TV channels, where they obviously intend to influence a broad audience (Phoenix 2014; Precht 2014). Among the political parties, members of Die Linke (The Left), Alternative für Deutschland (Alternative for Germany) and the German Social Democrats support positions that are very close to the official line of Russia, including among them, prominent public persons such as former chancellor Gerhard Schröder (Gehrcke 2014; Gauland 2014; Greven 2014). Some organizations, such as the German-Russian Forum with their chairman Matthias Platzeck and the Committee on Eastern European Economic Relations headed by the former Metro-Manager Eckhard Cordes, also criticize—in a significantly biased style—the policy of the German government towards Russia and show strong and unquestioned support for Russian positions (Zeit Online 2014; Cordes 2014).

A central topic of the Russian foreign media and their supporters is to discredit the German media by and large. The German media are generally accused of 'keeping the truth secret'—as suggested by *RT Deutsch*'s daily program "The Missing Part"—and are openly suspected of being ruled by intelligence services and transatlantic circles. As a result, citizen groups have formed with the explicit purpose of overrunning German media members with complaints, eventually to put them out of service. The number of complaints, submitted for example by the Association of the Permanent Public Conference of the public-service media based in Leipzig, continues to grow (Ständige Publikumskonferenz n.d.). The sheer number of complaints has significantly affected the ability of editorial offices to function (Niggemeier 2015). Paid web-activists hired by the *Agency for Internet Resea*rch in

St. Petersburg block discussions on websites with their comments (Rosbach 2014). These actors combine criticism of the media with strong favor for Russia in the Ukraine-conflict. This can be seen, for example, when the Permanent Public Conference blamed the German channel *ARD* for characterizing Russia as a conflict party in Ukraine and thereby directly promoted the Russian narrative of an 'internal civil war' (Ständige Publikumskonferenz 2014).

The instruments of Russian soft power in Germany include not only Russian state media and their cooperation partners but also Russian political state organizations, such as the Russian embassy in Berlin and the Agency for Cooperation with Russians abroad, Rossotrudničestvo. The Russian ambassador to Germany, Vladimir Grinin, actively takes part in the German media discourse regarding the Ukraine conflict (Botschaft der Russichen Föderation 2014a, 2014b, 2014c). The embassy in Berlin is in close contact with German politicians such as Alexander Gauland, vice-leader of the right-wing party Alternative for Germany and other party members who actively support Russian official positions and conduct "strategic consultations" in the embassy (Spiegel Online 2014). Rossotrudničestvo tries to spread an "objective view" of Russia abroad and organizes trips to Russia to inform German students about Russia and its foreign policy (Dornblüth 2014b, "O Rossotrudničestve" n.d.).

4. Russian Media in Germany and their Coverage of the Ukraine Crisis

Activities of Russia's Network Actors
In Germany, the Russian state media cooperate with right and left populist partners. One important actor is Jürgen Elsässer, chief editor of the monthly magazine *Compact*. Elsässer is not only an alleged 'expert' who is frequently present in Russian media, but he also disseminates the Russian version of the Ukrainian conflict in Germany, for example, when speaking about the Kiev coup regime and its Western backers (Compact TV 2014a).

Elsässer's activities are based on a well-developed political network. He is in close contact with Russian culture institutions in Berlin and Paris as well as with members of German political parties such as the Christian Democratic Union (CDU), the Social Democratic Party (SPD), and the Alternative für Deutschland (AfD). He is said to maintain good relations with Putin's close associate Vladimir

Yakunin, the former president of Russian railways, and he was one of the main speakers at the so-called 'Conference for Peace with Russia' in November 2014 in Berlin (Dassen 2014). Elsässer actively contributes to the development and distribution of anti-semitic statements and conspiracy theories. This became obvious when he publicly declared Germans as 'victims of the international financial system' and tried to mobilize against the presence of American troops in Germany. With the help of these conspiracy theories and the fundamental hostility to the USA, he has created a connection to leftist groups such as the movements of the 'Vigils' and the 'Monday demonstrations'. In more than one hundred German cities, these protesters campaign against the German government and its allegedly militant 'military policy'. During his performances, Elsässer declares himself an activist for peace who tries to defend Russia against the (supposedly) 'aggressive West' and to 'protect the German people from war'. Elsässer considers himself as a so-called 'Putin-Versteher' ('Putin-understander')—an ambivalent term that has gained prominence in the German public debate. The term "Versteher" originally referred to people who heavily sympathized with certain positions in a very naïve way. Hence, Versteher used to be a mocking term. During the Ukraine-Crisis, however, people started to declare themselves as 'Russland- (or Putin-) Versteher', emphasizing that they—and only they—are the ones who really understand (and appreciate) Russian politics. Needless to say, 'Versteher' do not express doubts or a preference for debate because they claim to know the truth.[iii] Elsässer has declared that he is convinced that most Germans are 'Putin understanders' but are unfortunately misled by "the Merkel system and its nasty journalistic followers" (Compact TV 2014b).

Elsässer's network activities are manifold. He actively advertises for the Russian mass media, particularly the new website *RT Deutsch*, and supports Russian policy positions in various ways (Compact TV 2014c): in his monthly show *Compact live* in Berlin, the Monday demonstrations, his speeches at demonstrations of Pegida (Patriotic Europeans against the Islamization of the Western World) and Legida (the Leipzig based branch of Pegida), special book presentations such as "Putin's Speeches" at the cultural institute "Russisches Haus", and his yearly so-called conference of sovereignty. Among the main speakers at the above-mentioned peace conference were the former German Minister of Research and Technology Andreas von Bülow (SPD) and the former state secretary in the ministry of defense Willy Wimmer (CDU). The guest of honor was Egon Bahr, a former minister in the government of Willy Brandt and one of the architects of the German *Ostpolitik*, which is publicly associated with the still popular slogan "change through rapprochement". In his conference speech, Bahr stressed a 'misunderstanding' in German society concerning Russia: "Some people are afraid of Russia", but these fears, Bahr assured, were groundless (Dassen 2014). This not only contradicts the general awareness of a rising danger of conflicts in the post-Soviet sphere but also publicly relieves Russia from any suspicion of responsibility for this danger.

An Effective Media Network or a Tiger Turned into a Rug?
Because the Russian international media campaign "Sputnik international" was launched just a year ago, it is too early to draw final conclusions about its effectiveness. The new label Sputniknews is still in the phase of being established. *SNA-Radio* (SNA—Sputnik-News-Agency), like *RT*, operates with an abbreviation and presents itself as an independent news source. Most German audiences are therefore not able to immediately recognize that the source of information is financed by the Russian state. On the level of the German Länder, *SNA-Radio* operates under the name *Mega-Radio*. The broadcasting can be heard on websites via Livestream or by digital radio DAB+. *Mega-Radio* broadcasts in Berlin, Brandenburg, and Hessen.[iv] In summer 2015, the International Information Agency *Rossiya Segodnia* tried to buy broadcasting time on German radio stations to extend the *Sputniknews* audience (Hans 2015).

Overall, *RT Deutsch* suffers from poor coverage. In December 2014, most of the articles on the website had less than 2,000 users and the daily program "The Missing Part" had less than 4,000 viewers. After February 2015, user numbers were hidden (Spahn 2016: 56–57). In September 2015, "The Missing Part" was reduced to three times per week, an indication of either the lack of acceptance of the program or financial problems. Since February 2016, there has been only one program per week.[v] Representatives of the Russian state media in Germany tend to appear on public German TV. Leading Russian journalists such as Igor Rodionov, the chief editor of *RT Deutsch* and *Ruptly TV*, and Dmitrii Tulchinskii, the head of *Rossiya Segodnia*, might thus receive a much broader audience when attending popular TV talk shows moderated by popular German talk show hosts, such as Anne Will, Günter Jauch, and Michel Friedman (N24 Talk 2014; Tulcinskij cited by Kerneck 2014).

Furthermore, the audience of the so-called 'Querfront movement' of Jürgen Elsässer and Ken Jebsen is quite limited. The magazine *Compact* has a circulation of 30,000 copies. The range of Ken Jebsen's *Ken FM* is wider and has 81,600 subscribers (Lauer 2014).[vi] However, due to public activities and cooperation with Monday demonstrations, Vigils for Peace and the Pegida movements, the scope is continuously extending according to information published by Elsässer and Jebsen themselves (Compact TV 2016).[vii] An objective rating does not yet exist. More effective than the Russian state media and their cooperation partners themselves are public persons of trust who appear on television and nation-wide media in Germany, such as Gerhard Schröder, Matthias Platzeck, Gabriele Krone-Schmalz and Jakob Augstein. All of them have a significantly broader impact on the German public through their presence in nation-wide TV channels, radio programs and the printed press. In fact, these German supporters are the sharpest weapon in Russian information warfare (Spahn 2016: 106).

Russian Information Policy with Regard to Ukraine
The Russian state media in Germany offer a distorted presentation of actualities by using selective facts and falsifications. As an example, below the *RT Deutsch* report heading "New NATO-Game in Ukraine: I can see something, but you can't", the following text is presented:

> According to NATO-commander in Europe, Philip Breedlove, the transfer of Russian military technics into Eastern Ukraine has recently been observed. The UN and Russia deny this allegation. However, what NATO and OSCE confirm, the UN cannot affirm. On Friday the UN spokesman, Stephane Dujarric, stated that a transfer of Russian troops by the UN could not be confirmed. The Russian ministry of defense in Moscow has also rejected the allegation that the Russian military has intervened in Ukraine as inaccurate (RT Deutsch 2014b).

The aim of this report is to deny the existence of Russian military convoys in Ukraine otherwise proved by NATO's photographic material. This report contains a falsification. At the briefing of UN spokesman Stephane Dujarric on Friday, 7 November, a journalist asked, "Is the UN in the position to independently verify these reports?" Dujarric answered, "On the troop movement, no, we're not, at this point from here, able to verify it." This statement was translated in German as "to confirm" (German: "bestätigen") (United Nations 2014).

Another report is entitled "Because he's Russian – star conductor Gergiev's invitation canceled" (RT Deutsch 2014c). The report shows the alleged discrimination of conductor Valeriy Gergiev because of his nationality. *RT Deutsch* copied a report of the German tabloid *Bild Zeitung* without verification (Bild Online 2014). Festival director Robert Leonardy denied that report: "We haven't invited him, so we couldn't cancel his invitation – we are not political." In addition, the director of the music festival stated that Gergiev was not worth considering because of his closeness to Putin (Deutschlandradio Kultur 2014).

Another example shows how important information is hidden, as was the case while the annexation of Crimea was being carried out. Three statements by *Voice of Russia* at different points at different times illustrate this strategy:

> "While Moscow has made no mention of an annexation of Crimea, they regard recent events in Kiev as an unconstitutional coup that has lead Ukraine into chaos" (Stimme Russlands 2014a, on 4 March 2014).

> "Immediately after the president's speech, an intergovernmental treaty on the integration of Crimea into the Russian Federation was signed" (Stimme Russlands 2014b, on 3 March 2014).

> "President Vladimir Putin appreciated the professionalism of the Russian military during the events on Crimea in spring: The military has saved the inhabitants of the Black-Sea-peninsula from bloodshed" (Stimme Russlands 2014c, on 19 December 2014).

The actors within Russian information policy—the Russian media as well as their German supporters—share a single line of argument that varies solely in the details concerning the beginning and the reasons for the Ukrainian crisis. Several controversial issues, so-called agonal centers within the framework of the linguistic discourse-analysis, dominate the Russian narrative. Some of these are "Crimea has always been Russian", "NATO threatens Russia", "the regime change in Kiev of February 2014 was a coup financed by the USA", "fascists or radical nationalists control Ukraine", "Russians and Russian-speaking citizens are being suppressed and thus need Russia's protection", "Ukraine isn't a real state", and "Russians and Ukrainians are one people" (for details on the analysis and sources, see Spahn 2016: 91–102).

These arguments support and promote the Russian narrative of the Ukrainian crisis. First, Russia is portrayed as threatened by NATO's enlargement, which is underlined by the imputation of NATO's (alleged) intention to allocate missiles in Ukraine. Second, the regime change in Kiev in February 2014 is depicted as a coup financed by the USA that brought fascists or radical nationalists to power. This is linked to another agonal center, which is the often repeated assertion that fascists or radical nationalists rule in and dominate Ukraine. President Putin confirmed this view when he claimed in an interview with the first German public channel ARD: "There are people out there with swastikas on their sleeves. We are seeing SS symbols on the helmets of the troops fighting in eastern Ukraine." In the same interview, Putin stated that he was worried about "ethnic cleansing" carried out in Ukraine (ARD 2014). This thesis of 'fascism in Ukraine' is actively spread in Germany by the Russian state media and their cooperation partners, such as Elsässer, as well as by politicians of the left party "Die Linke" (Gehrcke 2014a, 2014b; Compact TV 2014a).

These findings lead to the thesis that Russian media policy in Germany is based on the narrative of Russian authorities, who claim a 'necessity to defend Russia' and to intervene in Ukraine to safeguard Russian interests with regard to geopolitics, the protection of its own sphere of influence, and the preservation of the Black Sea Fleet in Crimea. The same applies to Eastern Ukraine. Russia publicly defines itself as the 'protector' of the Russian-speaking population in Ukraine. According to the Russian narrative, the annexation of Crimea and the separation of the so-called Peoples' Republics in Eastern Ukraine reflect the will of the people living in these regions. From this perspective, the West is accused of having provoked the crisis, and Russia reacted to the Western and nationalist threat. This reasoning transforms Russia from aggressor to victim. The narrative aims at persuading the West to respect Russia's interests, i.e., to recognize the post-Soviet region as an exclusive Russian sphere of influence (Spahn 2016: 89).

The Russian claim that the West should respect Russian interests and recognize the post-Soviet area as a sphere of exclusively Russian interest is another controversial issue. This claim is supported by journalists and politicians such as Jakob Augstein and former chancellor Gerhard Schröder. The Russian claim to power contradicts the post-Soviet countries' right to independence, territorial integrity and free choice of allies and thus is contrary to international law (Greven 2014; Augstein 2014).

In sum, Germany-based Russian media depict Ukraine as a geopolitical object that has been (unjustifiably) withdrawn from the Russian sphere of influence by the USA and EU. The Russian claim to power has its roots in an imperial tradition and national identity that regards Ukrainians as a part of the Russian people. One of the corporate opinion leaders founded by the Russian president and consulting the presidential administration is the Russian Institute for Strategic Studies. Its director, Leonid Reshetnikov, stated in an interview, "Russia proceeds towards renaissance of the Eastern orthodox civilization". He continued by stating that Russia is taking the place "determined [for it] by God and history" and that "Russia will be a global power again" (Russian Institute for Strategic Studies 2014). Like president Putin, Reshetnikov regards Ukraine as an artificial entity that in fact is "Malaya Rossiya" ("Little Russia"). From his point of view, the cause of the crises is the "artificial foundation of Ukraine". He underlines that Ukrainians are "our people" (ibid.). The theory of the all-Russian nation dates back to the 18th century, serving to justify the integration of the Eastern Slavonic regions of Ukraine and Belarus into the Russian Empire (Spahn 2014: 258–272).

Effectiveness with Regard to the German Public
How effective has Russian information policy been regarding its impact on the German public? It is too early to draw final conclusions because the international media campaign was only launched in 2014. Nevertheless, certain preliminary remarks can be made. According to an opinion poll carried out by the Institute for Public Opinion Research Allensbach, 55% of Germans hold Russia responsible for the conflict in Ukraine, followed by 34% who accuse the separatists of causing the conflict (Petersen 2015). Only a fifth of respondents said that Ukraine is responsible for the crisis. The USA and the EU were named by 17% and 6%, respectively. In regard to the cause of the crisis, two thirds of the respondents agreed with the statement "Russia supports separatists in Eastern Ukraine by delivering military equipment and weapons" (ibid.). 61% think that "Russia is trying to conquer Ukraine", 51% believe that the conflict in Eastern Ukraine occurred only because president Putin intended it (ibid.).

Key statements of the Russian narrative of the Ukraine conflict, however, are supported by a relative minority. 20% of the respondents believe that the current Ukrainian government came to power by a coup, and another fifth is convinced that the conflict in Eastern Ukraine escalated because of Western intervention. Only 7% believe that Russia has protected people in Eastern Ukraine from suppression by the Ukrainian government (ibid.). There is a remarkable difference between the supporters of different political parties. Only 7% of CDU/CSU voters, 4% of SPD voters, and 3% of Green Party voters believe that Russia has protected people in Eastern Ukraine from suppression—in contrast to a fifth of the voters of "Die Linke" and 15% of supporters of the right-wing populist party "Alternative für Deutschland" (ibid.).

The support of one fifth of the German population might be interpreted as an intermediate result of the Russian information policy in Germany, although a causal relationship cannot be substantiated by the data of this study. However, several stereotypes, such as "Ukraine isn't a real state", "NATO has surrounded Russia" and "the West supports fascists in Ukraine", are present—but not dominant—in the German discourse. There have been attempts to blur Russia's role as an aggressor in the conflict by presenting Ukraine and the West as the bad guys in the story. The cited data from the Allensbach survey shows that the immense effort with which the Russian media campaign on Ukraine has been pushed has not yet led to a substantial swing in opinion in Germany.

5. Conclusion

The beginning of the Ukrainian crisis was triggered by Russia violating Ukrainian sovereignty and territorial integrity by annexing Crimea, which led to Western sanctions against Russia. The purposefully spread Russian political narrative reverses this account, portraying the West (EU and the USA) as the aggressor and Russia as the victim. The real victim—Ukraine—is painted as a fascist regime and deemed an accomplice of the West that threatens Russians and the Russian-speaking population in Crimea and Eastern Ukraine. The function of this image is to justify the Russian intervention in Ukraine by portraying Russia as the protecting the power of the Russian-speaking population abroad. The image of an enemy is created by depicting the alleged fascist threat in Ukraine, playing off memories of the Second World War and the fight against fascist Germany. This enemy has presumably been created internally to consolidate Russian society and externally to politically mobilize people in Russia and abroad.

This article analyzed the multifaceted media network that has been set up to transport, disseminate and further these narratives in a broad public. It became obvious that media institutions cooperate with individual actors on different levels and in both Germany and Russia to promote the biased perspective of the Russian government. With this purposeful media network and campaigns, Russia reformulates the term of public diplomacy in favor of illiberalism. An interesting aspect here is the promotion of illiberalism through liberal political conditions. By establishing a regime of guided misinformation, the Russian foreign media profit from the freedom of press in Germany—something only partially existent in Russia (Gillert 2014)—to discredit the so-called mainstream media. Whereas in the Russian authoritarian system, the distribution of information is state-controlled, Russian leadership takes advantage of open societies, such as Germany, to sow doubt and insecurity (Müller von Blumencron 2015).

The second central question of this article was the effectiveness of the Russian campaign. Here, the analysis shows that the Russian regime has extended its ambitions to exert influence through the media beyond Russian borders. Russian domestic media are broadcast in a number of countries, particularly in former Soviet countries. Today, Russian media are blocked in the non-occupied territories of Ukraine, but until 2014, Russian state media were able to disseminate messages and interpretations from the Russian regime quite freely. However, Russia has now started a state media offensive for non-Russian speaking audiences in several countries. In this respect, it has started a transnational strategy. The effect of this strategy seems to be rather limited, at least in Germany. Still, many German politicians are reluctant to name basic facts, such as the Russian occupation of Eastern Ukraine, and instead talk about a civil war or Russian-backed separatists. All this is in line with the messages presented on Russian media and their influential German supporters. Whereas the range of Russian state media in Germany is very limited, well-known German politicians and journalists support the Russian narrative in nation-wide media outlets. These German supporters are, in fact, the sharpest weapon in the information war.

6. Bibliography

Albrecht, Erik. 2008. *Die Meinungsmacher. Journalistische Kultur und Pressefreiheit in Russland.* Köln: von Halem.

Amelina, Anna. 2006. *Propaganda oder Autonomie? Das russische Fernsehen von 1970 bis heute.* Bielefeld: transcript Verlag.

ARD. 2014. "Das Putin-Interview – wohin steuert der Kreml-Chef?" *ARD*, 16 November 2014. https://www.tagesschau.de/multimedia/video/video-40641.html

Augstein, Jakob. 2014. "S.P.O.N. – Im Zweifel links: Alien vs. Predator." *Spiegel online*, 20 November 2014. http://www.spiegel.de/politik/ausland/putin-platzeck-und-die-krim-krise-kolumne-von-jakob-augstein-a-1003994.html.

Bild Online. 2014. "Weil er Russe ist. Musikfestspiele laden Star-Dirigent aus." *Bild online*, 9 November 2014. http://www.bild.de/regional/saarland/festivals/star-dirigent-bei-saar-musikfestspielen-ausgeladen-38495094.bild.html.

Blum, Roger. 2014. *Lautsprecher und Widersprecher. Ein Ansatz zum Vergleich der Mediensysteme.* Köln: von Halem.

Botschaft der Russischen Föderation. 2014a. "Der Botschafter Vladimir Grinin nahm an der Podiumsdiskussion in Osnabrück teil." *Mitteilung der Botschaft der RF,* 5 November 2014. http://russische-botschaft.de/de/2014/11/05/der-botschafter-wladimir-grinin-nahm-an-der-podiumsdiskussion-in-osnabruck-teil/.

Botschaft der Russischen Föderation. 2014b. "Interview des Botschafters Wladimir Grinin für die 'Wiesbadener Kurier'." *Botschaft der Russischen Föderation in Deutschland,* 10 June 2014. http://russische-botschaft.de/de/2014/06/10/interview-des-botschafters-wladimir-grinin-fur-die-wiesbadener-kurier-2/.

Botschaft der Russischen Föderation. 2014c. "Beitrag des Botschafters. Interview für die Bild am Sonntag." *Botschaft der Russischen Föderation in Deutschland*,12 March 2014. http://russische-botschaft.de/de/2014/03/12/beitrag-des-botschafters/.

Bröckers, Mathias and Paul Schreyer. 2014. *Wir sind die Guten – Ansichten eines Putinverstehers oder wie uns die Medien manipulieren.* Frankfurt am Main: Westend-Verlag.

Brunner, Simone. 2014. "Russia Today macht Antiamerikanismus weltweit sexy." *Profil,* 18 October 2014. http://www.profil.at/gesellschaft/medien-russia-today-antiamerikanismus-378226.

Chasov-Kassia, Sergej and Sara Silverman. 2014. "Novosti s moskovskim akcentom." *Belarusskaja Pravda*, 5 October 2014. http://belprauda.org/novosti-s-moskovskim-aktsentom/.

Compact TV. 2014a. "«Krieg gegen Russland – wie die NATO nach Osten marschiert» - COMPACT Spezial #4 – Heftvorstellung." 1 October 2014. Accessed on 2 November 2014. https://www.youtube.com/watch?v=P4-fdgWQNFg.

Compact TV. 2014b. "Die Deutschen sind das Volk der Putinversteher" - Jürgen Elsässer - Washingtonplatz/Berlin 20.9.14." 21 September 2014. Accessed on 2 November 2014. https://www.youtube.com/watch?v=YDCHYNSo5Jo.

Compact TV. 2014c. "RT auf Deutsch – Nachrichten gegen die Mainstream-Propaganda." *Compact TV*, 4 September 2014. Accessed 25 October 2014. https://www.youtube.com/watch?v=d5GMVCGt6zQ.

Compact TV. 2016. "Elsässer vor 5.000 Merkel-Gegnern in Zwickau." Last modified 23 February 2016. https://www.youtube.com/watch?v=PgWeaqbdnFY.

Cordes, Eckhard. 2014. "Sanktionen kreieren Wagenburg-Mentalität" Interview by Tobias Armbrüster. *Deutschlandfunk*, 19 December 2014. http://www.deutschlandfunk.de/russische-wirtschaft-sanktionen-kreieren-wagenburg.694.de.html?dram:article_id=306654.

Dassen, Marc. 2014. "Dritte Compact-Souveränitätskonferenz. 2014. Frieden mit Russland." *Compact Online*. 22 November 2014. https://www.compact-online.de/dritte-compact-souveraenitaetskonferenz-frieden-mit-russland-22-11-014/.

Deutschlandradio Kultur. 2014. "Musikfestspiele Saar: Kein Engagement für Putin-Freund Gergiev." *Deutschlandradio Kultur*, 10 November 2014. http://www.deutschlandradiokultur.de/musikfestspiele-saar-kein-engagement-fuer-putin-freund.265.de.html?drn:news_id=420059

Dornblüth, Gesine. 2014a. "Die Medienoffensive des Kreml." *Deutschlandfunk*, 11 November 2014. http://www.deutschlandfunk.de/russland-die-medienoffensive-des-kreml.1773.de.html?dram:article_id=302804.

Dornblüth, Gesine. 2014b. "Professor Haag lobt Russland." *Deutschlandfunk*, 21 October 2014. http://www.deutschlandfunk.de/moskaus-imagearbeit-professor-haag-lobt-russland.1773.de.html?dram:article_id=300902.

Ennis, Stephen. 2015. "Russia in 'information war' with West to win hearts and minds" *BBC*, 16 September 2015. http://www.bbc.com/news/world-europe-34248178.

Felder, Ekkehard. 2012. "Pragma-semiotische Textarbeit und der hermeneutische Nutzen von Korpusanalysen für die linguistische Mediendiskursanalyse." In *Korpuspragmatik. Thematische Korpora als Basis diskurslinguistischer Analysen*, edited by Ekkehard Felder, Marcus Müller and Friedemann Vogel, 115–174. Berlin, Boston: De Gruyter.

Franke, Ulrike. 2015. "War by Non-Military Means. Understanding Russian Information Warfare." *FOI-R-4065-SE*, March 2015.

Gauland, Alexander. 2014. "Gauland: Putin findet modernen Weg zu traditionellen Werten." Interview by Armin Siebert. *Stimme Russlands*, 27 November 2014. de.sputniknews.com/german.ruvr.ru/2014_11_27/Gauland-Putin-findet-modern en-Weg-zu-traditionellen-Werten-7852/.

Gehrcke, Wolfgang. 2014a. "Nie wieder Krieg. Nie wieder Faschismus. Internationale Solidarität – das gilt auch für den Ukraine-Konflikt." Last modified 8 May 2014. http://www.wolfgang-gehrcke.de/de/article/1199.nie-wieder-krieg-nie-wieder-faschismus-internationale-solidaritaet-das-gilt-auch-fuer-den-ukraine-konflikt.html.

Gehrcke, Wolfgang. 2014b. "Maidan landet im Sumpf des Nationalismus." Pressrelease of the parliamentary group of the party "Die Linke", 26 October 2014. http://www.linksfraktion.de/pressemitteilungen/maidan-landet-sumpf-nationalismus/.

Gillert, Sonja. 2014. "Die erschreckende Lage der Pressefreiheit." *Die Welt*, 16 December 2014. http://www.welt.de/politik/ausland/article135414206/Die-erschreckende-Lage-der-Pressefreiheit.html.

Gläser, Jochen and Grit Laudel. 1999. *Theoriegeleitete Textanalyse? Das Potential einer variablenorientierten qualitativen Inhaltsanalyse.* Berlin: WZB, Arbeitsgruppe Wissenschaftstransformation.

Gläser, Jochen and Grit Laudel. 2004. *Experteninterviews und qualitative Inhaltsanalyse als Instrumente rekonstruierender Untersuchungen.* Wiesbaden: VS Verlag für Sozialwissenschaften.

Greven, Ludwig. 2014. "Putin verstehen mit Gerhard Schröder." *Zeit online*, 9 March 2014. http://www.zeit.de/politik/ausland/2014-03/ukraine-russland-putin-schroeder.

Hans, Julian. 2015. "Liniengrüße aus Moskau." *Süddeutsche Zeitung,* 2 September 2015. http://www.sueddeutsche.de/medien/russische-propaganda-in-deutschland-liniengruesse-aus-moskau-1.2630243.

Herman, Eva. 2014. "Aufruf an alle Journalisten zum Tag der Wahrheit." 22 November 2014. https://www.youtube.com/watch?v=GLpFrWbCVQ4.

Hutchings, Stephen and Natalija Rulyova. 2009. *Television and Culture in Putin's Russia.* London: Routledge.

Kerneck, Barbara. 2014. "Putins Plaudertaschen." *TAZ*, 12 May 2014. http://www.taz.de/!138215/.

Lauer, Stefan. 2014. "RT kommt nach Deutschland und die Herrschaft der Mainstreampresse ist vorbei." *Vice*, 22 August 2014. http://www.vice.com/de/pr int/rt-kommt-nach-deutschland-die-herrschaft-der-mainstreampresse-ist-vorbei-putin-elsaesser-compact-320.

Lenta.Ru. 2013. "Glagolom zeč'." *Lenta.Ru*, 9 December 2013. http://lenta.ru/ar ticles/2013/12/09/ria/.

Makarychev, Andrey. 2012. "Communication and Dislocations: Normative Disagreements between Russia and the EU." In *Constructing Identities in Europe. German and Russian Perspective*, edited by Reinhard Krumm et al., 48–56. Baden-Baden: Nomos.

Meister, Stefan and Jana Puglierin. 2015. "Perzeption und Instrumentalisierung. Russlands nicht-militärische Einflussnahme in Europa." *DGAPkompakt*, October 2015.

MIA. n.d. "Rossiya Segodnia". Accessed 12 November 2014. http://ria.ru/docs/ about/index.html.

Müller von Blumencron, Mathias. 2015. "Der ungleiche Kampf um die Deutungshoheit." *Frankfurter Allgemeine Zeitung,* 8 February 2015. http://www.faz.n et/aktuell/politik/sicherheitskonferenz-2015/der-ungleiche-kampf-um-die-deutu ngshoheit-13417093.html.

N24-Talk. 2014. "Der Westen gegen Putin?" 27 November 2014. http://www.n2 4.de/n24/Mediathek/Sendungen/d/5780524/der-westen-gegen-putin-.html.

Niggemeier, Stefan. 2015. "Beschwerden im Akkord: Wie eine selbst ernannte Zuschauervertretung ARD und ZDF zusetzt." *Krautreporter*, 8 January 2015. https://krautreporter.de/270--beschwerden-im-akkord-wie-eine-selbst-ernannte-zuschauervertretung-ard-und-zdf-zusetzt.

Nye, Joseph S. 1990. "Soft Power." *Foreign Policy* 80: 153–171.

"O Rossotrudničestve". n.d. http://rs.gov.ru/ru/about.

Petersen, Thomas. 2015. "Die Grenzen der Propaganda." *Frankfurter Allgemeine Zeitung*, 18 March 2015. http://www.faz.net/aktuell/politik/inland/allensbach-st udie-die-grenzen-der-russischen-propaganda-13489238.html?printPagedArticle =true#pageIndex_2.

Phoenix. 2014. "Im Dialog: Gabriele Krone Schmalz über Ukraine-Konflikt, Russland, Putin, Medien." 4 October 2014. Available at https://www.youtube.com/watch?v=LNc-QOe1teI.

Pomerantsev, Peter and Michael Weiss. 2014. "The Menace of Unreality: How the Kremlin Weaponizes Information, Culture and Money." *The Interpreter*, November 22 2014. http://www.interpretermag.com/the-menace-of-unreality-how-the-kremlin-weaponizes-information-culture-and-money/.

Precht. 2014. "Jakob Augstein Bei Precht." 30 November 2014. https://www.zdf.de/gesellschaft/precht/richard-david-precht-mit-dem-publizisten-jakob-augstein-100.html.

Reporter ohne Grenzen. 2013. "Der Kreml auf allen Kanälen. Wie der russische Staat das Fernsehen lenkt." Last modified 7 October 2013. https://www.reporter-ohne-grenzen.de/pressemitteilungen/meldung/rog-bericht-wie-der-russische-staat-das-fernsehen-lenkt/.

Rosbach, Jens. 2014. "Putins geheime Online-Armee." *Deutschlandfunk*, 22 May 2014. http://www.deutschlandfunk.de/ukraine-konflikt-putins-geheime-online-armee.1781.de.html?dram:article_id=287018.

RT Deutsch. 2014a. "Von der Leyens spezielle Entspannungspolitik: mehr Panzer." 12 November 2014. http://www.rtdeutsch.com/5898/inland/von-der-leyens-spezielle-entspannungspolitik-mehr-panzer-gegen-russland/.

RT Deutsch. 2014b. "Neues Nato-Spiel in der Ukraine: Ich sehe was, was du nicht siehst." 12 November 2014. http://www.rtdeutsch.com/6068/international/neues-nato-spiel-in-der-ukraine-ich-sehe-was-was-du-nicht-siehst/.

RT Deutsch. 2014c. "Weil er Russe ist – Stardirigent Gergiev ausgeladen." 11 November 2014. http://www.rtdeutsch.com/5903/inland/weil-er-russe-ist-stardirigent-gergiev-ausgeladen-von-saar-festival/.

RT Deutsch. N.d. "Der fehlende Part." https://deutsch.rt.com/programme/1-der-fehlende-part/

Russian Institute for Strategic Studies. 2014. "Interview with L.P. Reshetnikov on Greek TV." 10 November 2014. Accessed on 26 February 2015. http://riss.ru/my-v-smi/3844-direktor-risi-l-p-reshetnikov-dal-intervyu-grecheskomu-televideniyu#.VPWnRPmG-8A.

Sergunin, Alexander and Leonid Karabeshkin. 2015. "Understanding Russia's Soft Power Strategy." *Politics* 3-4: 252–254.

Spahn, Susanne. 2014. "Warum die ostslawische Gemeinschaft der Russen, Belarussen und Ukrainer gescheitert ist." In *Post-Panslavismus. Slavizität, Slavische Idee und Anti-Slavismus im 20. und 21. Jahrhundert*, edited by Agnieszka Gasior, Lars Karl and Stefan Troebst, 258–272. Göttingen: Wallstein-Verlag.

Spahn, Susanne. 2016. *Das Ukraine-Bild in Deutschland: Die Rolle der russischen Medien. Wie Russland die öffentliche Meinung in Deutschland beeinflusst*. Hamburg: Verlag Dr. Kovač.

Spiegel Online. 2014. "Strategiesitzung in der Botschaft. AfD sucht Rat aus Russland." 7 December 2014. http://www.spiegel.de/politik/deutschland/afd-sucht-rat-aus-russland-strategiesitzung-in-der-botschaft-a-1006983.html.

Sputnik News. 2014. "Rossiya Segodnia startet neues Mediaprojekt – Sputnik." Accessed 12 November 2014. https://de.sputniknews.com/politik/20141110269973566-Rossiya-Segodnya-startet-neues-Mediaprojekt--Sputnik/.

Ständige Publikumskonferenz der öffentlich-rechtlichen Medien e.V. n.d. "Programmbeschwerden." Available online https://publikumskonferenz.de/forum/viewforum.php?f=30.

Ständige Publikumskonferenz der öffentlich-rechtlichen Medien e.V. 2014. "ARD - Kiew gedenkt der Maidan-Proteste." 18 December 2014. Available online https://publikumskonferenz.de/forum/viewtopic.php?f=37&t=311

Stimme Russlands. 2014a. "Wladimir Putin: 'In der Ukraine hat sich gewaltsame Machtergreifung ereignet.'" 4 March 2014. http://de.sputniknews.com/german.ruvr.ru/2014_03_04/Wladimir-Putin-In-der-Ukraine-hat-sich-gewaltsame-Machtergreifung-ereignet-1029/.

Stimme Russlands. 2014b. "Wladimir Putin hielt Rede über Krim-Aufnahme." 18 March 2014. http://de.sputniknews.com/german.ruvr.ru/2014_03_18/Wladimir-Putin-hielt-Rede-uber-Krim-Aufnahme-6799/.

Stimme Russlands. 2014c. "Putin dankt Militär für Professionalität während der Krim-Ereignisse." 19 December 2014. http://de.sputniknews.com/german.ruvr.ru/news/2014_12_19/Putin-dankt-Militar-fur-Professionalitat-wahrend-der-Krim-Ereignisse-1033/.

Trautmann, Ljuba. 2002. *Die Medien im russischen Transformationsprozess – Akteur oder Instrument der staatlichen Politik*. Frankfurt: Lang.

Ulfkotte, Udo. 2014. *Gekaufte Journalisten. Wie Politiker, Geheimdienste und Hochfinanz Deutschlands Massenmedien lenken.* Rottenburg: Kopp-Verlag.

United Nations. 2014. *Daily Press Briefing By The Office Of The Spokesperson For The Secretary-General.* 7 November 2014. http://www.un.org/press/en/2014/db141107.doc.htm.

Vanderhill, Rachel. 2013. *Promoting Authoritarianism Abroad.* Boulder, Colorado: Lynne Rienner Publ.

Vertovec, Steven. 2009. *Transnationalism.* London, New York: Routledge.

Zeit Online. 2014. "Platzeck fordert Anerkennung der Krim-Annexion." 18 November 2014. http://www.zeit.de/politik/ausland/2014-11/platzeck-russland-ukraine.

---

i   For example this report of RT Deutsch, where the German defense minister Ursula von der Leyen is heavily criticized for allegedly aggravating the relations to Russia (RT Deutsch 2014a).

ii Gabriele Krone-Schmalz' books are listed on her personal website, [http://www.krone-schmalz.de/buecher.html].

iii The play on words rests on the fact that the German verb "to understand" refers to both comprehension and appreciation.

iv For the website of Mega-Radio, see [http://www.digitalradio.de/index.php/de/berliner-luft/item/mega-radio-sna].

v   For the online program of "Der fehlende Part", see [https://deutsch.rt.com/programme/1-der-fehlende-part/] (as of 6 October 2015, and 5 May 2016).

vi For the website of Ken FM, see [http://kenfm.de/].

vii Jebsen's KenFM is one of the main activists of the Monday demonstrations/vigils for peace-movement, [https://www.mahnwache.info/aktivisten/kenfm.html].

Ukrainian Nation Building and Ethnic Minority Associations: The Case of Southern Bessarabia[i]

Simon Schlegel

In rural south-western Ukraine, a multi-ethnic population is reflected in a high number of ethnic associations that represent these minority groups vis-à-vis the Ukrainian state. In recent years, these associations have formed a flourishing network of transnational ties to the minority groups' historical homelands. The aim of this study is to ask how ethnic associations use their connections abroad in local politics. How does their usage of ethnicity change the category's significance? The study results from field research in the small town of Izmail and its surroundings. Research methods included interviews with educators and activists as well as biographical interviews. It also heavily draws on participant observation and a study of the local press. The empirical part describes various strategies of using ethnic differences in local politics. What they have all in common is that they distribute resources from a patron to clients. The efficiency of this distribution process can be enhanced by serving clients through clearly bounded groups with internal hierarchies. Ethnicity offers an ideal category to form such groups. Resources can be channeled down along the hierarchies within ethnic associations. Therefore, it is beneficial for both patrons and clients to sharpen ethnic boundaries. Clients with unclear ethnic identities can hardly profit from patron's transnational connections and the resources gained through them. Because the Ukrainian state often fails to offer ethnic minorities the same opportunities as transnationally acting patrons, the solidarities among minorities tend to be split between a civil Ukrainian identity and a transnational ethnic identity.

1. Introduction

Writing before the Orange Revolution and long before Maidan, Andreas Kappeler (2000: 274) observed that Ukrainian political leaders have repeatedly stressed the importance of a political rather than an ethnic Ukrainian identity. Kappeler predicted that the shift from an ethnic to a civic conception of the Ukrainian state could only be achieved under conditions of democracy and the rule of law. These conditions, despite all of the flares of civil society activism that Ukraine has since seen, have not yet fully emerged. Accordingly, thus far, no serious political force has promoted a non-ethnic or even a post-ethnic conception of the Ukrainian state in which different languages and cultures influence each other and in which this exchange will eventually change what it means to be Ukrainian (Hrystenko 2008).

Ukraine is by constitution a multiethnic state. Its fundamental laws acknowledge the need to protect minority cultures and languages. However, the underlying concept of a nation state that is based on a clearly bounded ethnic majority that coexists with some equally clearly bounded minority groups is problematic for two reasons: It constantly runs in contradiction with the more complicated social reality of Ukraine's notoriously blurred ethnic boundaries, and it continues to exclude and estrange the substantial (and difficult to measure) portion of the Ukrainian population whose identities are not, or are not exclusively, Ukrainian.

In this study, I ask why ethnic distinctions retain so much political significance despite the fact that the formal preconditions for a civic Ukrainian identity have lasted for a quarter of a century. The article is based on fieldwork in southern Bessarabia, which is a region of Odessa Oblast. This research suggests that there is a widespread conceptualization of Ukraine as a society of separate ethnic units, each of which retains its own political relationship to the state. One must therefore ask whether this conceptualization stems from the needs of clientelistic politics and the lucrative transnational connections that are maintained by some patrons based on their ethnicity. In this essay, I consider the impact of local politicians' transnational ties on how ethnicity is performed and conceptualized in Ukraine.

Southern Bessarabia is a peripheral and multiethnic region, which is far from being representative of the rest of Ukraine. However, there are two factors on the regional level that mirror national politics: firstly, contested ethnic and linguistic identities are dominant topics in the political process; and secondly, ethnic ties transcend state borders and are often based on transnational solidarities. On the local Bessarabian level such connections are mostly limited to other regions of South-Eastern Europe, while on the national Ukrainian level, connections to Russia and to the Ukrainian diaspora inscribe ethnic identities in a number of geopolitical conflicts.

Field research was conducted between September 2012 and December 2013. The methods that were employed included 34 in-depth biographical interviews, mainly with elderly rural inhabitants of the region. These informants were Russian,

Ukrainian, Bulgarian, Gagauz and Moldovan. However, many of the interviewees had blurred ethnic identities. The biographical interviews were meant to determine how, at different times in the respondents' lives, their ethnic identity fostered or impeded their opportunities. A second strand of the research consisted of 16 semi-structured interviews with local politicians, scholars, teachers, and activists. The research further included a participant observation study of the parliamentary elections in October 2012, folklore performances, and a series of village festivals. Finally, a systematic study of local newspapers was used to analyze local discourses about ethnicity.

2. Clientelism and Transnational Connections on the Ukrainian Periphery

The region of southern Bessarabia was chosen as a field site for its extraordinary ethnic diversity. This diversity bears witness to a history of frequently shifting borders. The states that ruled over this region have formed and reformed its population according to their needs. This paper focuses on two minorities: the Bulgarians of southern Bessarabia and their long-time neighbors, the Gagauz, who speak the Turkic Gagauz language and who are predominantly Orthodox Christians. These minority groups are the descendants of "Transdanubian settlers," peasant colonists from the territory of modern day Bulgaria. They arrived in the region around 1812, when the Ottoman Empire was compelled to cede Bessarabia to Russia (Kushko & Taki 2012: 164). Since then, these two groups have lived through political sea changes such as the annexation of Bessarabia to Romania in the interwar years, the integration into the Russian-dominated Soviet Union between 1944 and 1991, and the turmoil of independent Ukraine since 1991. Bessarabian Bulgarians and Gagauz have lived in close proximity and in perpetual cultural exchange with their Moldovan, Ukrainian, Russian, and Albanian neighbors. Up to the deportations and ethnic cleansing of World War II, Jews and Bessarabian Germans were also part of the ethnic mosaic. However, the notion of clear and stable ethnic boundaries between all of these groups has been well preserved through the vicissitudes of history. More permeable state borders since 1991 have allowed representatives of these groups to seek political support and resources beyond Ukraine in their ancestral homelands, thereby building transnational patron-client ties to Bulgaria and Turkey based on a distinctly ethnic agenda.

The ethnic minority communities of southern Bessarabia are not composed of migrants who have left their home, and they are certainly not "transmigrants," the epitomization of transnationalism. Nevertheless, they clearly "build social fields that link together their country of origin and their country of settlement" (Glick-Schiller, Basch & Blanc-Szanton 1992: 1). In the conception of Portes, Guarnizo and Landolt (1999: 217) transnationalism is a matter of scale. In their view, the "critical mass and complexity" of transnational ties, which are sufficient to justify a new field of study, have emerged only recently and thus do not apply to the Tsarist, Romanian, or Soviet periods. However, the history of the "Transdanubian settlers" suggests some degree of transnationalism long before the concept became a tool for the analysis of globalization. While in the Soviet years there were hardly any transnational ties across the closely guarded borders, in the 19th century, the settlers from across the Danube remained highly mobile. In times of insecurity, many of them made use of their connections to the old country and to members of their diaspora elsewhere to seek refuge from famine, war, and the perceived threat of becoming serfs.[ii]

While transnationalism hinges on modern capitalism and the modern infrastructures of transportation and communication (Glick-Schiller et al. 1992; Portes et al. 1999), these communities draw part of their identity from narratives of a past way of life between old and new places, which is a narrative that is revived in modern transnational connections. Following a narrative that serves existing state or institutional orders is a method that is suggested by George Marcus (1995: 109) for multi-sited ethnographic studies. In the following discussion of the transnational ties that have been revived in the past three decades among the ethnic minorities of southern Bessarabia, it is not merely the people or the money that I follow, but the identity-forming narrative of belonging to a transnational group.

Another key concept for my argument is clientelism. In the context of this study, clientelism means the exchange of resources for political support between two prototypical figures, the powerful patron and his or her clients, who need material support or protection and who in exchange are willing to support their patron at the ballot box. Therefore, clientelism is "the proffering of material goods in return for electoral support, where the criterion of distribution that the patron uses is simply: did you (will you) support me?" (Stokes 2009: 649). Such a system prioritizes the maintenance of political power for those who hold it, and it is judged by what it achieves, not by what it stands for (Scott 1969: 1144). Clientelism is not meant to create social equality or rule of law. It is primarily a system for the distribution of resources (Roniger 1994: 10; Weitz-Shapiro 2012: 569).

Most local politicians in southern Bessarabia fit this characterization quite well. They draw their power from their role as benefactors, who generously offer support and understanding. In the 2012 parliamentary election campaign, the Party of the Regions, which at that time ruled most of Ukraine, including southern Bessarabia, chose the campaign motto "the power of benefaction."[iii] All along the Odessa ring road, uniform billboards appeared promoting the Party's good services to the population, from repairing roads to providing free medical examinations for the province's children. Politicians are no longer elected because they represent and exemplify an ideology but because they understand the people's needs and have the means to satisfy them. The image of generosity can be substantiated in public by highlighting a patron's gifts, by publicizing them in local newspapers and on social media and through gifts that are made by patrons at festivals. During the fieldwork for this study in rural southern Bessarabia, examples of such gifts to the communities included IT infrastructure for schools and culture houses, donations to sports clubs, or icons for churches. Many of the people who were interviewed for this study valued politicians more for what they did for the community than the political ideas that they propagated.

Ethnicity has long been an important factor in this region, even before this category could be used to form transnational connections. In the Soviet years, ethnicity was an ascribed passport category. Terry Martin (2000: 168) called it a "constant routine of ethnic labeling" that "inadvertently indoctrinated the Soviet population in the belief that ethnicity was an inherent, fundamental, and crucially important characteristic of all individuals." Thus, it is no surprise that when the promise of a harmonious, classless Soviet society began to falter, ethnicity became one of the few categories on which new forms of political representation could be built. In this period, ethnic movements began to gather momentum all over the Soviet Union.

3. Investing in Transnational Connections

In southern Bessarabia, with its colorful ethnic mosaic, hardly any of the newly emerging ethnic associations have seriously aspired to independence or territorial autonomy from Ukraine. Because there are no clearly defined ethnic territories in southern Bessarabia, and because the Bulgarians and Gagauz live on both sides of the Moldovan-Ukrainian border, most of the Gagauz and Bulgarian activists in the Ukrainian part of Bessarabia soon realized that any form of autonomy arrangements would be difficult to put into practice. Most activists understood that moving borders to make them congruent with ethnic boundaries was overly ambitious and might trigger an uncontrollable dynamic. The only organization that seriously promoted such plans was the Bulgarian *Cyril and Methodius Society*. The idea behind this risky effort was to secure resources for the development of Bulgarian culture and language that would not require support from the Ukrainian authorities. However, the endeavor never managed to attract the attention of the authorities in Kyiv or to mobilize support among the Bulgarians and the Gagauz.[iv]

An earlier project to create a Bulgarian-Gagauz autonomous Soviet Republic in 1989 had already been halted by opposition from within the Bulgarian associations in Moldova. The organization *Vozrozhdenie* (Renaissance), which was based in Chișinău, dismissed the project as "absurd." The statement made clear that the Bulgarians already had a state: Bulgaria (Shornikov 2012: 784). Bulgarian and Gagauz activists scaled down their demands of autonomy and instead began to form associations in close collaboration with activists and politicians in Bulgaria. The transnational bonds that were built on ethnic ties formed the material basis for the cultural aspirations of ethnic minorities, such as having their own cultural centers, their own folklore festivals, language lessons in schools and Sunday schools, library collections in their respective languages, radio and newspapers in minority languages, as well as regular cultural exchange with their countries of origin.

All of the ethnic groups in southern Bessarabia, even the smallest, are represented vis-à-vis the Ukrainian state by ethnic associations. The larger these ethnic groups are and the more actively they maintain connections to their respective countries of origin, the more ethnic associations have emerged. The most active ethnic associations represent the roughly 150,000 Bulgarians who live in Odessa Oblast.[v] In Izmail, which is southern Bessarabia's largest town, there are three different Bulgarian associations, the *Cyril and Methodius Society*, the *Society of St. Sophia*, and the *Society of Bulgarian Families*. There are also nationwide organizations such as the *Association of Bulgarians in Ukraine*, which is headed by Anton Kisse, a member of parliament, or the *Congress of Bulgarians*, which also exists in other countries with Bulgarian diasporas. Such organizations aim to secure the interests and constitutional rights of ethnic minorities and to foster their culture and native language.[vi] The region's 28,000 Gagauz are represented by the *Union of Gagauz in Ukraine*.

In summer 2012, the Ianukovich government adopted legislation allowing municipal and rayon authorities to use local languages in the administration if one such language was considered to be native by more than 10% of the local population (RBK Ukraina 2012). The *Association of Bulgarians in Ukraine* petitioned to make Bulgarian an officially recognized language in Izmail, where Bulgarians make up about 10% of the population. The petition was not even considered by municipal authorities. In contrast, Russian was given the status of an official language locally by municipal authorities (Zerkalo Nedeli 2012; 2013).

This decision merely provides the legal ground to the long established practice of using Russian in all realms of public life. However, the *Cyril and Methodius Society* announced that they would bring their case to court (UNIAN 2012). Bulgarian folklore groups in protest boycotted the celebrations of the 2012 annual city day. The head of the *Cyril and Methodius Society*, Vladimir Petrov, was cited as saying that Bulgarians refused to celebrate along with authorities who denied them the right to speak their native language (Novinite 2012). Again, the motion failed to attract enough protest to challenge the Ukrainian authorities. Most Bulgarians and Gagauz have long been accustomed to managing their administrative affairs in Russian. Therefore, the fact that they could not address the state in their ancestral language could hardly be cited as a widely felt grievance. One also must bear in mind that in Ukraine, people often indicate the language of the group which they identify with as their native language, not necessarily the language that they learned first or use most frequently (Arel 2006: 9; Kulyk 2006: 126; Hrystenko 2008: 200). Since 2006, when the European Charter for Regional or Minority Languages entered into force in Ukraine, schools in villages where one minority language is clearly predominant teach these languages as a compulsory subject, along with Ukrainian and English. Nevertheless, Russian remains the language of instruction in such schools.[vii]

Other conflicts between local ethnic associations and subunits of the Ukrainian state similarly failed to mobilize many people. In general, such conflicts were not caused by the state's attitude towards ethnic minorities and their languages but by disputes between state authorities and minority organizations over resources and property. In three documented incidents in Odessa Oblast ethnic associations entered into conflict with the state over real estate that municipalities rented or leased to them: In 2008, the city of Odessa, the provincial capital, attempted to drive the Cultural Center of Bulgarians out of a building that it had been using for many years. In an angry letter to a local newspaper, the chair of the Bulgarian *Society of St. Sophia* hinted that the building, a historic cinema in the heart of the old town, had increased in value after it had been renovated with financial support from Bulgaria (Pridunaiskie Vesti 2008). The *Association of Bulgarians in Ukraine*, with support from mayors of Bulgarian villages in southern Bessarabia, wrote to the Parliamentary Commission for Human Rights and Protection of Minorities and stated that the incident had harmed interethnic relations in Ukraine as well as Ukraine's reputation in Europe (ibid.).

In a similar incident in Izmail, the Bulgarian *Cyril and Methodius Society* entered into conflict with city authorities over a building that the *Society* had renovated and used for 20 years before the municipality wanted to sell it.[viii] In March 2013, the Ukrainian ethnic association *Prosvita* and the Greek organization *Ellada* teamed up to publically lament that the office space that the municipality of Izmail leased to them lacked basic sanitation and that a city official used parts of the space rented by these organizations as a private apartment. In a bitter letter to the Izmail weekly *Kur'er Nedeli,* the head of *Ellada*, Tatiana Mitaki, expressed the suspicion that "someone had decided to drive the Greeks out" (Kur'er Nedeli 2013). In all of these cases, representatives of ethnic associations framed their conflicts with the state as cases of ethnic discrimination, thereby emphasizing their role as representatives of entire ethnic groups. Such activism is important, even if it is not ultimately rewarded with political success, to remain notable among the local population but also among sponsors beyond Ukraine's borders. These disputes between the Ukrainian state and ethnic associations highlight the importance that transnational ties have recently gained as a field of political engagement (Vertovec 1999: 454–5). In the Bessarabian case, even local politics can take place in a transnational arena.

Both Bulgarian and Gagauz organizations retain active contacts to Bulgaria, to where the two groups trace their historical roots. The Gagauz are also courted by organizations in Turkey, which treat them as their ethnic brethren. Both countries, through ethnic associations, provide education opportunities such as scholarships. Many language or history teachers who teach the extracurricular courses that are offered by ethnic associations have themselves studied abroad. The teachers in Izmail's Bulgarian Sunday school, for instance, have all received part of their education in Bulgaria, and they are proud that many of their pupils will eventually have a chance to study in Bulgaria.[ix] Additionally, Bulgaria offers the prospect of citizenship and thereby opportunities for business relationships and migration within Europe (Demirdirek 2008: 100).

However, both education and citizenship rights require the navigation of a complex, transnational bureaucratic jungle. People who hope to gain an education or citizenship in Bulgaria must invest time and money. It can be a tricky endeavor to prove that one's roots lie in Bulgaria, particularly for ethnic Gagauz. Securing one of the 110 university places that Bulgaria annually reserves for Ukrainian citizens requires not only proficiency in Bulgarian but also specialized knowledge of Bulgarian history, culture and literature (Topor 2015).

Ethnic associations can provide assistance and education for those who are willing to invest in acquiring proficiency in a minority language and sharpen their ethnic identity. Efforts by a state to strengthen the national identity of its diaspora, often through the collective enjoyment of cultural goods, have been identified as an important form of transnational activities (Portes et al. 1999: 221). The foreign state that provides such opportunities reinforces the identity of its diaspora. For the diaspora, such opportunities also mean a chance to enhance their prospects: Whereas citizenship in Bulgaria requires administrative proof of Bulgarian ancestry, scholarships do not usually cite ethnicity as an eligibility criterion. However, young people who have invested into the Bulgarian or Gagauz languages clearly have an edge over students who must learn an entirely new language. Therefore, ethnic associations cite educational opportunities as an incentive for the extracurricular courses that they offer. The website of the Bulgarian Agency for Bulgarians Living Abroad, which is the authority that is in charge of residence permits and facilitated naturalization, lists ethnic associations that can provide the education and administrative assistance that are needed to turn Bulgarian ancestry into an asset.[x]

Thus, ethnic associations can turn their transnational ties into individual gains if individuals invest in ethnic minority identity and acknowledge the association's role as their political representative. Ethnic associations can only play this role as long as their activities are well-regarded by the state in which they operate and by other ethnic groups' associations. They provide services and opportunities that the Ukrainian state is unable or unwilling to provide. This division of labor is mutually beneficial. It allows ethnic associations to claim representation for minority groups and the state to outsource some of its core functions to ethnic associations. With this arrangement, the Ukrainian state can afford laws on minority language education that entail few obligations (Hrystenko 2008: 213). This mutually beneficial relationship is reenacted regularly at public events, where representatives of the state and of ethnic associations regularly exchange pleasantries, using a well-rehearsed rhetoric of interethnic harmony.

4. Strategies for Addressing Ethnicity in Local Politics

In many regions, ethnic associations are a blessing for the clientelistic mode of local politics. To build the trusted relationships that are needed in clientelism, one needs to obtain a great deal of information about one's counterparts. Such information is often difficult to find, and ethnicity can sometimes offer an information shortcut. This allows clients to better predict how potential patrons might act in the future and which group of people they will favor. In many settings, costless information about an individual's ethnic identity is readily available (speech, name, sometimes dress), whereas information about other, non-ethnic characteristics (class, profession, income) is more difficult to attain (Chandra 2004: 33–38).

However, in post-Soviet Ukraine, ethnicity provides a poor information shortcut. This includes southern Bessarabia, where language may provide a clue, but where most people can conceal their native language at will by speaking Russian. Family names are commonly believed to carry information about a person's ethnicity, but in fact, they are often inconclusive indicators. Accordingly, to learn about a person's ethnic identity is by no means costless. Therefore, in southern Bessarabia and other areas of the former Soviet Union, another type of information-shortcut has evolved: While neither a name nor accent is decisive, an individual's behavior may provide information to help to determine ethnic identity. Behavior is an important means by which people are made to be recognizable as "one's own kind" (*svoy*) or "one of us" (*nash*).

The labels *nash* and *svoi* have become one of the most important criteria for belonging in a turbulent post-Soviet society. Both labels roughly have the same meaning, and in Ukraine, they are not necessarily tied to national or ethnic identities. More than an ethnic label, being *svoy* or *nash* implies trustworthiness, which is a highly valued characteristic in an economy of shortage (Wanner 1998: 52–56). People who are *svoy* will very likely not cause problems and act in a predictable, comprehensible way (Yurchak 2006: 109). Being *svoy* and behaving in a *svoy* manner helps both patrons and clients to shape realistic expectations about how their counterpart will act. One important way in which *svoy* is performed in southern Bessarabia is to refer regularly to ethnicity and to innate ethnic characteristics. Another way, which was established during the advent of Soviet rule, is to proudly refer to ethnic diversity and interethnic tolerance in the region.[xi] Even today, hardly any political speech fails to mention how ethnically diverse Bessarabians are and how well they nevertheless get along with each other. When patrons speak publically, they emphasize their tolerance towards other ethnic groups as much as their generosity. In contrast, stirring up conflict between ethnic groups would not be seen as the behavior that one would expect from "one's own kind." In fact, the respondents repeatedly associated stirring up ethnic conflict with far-away places that are associated with ethnic strife, such as Kosovo or Western Ukraine.

Although ethnic boundaries do not impede the trusted ties that reach across them, they play a crucial role in the clientelistic mode of doing politics. They provide clearly bounded groups that represent all of the clients that are represented within them. Ethnic groups are certainly not the only possible receiving groups in the clientelistic exchange. Any group that can channel down resources that are received from a patron is in principle qualified as a beneficiary. In the parliamentary campaign of 2012, for instance, churches, unions, the staff of large employers, or sports clubs were all served with the resources of local politicians. However, in the face of competition with other patrons, there are always high incentives to mobilize as many different types of receiving groups as possible. Therefore, patrons and aspiring patrons can usually not afford to forgo ethnic associations.

The usage of ethnic boundaries in clientelistic politics depends on ethnic group consciousness, interethnic relations, and the ethnic composition of the region. This point can be illustrated by examples that are taken from the Ukrainian parliamentary elections in October 2012 in which different patrons employed different strategies to win a parliamentary mandate.

In one strategy, a candidate who was faced with an ethnically diverse electorate did not employ his own ethnicity. In a neighboring electoral district, another candidate primarily mobilized within an ethnically Bulgarian electorate and therefore made his own Bulgarian identity one of his major selling points. In Izmail, which is a city with no clear ethnic majority, the municipal authorities cater directly to ethnic groups, but they are careful to spread the benefits evenly.

The first of these strategies was employed by the incumbent Party of the Regions candidate in electoral district 143, Iuri Kruk. The district includes the city of Izmail, where Russians are the single largest group (43%), closely followed by

Ukrainians (38%). In the rural areas of this electoral district, Moldovans, Bulgarians, and Ukrainians each make up approximately one-fourth of the population, while Russians and other groups comprise the last fourth.[xii] In such a setting, it is difficult to address the ethnic identity of voters. During the election campaign, Iuri Kruk never revealed his own ethnic identity. He was visible in the region in the weeks leading up to the election, when he served numerous patron-client networks with real or promised resources. Most visibly, he inaugurated a freshly repaved road in Izmail during city-day celebrations; he promised better perspectives to the workers of Izmail's Danube river port; he had playground facilities repainted all over Izmail and placed a sign with his name at each site; and he sponsored the renovation of several churches in the area, for which he was awarded a high religious distinction just days before the election (Kur'er Nedeli 2012). None of this prevented Kruk from also using ethnic networks. For instance, he sponsored a local Bulgarian group's trip to a village to which they trace historic kinship ties in eastern Ukraine.[xiii] Kruk's strategy worked. He was re-elected to the national parliament.[xiv]

In the neighboring electoral district 142, the eventually successful candidate, Anton Kisse, employed a much more visible ethnic strategy. Because in this electoral district Bulgarians are the majority,[xv] Kisse could wholeheartedly use his Bulgarian ethnicity during the election campaign. Not only does Kisse often mention his ethnic belonging, he is also the prominent head of the *Association of Bulgarians in Ukraine*, and he uses social media to broadcast his strong ties to Bulgaria. He had already proven his firm Bulgarian identity by authoring the widely distributed book *The Renaissance of the Ukrainian Bulgarians* (Kisse 2006). One week before the election, hundreds of people came to Bolgrad, which is the main Bulgarian town in the region, to see Mr. Kisse inaugurate a monument, the construction of which he had organized and sponsored. The monument stands in memory of volunteer Bulgarian militias (*opolchentsy*), who supported the Russian army in the Russo-Turkish war of 1877–78, the war that eventually led to Bulgarian independence from the Ottoman Empire. The spectators, who gathered around the monument in the square in front of Bolgrad's church, listened to speakers from local politics, the Orthodox Church, the military, the provincial capital, neighboring Moldova, and not least Bulgaria. They all praised the Bulgarian freedom fighters in whose memory the monument was erected and the patriotic spirit of the candidate, Anton Kisse. The week after, Kisse was elected within a comfortable margin, even against an incumbent candidate from the then still-powerful Party of the Regions.

The municipal council of the city of Izmail employed yet another strategy to address ethnic diversity. Careful not to side with one ethnic group, for many years, city officials have placed "interethnic harmonization" at the center of their activities. In a special program that was dedicated to the city's "more than eighty ethnic groups," the municipal administration offered financial and administrative resources for a number of ethnic groups. These include Poles, Greeks, Ukrainians, Jews, Russians, Germans, and Bulgarians, each of whom have ethnic associations that are based in Izmail. Each of these associations organizes their own "day of national culture" over the course of the year. It is an explicit goal of the program to "preserve the ethnic uniqueness" of these groups and to "ensure their harmonic relations by way of supporting their officially registered ethno-cultural societies."[xvi]

The diversity of political strategies in addressing ethnicity illustrates that ethnicity is an important group denominator, particularly in a region where there are many ethnic groups to satisfy. However, it is important to note that supporting one group does not automatically mean the renunciation of other groups. Indeed, the opposite may be true. The more visibly a patron supports one ethnic group, the more attractive he becomes for other groups as a potential patron. Anton Kisse, who is the most prominent patron of ethnic Bulgarians in Ukraine, also supports a Gagauz association. Gagauz form the second largest ethnic group in his electoral district. In fact, Kisse held a much applauded speech at the annual "Day of Gagauz Culture" festival in Odessa, where he praised both groups' unity.

A second important conclusion to be drawn from the different political strategies that are described above is that they would all cease to work if ethnic boundaries were fuzzy. Therefore, patrons who want to use their ethnicity as a mobilization strategy invest in two ways: They sponsor ethnic associations whose task it is to sharpen ethnic group boundaries, and they invest in transnational ties to ethnic group's ancestral homelands, which equips ethnic associations with resources, opportunities, and prestige.

5. Political Representation and the Urge for Clear-Cut Ethnic Identities

After voters have elected a particular patron, they must maximize the value of their electoral investment by pressuring the patron to deliver on his pre-electoral promises and by ensuring that a share of the patron's favors reaches them *personally*. In contrast, patrons face the problem that they can serve their clients with political favors, but they do not know whether such clients will actually support them at the ballot box. Moreover, patrons are interested in recruiting as many clients as possible while disseminating as little of their limited resources as possible (Chandra 2004: 54–56). Both problems can be solved by forming groups and sharpening group boundaries. Ethnic markers are one category that can be useful in this context. Patrons, who draw their power from representing communities that are held together by allegedly inborn ethnic solidarity, cannot have a meltdown of ethnic boundaries. If this category were to dissolve, or worse even, merge with a group that is represented by their political rivals, they would need to find another way to legitimize their power.

The three political strategies that are described above demonstrate that in ethnically diverse areas, such as southern Bessarabia, local politicians who represent a multiethnic electorate have no business telling people with which ethnic group or language to identify. Such actions would clearly harm their political standing. Local politicians support ethnic associations and use ethnicity as a constant reference category not because they are ethnic nationalists but because they need to structure their client base into well-arranged subgroups. Only with such subgroups can they efficiently channel the resources that they gain from their transnational fundraising activities. This brings us to a mechanism that takes place in multiethnic clientelistic societies and that is crucial in maintaining ethnic group boundaries. This mechanism is based on a dilemma that both patrons and clients face equally: they must ensure that they can force their counterpart to cooperate. For patrons, this is much easier if they do not engage with individuals but with clearly bounded groups with internal hierarchies. For clients, an incentive to sharpen group boundaries begins with the notion that those who are unattached to existing categories are often excluded from political representation.

In addition to ethnic groups, many other social categories qualify for clientelistic exchange, most notably religious groups or speaker communities of particular languages. Those who do not belong to any of these categories have no organizations and no figureheads to speak for them. There are no institutionalized links between ethnically or religiously unattached people to create a sense of community. Clientelism relies on the voter's belief that his or her decision at the ballot box will result in *personal* material gains or losses (Weitz-Shapiro 2012: 569). However, once they choose the option that they think will gain them a material advantage, clients must form groups to ensure that their patrons will deliver. If a client becomes a member of a recognizable group, such as a clearly bounded and well-represented ethnic group, there is still no guarantee that he or she will *personally* receive favors from the patron. However, it significantly increases his or her chances because *some members* of the group will be served; otherwise, the group as a whole can punish uncooperative patrons by shunning them the next time they need support. Therefore, to be a part of a group is in any case more beneficial than being a free-floating client (Chandra 2004: 54).

A good illustration of the situation for those with ambiguous ethnic identities can be found in the speakers of mixed languages. In Ukraine, the types of language varieties that dissolve the boundary between the Ukrainian and the Russian standard languages are called *Surzhyk* (Bernsand 2001). *Surzhyk* is frequently deplored in public, especially by the many zealous organizations that promote the standardized language varieties of Russian or Ukrainian. Although they are many, speakers of *Surzhyk* have no organizations that claim to represent them. Similar to the speakers of mixed languages who lack representation, people with ambiguous ethnic associations are out of the focus of ethno-politicians. Imagine the absurdity of an association for the ethnically mixed, or a club that represents the interests of the unaffiliated, or a museum for the folklore of the sovietized masses. No such organizations exist, and no one claims *common characteristics* with people who have no clear ethnic affiliation. Moreover, people with fuzzy ethnic identities have no "historic homeland" and therefore cannot serve as the basis of transnational ties. People who do not claim common characteristics with a large group have a difficult time claiming that they share characteristics with a patron. This is why they are difficult to exclude from a receiver group that is defined by ethnic boundaries. If a patron calls on his clients to mobilize on the grounds of their ethnic identity, as Anton Kisse did with his monument for Bulgarian freedom fighters, he had no claim to have served these unattached clients.

The patron, therefore, cannot demand or ensure the political support of free-floating clients. Thus, the efficiency of the clientelistic exchange can be seriously damaged by free-floating clients. In secret ballots, the political decision of an individual voter can only be established at great cost. If difficult-to-control, free-floating individuals still manage to profit from a patron's favors, they also become free riders at the patron's expense. However, by relying on clearly defined groups, they can be more easily excluded. If the patron relies on a group and its inner hierarchy, the actual voting behavior of single group members can be controlled more efficiently through intermediaries, for example, large employers or the representatives of ethnic associations.

The ethnic associations in Bessarabia, along with many other organizations such as churches or language promotion groups, serve as facilitators for the clientelistic exchange between local patrons and their clients. Their most crucial task in the clientelistic system is to define who is a member of a particular ethnic group and who is not. Thus, they shape the concept of what it means to be Bulgarian, Gagauz, Russian, or Ukrainian, but they also ensure for the patrons that they do not have to engage with free-floating individuals who exist somewhere at the frayed margins of a poorly defined group. Both the resources that are used by these associations and the identity concepts on which they rely are created in an intense transnational exchange with the regions to which these minorities trace their roots.

6. Conclusion

The idea that loyalty towards the state stems from ethnicity brings all of those who belong to an ethnic minority with ties to a foreign country under the suspicion that their loyalties are more transnational than national. Transnational identities, in Ukraine as elsewhere, challenge notions of ethnicity and nationalism. This defies the bounded categories of social scientists; however, it also poses a problem for politicians, whose powerbase is delimited by ethnic boundaries and state borders.

In southern Bessarabia, transnational ties can provide opportunities for employment and education that the state in this rural area fails to provide. For members of ethnic minorities such as the Bulgarians or the Gagauz, this results in an incentive to invest in their ethnic minority identity. Ethnic associations facilitate this investment. Local politics in this region can therefore no longer be explained by scrutinizing only Ukrainian state institutions. The scope of inquiry must be widened to include a transnational perspective. I have argued that the dominant model for recruiting voters is based on the distribution of resources from patrons to clients. This system fuels ethnic boundary maintenance by the associations that represent ethnic minorities.

To claim their role as representatives of entire ethnic groups, ethnic associations tend to frame the conflicts that they as organizations have with the state as being caused by ethnic discrimination. In some cases, ethnic associations use their transnational ties to enhance their bargaining power in such conflicts. Ethnic particularism and clientelism reinforce each other. The significance of this assessment lies in the fact that such a constellation makes it more difficult for non-ethnic organizations to be heard in local politics. It favors the public display of ethnic identities over a competition of political ideas. A Ukraine in which political affiliation is more decisive than one's ethnic or linguistic identity seems possible only once civil society forms a forceful counterweight to clientelism. Transnational ties can certainly help to achieve this, but only once they are based on more than ethnic agendas alone.

7. Bibliography

Arel, Dominique. 2006. "Theorizing the Politics of Cultural Identities in Russia and Ukraine." In *Rebounding Identities: The Politics of Identity in Russia and Ukraine*, edited by Dominique Arel and Blair A. Ruble. Baltimore: The John Hopkins University Press.

Batiushkov, Pompei Nikolaevich. 1892. *Bessarabiia – Istoricheskoe Opisanie.* St. Petersburg: Ministerstvo Vnutrenikh Del.

Bernsand, Niklas. 2001. "Surzhyk and National Identity in Ukrainian Nationalist Ideology." *Berliner Osteuropa Info* 17.

Chandra, Kanchan. 2004. *Why Ethnic Parties Succeed—Patronage and Ethnic Head Counts in India.* Cambridge: Cambridge University Press.

Demirdirek, Hülya. 2008. "In the Minority in Moldova: (Dis)Empowerment through Territorial Conflict." In *Europe's Last Frontier? Belarus, Moldova, and Ukraine between Russia and the European Union*, edited by Oliver Schmidtke and Serhy Yekelchyk. New York: Palgrave.

Derzhavin, Nikolai Sevast'ianovich. 1914. *Bolgarskiia Kolonii v Rossii, Tavricheskaia, Khersonskaia, i Bessarabskaia Gubernii.* Sofia: Derzhavna pechatnitsa.

Glick-Schiller, Nina, Linda Basch and Cristina Blanc-Szanton. 1992. *Transnationalism: A New Analytic Framework for Understanding Migration.* Annals of the New York Academy of Sciences, no. 645.

Hrystenko, Oleksandr. 2008. "Imagining the Community: Perspectives on Ukraine's Ethno-Cultural Diversity." *Nationalities Papers* 36 (2).

Istoriia gorodov i sel Ukrainskoi SSR. 1978. "Odesskaia Oblast". Kiev: Institut akademii nauk USSR.

Kappeler, Andreas. 2000. *Kleine Geschichte der Ukraine.* München: C.H. Beck.

Kisse, Anton Ivanovich. 2006. *Vozrozhdenie Bolgar Ukrainy.* Odessa: Optimum.

Klaus, Aleksandr Avgustovich. 1869. *Nashi Kolonii - Opyty i Materialy Po Istorii i Statistiki Inostrannoi Kolonizatsii V Rossii.* St. Petersburg: Tipografiia V.V. Nuswal'ta.

Kulyk, Volodymyr. 2006. "Normalisation of Ambiguity—Policies and Discourses on Language Issues in Post-Soviet Ukraine." In *History, Language and Society in the Borderlands of Europe—Ukraine and Belarus In Focus,* edited by Barbara Törnquist. Plewa, Malmö: Sekel.

Kushko, Andrei and Viktor Taki. 2012. *Bessarabiia v sostave Rossiiskoi Imperii (1812–1917).* Moskva: Novoe Literaturnoe Obozrenie.

Marcus, George E. 1995. "Ethnography in/of the World System: The Emergence of Multi-Sited Ethnography." *Annual Review of Anthropology* 24.

Martin, Terry. 2000. "Modernization or Neotraditionalism? Ascribed Nationality and Soviet Primordialism." In *Russian Modernity—Politics, Knowledge, Practices,* edited by David L. Hoffmann and Yanni Kotsonis. New York: Macmillan Press.

Portes, Alejandro, Luis E. Guarnizo and Patricia Landolt. 1999. "The Study of Transnationalism: Pitfalls and Promise of an Emergent Research Field." *Ethnic and Racial Studies* 22 (2).

Roniger, Luis. 1994. "The Comparative Study of Clientelism and the Changing Nature of Civil Society in the Contemporary World." In *Democracy, Clientelism, and Civil Society,* edited by Luis Roniger and Ayşe Güneş-Ayata. London, Boulder: Lynne Rienner.

Shornikov, Petr Mikhailovich. 2012. "Diskussii po voprosu o sozdanii avtonomii na iuge Moldavii i v pridunaiskikh zemliakh Ukrainy." In *Gagauzy v mire i mir Gagauzov Tom 2,* edited by Mikhail N. Guboglo. Komrat: Izpolkom ATO Gagauziia.

Scott, James C. 1969. "Corruption, Machine Politics, and Political Change." *The American Political Science Review* 63 (4).

Skal'kovskii, Apollon Aleksandrovich. 1850. *Opyt Statisticheskago Opisaniia Novorossiiskago Kraia Chast' I.* Odessa: Tipografiia Frantsova i Nitche.

Stokes, Susan C. 2009. "Political Clientelism." In *The Oxford Handbook of Political Science,* edited by Robert E. Goodin. Oxford: Oxford University Press.

Svin'in, Pavel Petrovich. 1816. *Opisanie Bessarabskoi Oblasti* - Sostavleno Vedomstva Gossudarstvennoi Kollegii Innostrannykh Del Nadvornym Sovetnikom Pavlom Svin'inym, 1816 Goda, 1-go Iunia.

Vertovec, Steven. 1999. "Conceiving and Researching Transnationalism." *Ethnic and Racial Studies* 22 (2).

Weitz-Shapiro, Rebecca. 2012. "What Wins Votes: Why Some Politicians Opt out of Clientelism." *American Journal of Political Science* 56 (3).

Wanner, Catherine. 1998. *Burden of Dreams—History and Identity in Post-Soviet Ukraine.* University Park PA: The Pennsylvania State University Press.

Yurchak, Alexei. 2006. *Everything Was Forever, until it Was No More—the Last Soviet Generation.* Princeton: Princeton University Press.

Newspaper Articles

Kur'er Nedeli. 2012. "Mitropolit Vladimir vruchil orden Iaroslava Mudrogo narodnomu deputatu Ukrainy Iuriu Kruku." 20 October.

Kur'er Nedeli. 2013. "Kto v dome khoziain?" 8 March.

Novinite. 2012. "V Izmaile boikotiruiut Den' Goroda iz-za otkaza priznat' bolgarskii iazyk regional'nym." 28 September 2012. Accessed 19 June 2016. http://novinite.ru/article_print.php?id=533&show_logo=true.

Pridunaiskie Vesti. 2008. "Povorotnaia tochka." 7 February.

RBK Ukraina. 2012. "V Ukraine vstupil v silu zakon o iazykakh." 10 August 2012. Accessed 19 June 2016. http://www.rbc.ua/rus/news/v-ukraine-vstupil-v-silu-zakon-o-yazykah-10082012104900.

Topor. 2015. "V Bolgrade gotoviatsia k postupleniu v VUZy Bolgarii." 5 April 2015. Accessed 19 June 2016. http://topor.od.ua/v-bolgrade-gotovyatsya-k-postupleniyu-v-vuz-bolgarii-foto/.

UNIAN. 2012. "V Izmayili bolgary cherez sud vymahatymut' rehional'nii status dlia svoyeyi movy." 22 August 2012. Accessed 19 June 2016. http://www.unian.ua/society/686365-v-izmajili-bolgari-cherez-sud-vimagatimut-regionalniy-status-dlya-svoeji-movi.html.

Zerkalo Nedeli. 2012. "V Odesskoi oblasti bolgaram otkazali v prave na regional'nyi iazyk. Oni pozhaluiut'sia Ianukovichu." 17 August 2012. Accessed 19 June 2016. http://zn.ua/POLITICS/v_odesskoy_oblasti_bolgaram_otkazali_ v_prave_na_regionalnyy_yazyk_oni_pozhaluyutsya_yanukovichu.html.

Zerkalo Nedeli. 2013. "Ukrainskie bolgary budut dobavit'sia dlia svoego iazyka statusa regional'nogo." 13 June 2013. Accessed 19 June 2016. http://zn.ua/UKR AINE/ukrainskie-bolgary-budut-dobivatsya-dlya-svoego-yazyka-statusa-region alnogo-123960_.html.

---

i   The research for this contribution was enabled by generous funding from the Max Planck Institute for Social Anthropology.
ii A wave of rumors in 1814 and 1815 that Russia might introduce serfdom for Bessarabian peasants led to the flight of more than 3,000 families across the river Prut into Austrian Bukovina (Svin'in 1816: 211; Batiushkov 1892: 137; Kushko & Taki 2012: 157). Another wave of 3,000 Transdanubian Settler families returned to the Balkans after a series of poor harvests between 1830 and 1834 (Skal'kovskii 1850: 246). In 1856, after the Crimean War, a part of southern Bessarabia came under the rule of the United Principalities, a state that was formally still under Ottoman suzerainty; this led to yet another wave of emigration of Transdanubian Colonists, who resettled farther inside the Russian Empire (Klaus 1869: 294; Derzhavin 1914: 11).
iii The Russian original of the slogan was "Sila dobrykh del," which can also be translated as "the *force* of benefaction."
iv Interview with Vladimir Petrov, President of the *Cyril and Methodius Society*, Izmail, 21 April 2013.
v   All of the demographic information that is used in this article stems from the Ukrainian census of 2001, which is the latest available source. [http://2001.ukrcensus.gov.ua/rus/] (as of 19 June 2016).
vi See, for example, the website of the *Congress of Bulgarians in Ukraine* (2016), available online [http://kbg.org.ua/?page_id=30.] (as of 19 June 2016).
vii Interviews with school teachers from the town of Izmail (14 November 2012), Reni Rayon (12 July 2013, 30 July 2013) and Bolgrad Rayon (19 September 2013).
viii Interview with the association's president Vladimir Petrov, Izmail, 21 April 2013.
ix Interview in Izmail, 3 March 2013.
x   Darzhavna agentsiia za bulgarite v chuzhbina. [http://www.aba.government.bg/?country =73&org=1] (as of 19 June 2016).
xi Soviet party newspapers such as the local *Pridunaiskaia Pravda* began to celebrate the region's multiethnic population as early as 1949, for example, in one of the paper's New Year's editorials ("Na novom pod"eme," Pridunaiskaia Pravda, 1 January 1949). In the seminal reference book *The History of Towns and Villages of the Ukrainian SSR*, the section about southern Bessarabia began with a note that stated that it was a multi-ethnic but nevertheless very peaceful region (Istoriia gorodov i sel Ukrainskoi SSR 1978: 427).
xii Electoral district 143 comprises the city of Izmail, rayons Izmail and Reni, and parts of Bolgrad Rayon. All of these rayons are part of Odessa Oblast'. For the ethnic census data of

	these areas, see the Ukrainian census of 2001. [http://2001.ukrcensus.gov.ua/rus/results/general/nationality/odesa/] (as of 19 June 2016).
xiii	See Iuri Kruk's post (September 21 2012) on his Vkontakte account [https://vk.com/wall173409888?offset=1340] (as of November 12 2016)
xiv	A list of the results for the parliamentary elections 2012 by electoral districts, Central Election Commission. [http://www.cvk.gov.ua/pls/vnd2012/wp039?PT001F01=900] (as of 19 June 2016).
xv	Electoral district 142 comprises Rayons Artsis, Tarutino, Sarata, parts of Bolgrad Rayon, and parts of Kiliia Rayon. For the ethnic census data of these areas, see the Ukrainian census of 2001. [http://2001.ukrcensus.gov.ua/rus/results/general/nationality/odesa/] (as of 19 June 2016).
xvi	The 2015 budget for the "Program of harmonization of interethnic relations on the territory of Izmail and support of the ethno-cultural societies" was granted by the city council with decision No. 4871-VI on 16 January 2015, as published on the municipal council's homepage. [http://www.izmail-rada.gov.ua/2010-05-05-12-39-15] (as of 19 June 2016).

The Transnational "Neo-Eurasian" Network and its Preparation of Separatism in Ukraine 2005–2014

Veronika Borysenko, Mascha Brammer and Jonas Eichhorn

The article sheds light on the roots of the so-called 'Donezk People's Republic' (DNR) in Eastern Ukraine. Although the DNR was established only in 2014, the analysis reveals a striking continuity of ideational aspects and leading figures of the separatist republic that can be traced back to the formation of neo-eurasian organizations in the early 2000s. Based on the theories of Transnational Advocacy Networks (TAN) and uncivil society, we argue that a transnational movement of neo-eurasianist groups and organizations emerged in the Donbas which laid the foundations for the separation processes. A network analytical approach helps to disclose the movements' individuals, events and organizations which can be considered as being particularly influential in the creation of the DNR.

1. Introduction: the Long Roots of Separatism

During early spring 2014, pro-Russian separatists occupied several administration buildings in eastern Ukrainian cities and proclaimed an "Independent People's Republic" in Donetsk. These events quickly escalated. An armed conflict between separatists and Ukrainian security forces erupted and led to an ongoing war. At the same time, the two self-proclaimed republics, Donezk People's Republic *(Donezkaja narodnaja respublika, DNR)* and Luhansk People's Republic *(Luhanskaja narodnaja respublika, LNR)*, were established.

Although the separatist attempts surfaced in spring 2014, their roots go a long way back within the Donbas region. What is new is the intensity and the use of weapons to obtain a secession from Ukraine. However, a transnational network of organizations and persons that follows the aims that were later proclaimed by the separatists had already emerged a decade before Euromaidan. The goals of this network, which were formed both in the Russian Federation and in Ukraine, were to undermine Ukrainian sovereignty and territorial integrity and to obstruct the Ukrainian-EU rapprochement (Shekhovtsov 2017: 189).

A key player within that network was the organization Evrazijskij sojuz molodezhi (Eurasian Youth Association, ESM). Since its founding in 2005 in Moscow, it became active and frequently mobilized in Ukraine. The activities of the organization were centered around the idea of neo-Eurasianism, which postulates that Ukraine ultimately belongs to Russia and, on a larger scale, to Eurasia (Shekhovtsov 2014: 77f.). In our text, we enquire into the topography of this network, which consists of individuals, organizations and ideological frames. We argue that neo-Eurasianist movement structures have formed a central base of the establishment and proclamation of the DNR since 2014.

The analysis proceeds as follows. First, we introduce a concept that catches the characteristics of the Eurasian movement in Eastern Ukraine: the Transnational Advocacy Network Theory (TAN) as developed by Margaret Keck and Kathryn Sikkink (1999). Second, we present the ideological content of the movement—the roots and ideology of neo-Eurasianism. Third, we describe how the "Eurasian Youth Union" as the organizational body of the neo-Eurasian ideology and some of its partner organizations evolved in Ukraine since 2004. This description is conducted according to the criteria of a transnational advocacy network. This in-depth analysis is followed by a network analysis that identifies core persons, organizations and events of the neo-Eurasianist movement in Eastern Ukraine.

2. Theoretical Background:
Transnational Advocacy Networks (TAN) and Uncivil Society

The TAN theory of Keck and Sikkink (1999) arises from the concepts of civil society research, particularly with regard to the promotion of democracy, human rights or environmental protection. Keck and Sikkink define TANs as "forms of organization characterized by voluntary, reciprocal and horizontal patterns of communication and exchange" (Keck & Sikkink 1999: 91). They primarily address information-intensive topics and are less hierarchical than state structures and more efficient than market-based arrangements. Typically, political actors such as NGOs, media and authorities as well as individual firms, intellectuals, foundations, local social movements and parts of parliament are major actors in such networks. Their internal structures are often characterized by a high fluctuation of participants and financial resources and by a large number of formal and informal connections. Among NGOs, a particularly important role is played by educational formats such as round tables or conferences. The most important arena for TANs is the transnational pubic sphere. Here, social movements and NGOs can draw attention to the infringement of individual or human rights by state authorities.

The starting point of a TAN is often an unresolved conflict between the government and the social movement in which no mutually satisfactory approach is recognizable. In such a situation, movement activists expect concerted international action to help push their claims ahead. Newly created or already existing platforms such as international conferences may then be used to form, deepen or strengthen the existing networks. Consequently, one important precondition for their appearance consists in low costs of international communication and transport (ibid.: 93). Network members are not powerful political actors in a traditional sense, but they seek to bring issues to a public agenda, such as by establishing cognitive frames, as Snow et al. (1986) illustrated.

In their TAN model, Keck and Sikkink developed a typology that distinguishes four tactics of how network actors may try to alter information and value contexts of state politics:

- *Information politics* means the "ability to move politically usable information quickly and credibly to where it will have the most impact" (Keck & Sikkink 1999: 95f.). Network actors provide for the circulation of information (e.g., e-mail, flyers and pamphlets) within and outside the network. In addition, personal stories (testimonials) can be used to frame information and interpretations according to the topic of the TAN.
- *Symbolic politics* means the active framing of issues by activists to explain important events. By promoting symbolic interpretations, network activists create awareness for certain problems or claims (ibid.: 96f.). Symbolic politics often arise in situations that are marked by multivalent meanings, such as in a context of several language systems or competing historical narratives.
- *Leverage politics* means how advocacy networks can bring about policy change by both persuading and pressuring more powerful actors. Leverage can be combined with benefits; this would be material leverage with sanctions and public shaming in the case of moral leverage (ibid.: 97).
- Accountability politics is the attempt of the TAN to remind governments to implement their promises or announcements (ibid.: 94–98).

Keck and Sikkink further argue that advocacy networks may exert influence on different levels. Issue creation and agenda setting are the most basic levels, but they may also alter discursive positions of states or regional and international organizations. The influence on institutional procedures marks a higher level of influence and a successful policy change of 'target actors' such as states, organizations or even private actors (ibid.: 98).

The approach of Keck and Sikkink has been widely discussed in civil society research (see, among others, Worschech 2017, forthcoming). Usually, it is used in a context in which civic organizations advocate for a normatively 'desirable' common good, such as human rights protection. Keck and Sikkink's advocacy networks originally referred to a concept of civil society as the 'watchdog' of democracy and civil liberties. As noted in the following section, however, many activities of the networks in the Ukrainian Donbas are not marked by practices that can be characterized as civil. Rather, violence, the negation of civil liberties and the adherence to illiberal mind frames are widespread. Therefore, we combine the concept of an uncivil society with Keck and Sikkink's approach on transnational advocacy networks. Uncivil society is a concept that various scholars have used to include illiberal and/or undemocratic organizations in the idea of civil society as a sphere of autonomous societal organizations.

The concept can be found in different variations. Friedbert Rüb, a German political scientist who devised the concept in the context of the Yugoslav wars of the 1990s, argues that uncivil features are structural parts of any civil society (Rüb 2000: 185). Other authors relate "uncivil society" explicitly to certain regions, particularly to Eastern Europe (Kopecky 2003, Ruzza 2011). Similar to Rüb, Ruzza claims that organizations of "uncivil society" share features of civil society organizations, such as the conjunction to the political system via parties (Ruzza 2011: 146) and a brokerage function, because these organizations represent an alternative type of political participation (ibid.: 150). Ruzza also argues that "uncivil society" is related to anti-political views and to the rejection of checks and balances in contemporary democracies (ibid.: 143). Actors of uncivil society often explicitly reject the values and practices of civil societies, which situates civil and uncivil society in antagonistic positions. Uncivil societies aim to exclude certain persons from the political and symbolic community space; their actors often show violent, aggressive, xenophobic and anti-democratic behavior (ibid.: 148).

With this combined theoretical approach, we pursue two analytical targets: First, the concept provides us with theoretical guidelines for a descriptive analysis of our empirical phenomenon, the neo-Eurasianist movement and activities in Eastern Ukraine that are assumed to have prepared the ideological and motivational basis of the separatists' mobilization in 2014. Second, we examine the extent to which the concept of transnational advocacy networks is a fruitful analytical tool not only for human rights groups and related topics but also for the dark side of civil society.

3. Ideological Background: "Neo-Eurasianism"

What constitutes the ideological foundation of uncivil network behavior in Eastern Ukraine? The most significant frame to which groups and individual actors have referred to consists in a specific form of ideology that can be labeled as "neo-Eurasian". This concept, which was most influentially introduced by the Russian thinker Aleksandr Dugin, can be seen as a successor to the concept of Eurasianism, which was developed by Russian émigrés mainly to Paris and dates from the 1920s. Its core arguments can be found in the journal Smena Vekh. The authors of the journal argued that the Communist Revolutions of 1917 bore a certain logic as a reaction to an overly rapid modernization of Russia. In contrast to most other émigrés, who were often representatives of the gentry and had revanchist intentions, the Smena Vekh authors insisted on the interest of the Russian masses in social policies and national resurrection under Communist terms (Terras 1985: 427–428). In this context, Eurasianism bears a strong element of Russian nationalism in the slavophile tradition.

Significant aspects of the Eurasian idea are the evaluation of the Russian territory and consequent nationalism. Within the discourse on defining the Russian territory, Eurasianism aims to disengage from a Western course of development (Frank 2003: 201f.). Eurasianists argue against the division between the East and the West. Instead, they insist on climate zones shifting from north to south. Eurasia forms a climatic and botanical whole, with the chernozem ("black earth") zone considered the center around which the common culture has evolved. The Mongolian Empire of Genghis Khan is assessed positively and recognized as the predecessor of the Russian Empire (ibid.: 208). Already in the 1920s, Eurasianism deliberately refused Western-perceived geopolitics and its implicit economic and military purposes because they do not fit the Eurasian isolationist concept due to their global position (ibid.: 213–214). Another Eurasian feature is the originality of national cultures. Whereas cosmopolitanism and internationalism were seen as a European attempt to enforce their own Western standards globally, Eurasian intellectuals were concerned with the issue of nationalism as part of their criticism regarding the West and Russian culture. Eurasianism propagated a tolerant albeit imperial nationalism in a multi-ethnic, Christian empire under Russian supremacy (ibid.: 207, 215).

Neo-Eurasianism has developed in the late years of Perestroika and Glaznost and can be interpreted as a counter-movement to the reformist ideas of the late Soviet Union. Rather than orienting Russia towards ideas such as individual liberty, economic and political freedom, neo-Eurasianists argued that Russia is culturally closer to Asia than to the West and should therefore seek inspiration from frames that are based on collectivist ideas and power based on 'natural spaces'. In contrast to traditional Eurasianism, neo-Eurasianism strongly refers to ethnicity, in particular to the ethnogenesis of the Russian people as a rampart against Western influences.

The most influential figure of neo-Eurasianism is Aleksandr Dugin. Dugin, a publicist and scholar, was until recently the head of the "Center for Conservative Studies" at the Moscow State University MGU. He regularly appeared on Russian television and was a consultant for the Duma and the Kremlin (Jarzyńska 2014). Dugin's specific concept of neo-Eurasianism comprises several ideological parts. His ideas are based on the theories of the European New Right that have emerged since the 1960s (Shekhovtsov 2009: 700), from German fascism (Shekhovtsov 2008: 498) and on the imperial-geopolitical ideologies of the interwar period (1918 – 1939). Despite Dugin's hostility to any Western influences, his thoughts have a strong root in the history of Western European thought (Umland 2007: 144). Major elements of Dugin's neo-Eurasianism are opposed to classical Eurasianism, for example, with regard to the role of geopolitics and the vicinity of society to the state (Frank 2003).[i] Although Eurasianists from the interwar period were hostile to Nazism, Dugin refers positively to National Socialism in Germany (Umland 2007: 155f.). Dugin draws further influences from traditionalism, National Bolshevism, the Conservative Revolution, occultism and mysticism (ibid.: 181).

As already mentioned, Aleksandr Dugin was active as a Kremlin consultant and well networked with Russian state authorities. Some patterns of neo-Eurasianism have influenced the Russian elite and foreign policy. For example, Putin's second presidential appointment marked a clear trend to promote proximity to "neo-Eurasian" ideas by leading Russian politicians' and their close-standing people's use of certain expressions in public speeches. They often underline the civilizing mission of Russia or refer to the idea of the "Russian world", and the rhetoric itself is generally more "anti-Western" (Jarzyńska 2014: 4). In general, however,

Russian foreign policy to date does not seem to be significantly influenced by the ideology of neo-Eurasianism, despite these rhetorical overlaps (Luks 2015).

However, the ethnogenetic guise of neo-Eurasianism in combination with a positive image of Russian-led geopolitics clearly questions the right of Ukraine to self-determination and independence. Consequently, in Dugin's framework, Ukraine belongs to Eurasia:

> The sovereignty of Ukraine represents such a negative phenomenon for the Russian geopolitics that it can, in principle, easily provoke a military conflict. [...] Ukraine as an independent state with some territorial ambitions constitutes an enormous threat to the whole Eurasia, and without the solution of the Ukrainian problem, it is meaningless to talk about the continental geopolitics. [...] Considering the fact that a simple integration of Moscow with Kiev is impossible and will not result in a stable geopolitical structure [...], Moscow should get actively involved in the re-organization of the Ukrainian space in accordance to the only logical and natural geopolitical model.[ii]

Subsequently, Dugin also considers the invasion of Ukraine to be the Kremlin's fundamental duty and necessary to fulfill Russia's Eurasian mission (Shekhovtsov 2014: 77f.). Aleksandr Dugin and his statements on current political and historical events are published on a regular basis. A major publication organ is the website evrazia.org, whose main function is the distribution of "neo-Eurasian" thoughts. The "neo-Eurasian" view is based on actual examples through numerous "analyses" of political and historical events. As shown below, Aleksandr Dugin himself participates in multifold network activities such as youth meetings, forums and summer camps, partly even with family members.[iii]

4. Empirical Analysis: Neo-Eurasian Networks in Ukraine

4.1 Movement history

We will now turn to our empirical phenomenon and analyze how the ideology of neo-Eurasianism is framed and by whom. Keck and Sikkink (1999) argue that transnational advocacy networks usually arise from conflicts between rulers and ruled that cannot be resolved within the political routine. To broaden and strengthen their network, movement activists try to find and use platforms such as international conferences. In the following section, we illustrate how the 'neo-Eurasianist TAN' evolved from a conflictive situation and grew through targeted network mobilization.

The Ukrainian "Orange Revolution" in 2004 – 2005 endangered the alleged neo-Eurasian belonging of Ukraine. Viktor Iushchenko had promised a clear turn of Ukraine to the West in general and to the EU in particular. This turning away from the so-called multi-vectoral foreign policy was taken with discomfort in some parts of Eastern Ukraine. The conflictive development resulted in the constitution of counter-frames, counter-movements and counter-organizations that opposed the 'Western pathway' of Ukraine. Whereas pro-European activists took root in many regions of Ukraine, Russophile organizations were established in both Ukraine and Russia. These connected with each other to resist the country's orientation to the West and the EU. Such organizations were the Evrazijskij sojuz molodezhi (ESM), *Nashi* ("Ours"), *Rossija Molodaja* ("Young Russia"), and *Molodaja gvardija* ("Young Guard") (Shekhovtsov 2017: 189). The ESM was established in Moscow as the youth organization[iv] of the *International Eurasian Movement* (MED) and the *New University* – a private university funded by the Russian state[v]—at the *Congress of the Intellectual Eurasian Youth*. The official ESM website states that the first task of the "young Eurasians" was to build a "neo-Eurasian" network in the post-Soviet territory to prevent a possible "colored revolution" and thus the collapse of the Russian state (Pershin n.d.). The Russian government supported these organizations because of its well-known opposition to the colored revolutions in countries such as Serbia (2000), Georgia (2003) and Ukraine (2004/05).

Between 2005 and 2007, offices of the ESM were established in many Ukrainian cities (e.g., Kyiv, Kharkiv, Sumy, and Sevastopol), which meant that more than half of the non-Russian ESM-offices were located in Ukraine (Zarifullin 2007). Concurrently, ESM representatives sought for contacts with various Ukrainian organizations and parties. The most important partners can be identified as follows (Shekhovtsov 2017: 191). The first is Natalia Vitrenko, the chairwoman of the Progressive Socialist Party of Ukraine (PSPU). She performed as a speaker in ESM summer camps and was a permanent member of discussion rounds organized by ESM in Ukraine and Russia. PSPU is a Ukrainian conservative pro-Russian, party opposing Ukraine's European and Euro-Atlantic integration and supporting the creation of a union between Ukraine, Russia and Belarus.[vi] The second network knot to be named is the so-called independent political entity called *Donetsk Republic* (DR). In November 2006, activists from ESM and DR—including Andrey Purgin, Aleksandr Curkan[vii] and Oleg Frolov—gathered signatures for a referendum to announce the founding of an independent political entity called the 'Donetsk Republic'. In 2008, both organizations adopted a declaration that officially proclaimed the 'Donetsk Federal Republic'.[viii] In 2007, the DR was prohibited by the SBU because of its extremist activities and was therefore not active until 2012.[ix]

When it became clear in 2012 that Ukraine was not going to join the Eurasian Union, conferences co-organized by the ESM were held with the aim of supporting the idea of the Eurasian Union in Ukraine. On 18 February 2012, a conference with the title "The Future of Donbas" took place in Luhansk with approximately twenty participants from Russia and Ukraine (Bredechin 2012). It concluded that Ukrainian integration into the Eurasian Union was highly important for the country. On 11 March 2012, the conference "Ukraine and Donbas for the Eurasian Union" took place in Rostov-na-Donu, where representatives of the ESM (e.g., Andrey Kovalenko, Head of the Moscow Department of the ESM) and the DR were present (Zarovnaja 2014). This resulted in the foundation of the NGO "Ukraine for the Eurasian Union" with Sergej Baryshnikov, a professor of the Donetsk National University and Dugin supporter, as chairman (Shekhovtsov 2017: 193). In July 2012, the conference "Regional Integration as Foundation for Eurasian Unity" took place, with leaders of DR and ESM (Purgin and Kovalenko) and other members of their organizations taking part. In November 2012, the conference "Donbas in the Eurasian Project" was held with nearly identical participants. Again, its goal was Ukrainian integration into the Eurasian Union (ibid.: 194).

Another important activity, which provided ideological training for the participants, was ESM summer camps. Many of the participating Ukrainian citizens later became regional coordinators of the ESM. As early as 2005, during the first ESM summer camp in a Moscow residential house, the future coordinators were carefully selected, trained and given the authority to represent the ESM in their cities and to coordinate local activities in the name of ESM (Pershin n.d.). Seminars and lectures were conducted and held by well-known political scientists, politicians and public figures from Russia and neighboring countries: Natalija Vitrenko, Oleksandr Svistunov, and Oleg Bachtijarov (Shekhovtsov 2017: 191). The summer camps had the following topics: behavior in riots and clashes; decision-making in critical situations; coordination of large groups; organization of protests; rallies, etc. In addition, participants could take part in lessons on self-defense or spatial orientation (ibid.).

Following our theoretical framework, the functioning of a TAN can be summarized as consisting of four central elements: information, symbolism, leverage and accountability politics. We will now discuss ESM activities according to these elements.

With regard to *information politics*, the official website of the ESM—titled the Official Portal of the Eurasian Youth Association/ *Offizial'nyj portal Evrazijskogo sojuza molodezhi* (http://www.russia3.ru)—can be considered the most important 'voice' of the advocacy network. Regular reports on the activities of the TAN, such as reports on the summer camps, book publications, and conference reports, are published on this website. Because of its structure as a portal, users can participate in the virtual exchange within the portal after registration. The activities of Aleksandr Dugin and his statements on current political and historical events are also published here on a regular basis. The combination of different sources and authors gives the feeling of community in which hierarchy does not play a large role. For example, it is easy to find photos where Dugin sits and speaks with participants of a summer camp around a campfire.

Another important internet site that ensures the information distribution of the neo-Eurasian TAN is the already mentioned portal Evrazija (www.evrazia.org), which also provides reports on summer camps of the ESM, political statements and literature recommendations on neo-Eurasianism. In particular, since 2014, it has focused strongly on the development of the so-called Luhansk and Donetsk People's Republics. Other important sources to be mentioned are the portal 'geopolitika.ru' and the TV channel "Evrazija TV" (www.evrazia.tv). The editor-in-chief of Evrazija TV, Leonid Savin, was a regular participant in the ESM's summer camps. The social networks vkontkte.ru and odnoklassniki.ru can be seen as parts of the TAN's information politics that, in a broader sense, provide exchange, linkage and in-group debates for neo-Eurasian activists and supporters.

Taken together, the neo-Eurasian activists seem to rely primarily on web-based information distribution channels. However, together with the networking activities such as summer camps and conferences, they are able to spread their ideas, interpretations and goals within and outside the network to those geographic and social places "where it will have the most impact", as Keck and Sikkink (1999: 95) described it.

As Keck and Sikkink argue, the *symbol politics* of a TAN means the active framing of issues by activists to provide explanations for important events. This symbolic dimension of the neo-Eurasian transnational movement can best be illustrated with the example of the flags of the so-called Donetsk People's Republics.

There are significant overlaps of the symbols used by the ESM, the organization 'Donetsk Republic' (DR) and the two contemporary separatist 'republics'. The ESM's flag shows some golden arrows that gravitate from a center to the periphery. According to several self-descriptions of the neo-Eurasian movement, these arrows symbolize the aim of widening Eurasian territory and the expansion of neo-Eurasianism.[x] This symbol is often used at ESM events on flags, t-shirts or armlets.

The symbols of the DR and the separatist republics are strikingly similar and strongly resemble the Russian state symbols with respect to their colors and the emblem of an eagle. Only the person on the eagle's chest is different and refers to heroes from Christian mythology. The DNR, however, uses nearly the same flag as the DR, only with some slight changes of the eagle's appearance. This example underlines the visual incorporation of the neo-Eurasian ideology into its graphical appearance and the strong reference of the subsequent organizations and the separatist republic to Russia as the core of Eurasia. Both are clear counter-framings that are set up as an alternative development path to Ukraine's orientation towards 'the West'. The ESM in particular provides the establishment of an own—non-Western—identity based on the neo-Eurasian ideology with references to 'imperial greatness'. The DR's and DNR's flags refer more to the Russian 'homeland' and Christian mythology.

In Keck and Sikkink's argumentation, *leverage politics* refers to a movement's ability to substantially influence politics, despite the movement's obvious unfavorable hierarchical position. In our case, leverage focuses on the disruption and destruction that the neo-Eurasian movement carries out against the integrity of Ukraine as both a society and state, which is supported by the resource allocation of the movement. An important role to overcome the TAN's weak position is played by the Russian state, which has supported the objectives of the TAN in Ukraine since 2005. As an initiator for the founding of the ESM, Russia has played a direct supporting role from the beginning. The ongoing funding of the ESM and similar organizations is difficult to prove, but it probably originates from formal and informal sources alike. According to the "Center for Political Economic Reforms", the Russian state's financial support for "neo-Eurasian" organizations marks a considerable share of the presidential funds.[xi] For some of the "neo-Eurasian" organizations, the funding increased significantly in 2013: the ESM (2013 – 2015: 18.5 million rubles), the "Institute for Eurasian Studies" (15 million rubles) and the foundation "Development of Eurasian Cooperation" (6.5 million rubles) were among those groups whose state-based resources grew. In 2013, the ESM received 2.5 million rubles alone for the project "Student Eurasian Intellectual Clubs".[xii]

As argued, Putin's second presidency stands for a clear trend to promote proximity to the "neo-Eurasian" ideology and practical politics. With the military intervention of Russia in Ukraine and the "connection" of Eastern Ukrainian territories and Crimea to Russia, at least one of the main objectives of the neo-Eurasian transnational advocacy network has been reached. Since then, the formerly ideational frame of the civilizing mission of Russia has become a realistic scenario for allegedly defective territories into the Russian world.

With regard to *accountability politics*, the uncivil character of our TAN becomes relevant. The normative orientation of Keck and Sikkink was developed for civil networks. Accountability refers to the sense of responsibility, the rule of law and striving for legitimacy, and it implies the acceptance of peaceful negotiations. Nationalist groups usually do not follow these patterns, but they were, in the Donbas case, able to exert normative pressure on Ianukovich and his government. In accordance with Russian aspirations, neo-Eurasian ideas were not rejected despite their obvious dangers for the sustainability of an independent Ukraine. Keck and Sikkink (1999: 97f.) note that network actors "try to make such statements into opportunities for accountability politics" and may expose the distance between discourse and practice once a government has publicly committed itself to a principle. The above-mentioned conferences in 2012 can be considered one attempt to create and use such a window of opportunity to raise a public requirement for a clear neo-Eurasian policy.

All of these activities underline that the neo-Eurasianist movement in Eastern Ukraine can be classified as a transnational network. When the activities extend across the existing national borders, they are characterized by anti-nationalism with regard to Ukraine and by aggressive nationalism in reference to Russian ideas and activities. Although knowledge-oriented texts about the ideas of neo-Eurasianism exhibit some type of scholarly claim, many forms of interaction are practice related, such as in the form of summer camps or paramilitary training events. This clear strategic and political objective of the movement indicates that 'advocacy' for a distinctive political aim is an important element of the transnational network. These are our reasons for analyzing and visualizing the major activities of the network around the Eurasian Youth Organization.

4.2 Network analysis

To complete our empirical analysis, we now conduct a social network analysis of the 'neo-Eurasianist TAN'. The analysis of linkages between actors and events can reveal the structures of power and influence in the network and may show which actors can be considered the main drivers, crosslinkers or information distributers in the movement. This is done by determining the most central events, organizations and persons that actively connect activists and shape ideas and political aims and thereby disclosing how the actors are interconnected.

Data and Method

The empirical starting point of the network analysis is those organizations and events where actors of the neo-Eurasianist movement met. These organizations and events can be regarded as 'social hubs' or platforms that link activists, help them share information, develop and promote framings and common understandings, formulate aims and mobilize people. In a first step, we extract information on these 'social hubs' from the observations and descriptions presented in four analytical texts (Shekhovtsov 2016, 2017; Mitrokhin 2014a, 2014b). From these descriptions of activities and events, we draw a first 'map' of relevant events and respective participants. In a second step, we purposefully collect information about the events, organizations and persons who participated in these events or were active in the respective organizations. Central sources were internet activities such as documentaries or interviews provided by the organizations on their homepages.[xiii] The data on activists' participation in different events and their engagement in neo-Eurasianist organizations are transformed into a two-mode network that shows the relevant events and organizations and the respective affiliations of activists.

The network analysis is based on the concept of centrality. Centrality and prestige measures mirror the participation of actors in processes of mutual influence. These measures can either count the direct or indirect ties of each actor (degree-centrality), thereby measuring how fast influence can be imposed, or they measure the *betweenness* of an actor, that is his/her capacity to connect two other actors and to restrict or broaden the information flow between them (Friedkin 1991; Freeman 1977, 1979). The general idea of prominence related to network embeddedness is that an actor is 'prominent' if she or he is involved in many relationships within the network. As a result of the network position, central actors have better access to information sources and can exert their influence better than less prominent actors within the network. (Jansen 2013: 127f.). We therefore analyze the degree-centrality to show which events and organizations are well attended and which individuals are well connected. In a later step, we additionally analyze the actors' betweenness-centrality to show which individuals link others exclusively, thereby constraining the flow of information and resources within the network.

All network calculations and visualizations are conducted with the program visone (visone project team 2001–2014).

Empirical Network Analysis

In a first step, we present a two-mode network that combines and equally shows network actors, their respective organizations and/or their participation in events. Based on network measures such as density and degree centrality, we describe the structuration of the network and detect possible fragmentations and prominent positions. Network density measures the ratio of the number of realized relationships to the number of possible relationships within a network (Jansen 2013: 110f.). In the case of the ESM network, the density calculation leads to a value of 0.426, which is in the (approximate) range of a strong-tie network (ibid.). Regarding the degree-centrality, an actor's centrality is higher if she/he maintains more direct connections in the network (ibid.: 139).[xiv] Our two-mode network of organizations and events shows five remarkably central organizations and events, as listed in table 1. Their high centrality indicates a high importance within the network due to their high number of members and participants; these organizations and events are the main social 'spots' where activists could meet. The particular affiliations of actors to these organizations and events are displayed in illustration 1.

Table 1: Most central organizations/events of the TAN (degree-based)

	Name	Degree-centrality
1.	Evrazijskij sojuz molodeži (ESM)	0.34
2.	Conference "Donbas in the Eurasian Project"	0.33
3.	Roundtable "The Future of Donbas"	0.3
4.	ESM Summer Camp 2006 (ESM SC 2006)	0.2
5.	Organization "Donetskaja respublika" (DR)	0.16

Illustration 1: Two-mode-network of the 'neo-Eurasianist TAN'

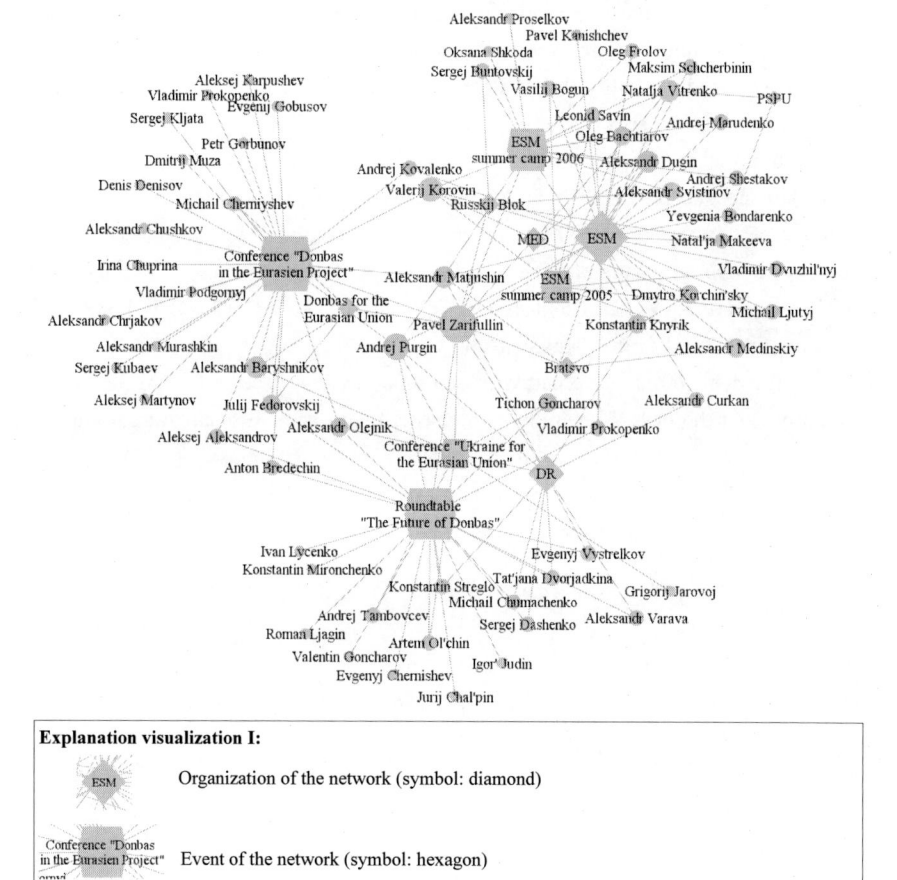

[Network diagram showing nodes including:]

Aleksandr Proselkov, Pavel Kanishchev, Oksana Shkoda, Oleg Frolov, Sergej Buntovskij, Maksim Schcherbinin, Aleksej Karpushev, Vladimir Prokopenko, Vasilij Bogun, Natalja Vitrenko, Evgenij Gobusov, PSPU, Sergej Kljata, Leonid Savin, Andrej Marudenko, Petr Gorbunov, ESM, Oleg Bachtiarov, Dmitrij Muza, summer camp 2006, Aleksandr Dugin, Andrej Kovalenko, Andrej Shestakov, Denis Denisov, Valerij Korovin, Aleksandr Svistinov, Michail Cherniyshev, Russkij Blok, Yevgenia Bondarenko, Aleksandr Chushkov, MED, ESM, Natal'ja Makeeva, Irina Chuprina, Conference "Donbas in the Eurasien Project", Aleksandr Matjushin, ESM, Vladimir Dvuzhil'nyj, Vladimir Podgornyj, Donbas for the Eurasian Union, summer camp 2005, Dmytro Korchin'sky, Aleksandr Chrjakov, Pavel Zarifullin, Konstantin Knyrik, Michail Ljutyj, Aleksandr Murashkin, Andrej Purgin, Aleksandr Medinskiy, Sergej Kubaev, Aleksandr Baryshnikov, Bratsvo, Aleksej Martynov, Julij Fedorovskij, Tichon Goncharov, Aleksandr Curkan, Aleksandr Olejnik, Vladimir Prokopenko, Aleksej Aleksandrov, Conference "Ukraine for the Eurasian Union", Anton Bredechin, DR, Roundtable "The Future of Donbas", Ivan Lycenko, Evgenyj Vystrelkov, Konstantin Mironchenko, Tat'jana Dvorjadkina, Konstantin Streglo, Grigorij Jarovoj, Michail Chumachenko, Andrej Tambovcev, Aleksandr Varava, Roman Ljagin, Sergej Dashenko, Artem Ol'chin, Valentin Goncharov, Igor' Judin, Evgenyj Chernishev, Jurij Chal'pin

---

Explanation visualization I:

ESM — Organization of the network (symbol: diamond)

Conference "Donbas in the Eurasien Project" — Event of the network (symbol: hexagon)

Konstantin Knyrik — actor of the network (symbol: ellipse)

- Size of symbols: The larger a symbol is, the higher the degree centrality value is
- Calculation and visualization by the program visone, using the following algorithm $d = \sum_j x_{ij} = \sum_j x_{ji}$ (Jansen, 2013: 137):

The network graph illustrates that nearly seventy actors of the movement are relatively densely linked but only via a few organizations and events. This underlines that this TAN is a rather strong network with a certain hierarchy and a developed mobilization basis.

In our second step, we focus on the actors of the network by transforming the two-mode network into a one-mode network. This one-mode network gives us the additional possibility to analyze not only the degree-centrality, but also the betweenness-based centrality that indicates an actor's capacity to control the information flow in the network and is an indicator of power and prominence. The calculation of the *degree*-centrality in the one-mode network reveals the following result: The most central actor by far is the above mentioned Andrej Purgin; he counts for a *degree*-centrality value of 1, which means that he is directly connected to all other actors. Purgin is therefore the most influential figure in the TAN. Further central figures are Aleksandr Matjushin (0.8), Valeryj Korovin (0.754), Tichon Goncharov (0.692) and Andrey Kovalenko (0.692).

The actor prominence pattern based on *betweenness*-centrality[xv] differs only slightly from the *degree*-centrality. The most central actor is again Andrej Purgin (0.146), followed by Valery Korovin (0.059), Aleksandr Matjushin (0.59), Andrey Kovalenko (0.045) and Tichon Goncharov (0.042; see illustration 2). These actors steer, navigate and control the network.

THE TRANSNATIONAL "NEO-EURASIAN" NETWORK   241

Illustration 2: One-mode network of the 'neo-Eurasianist TAN'

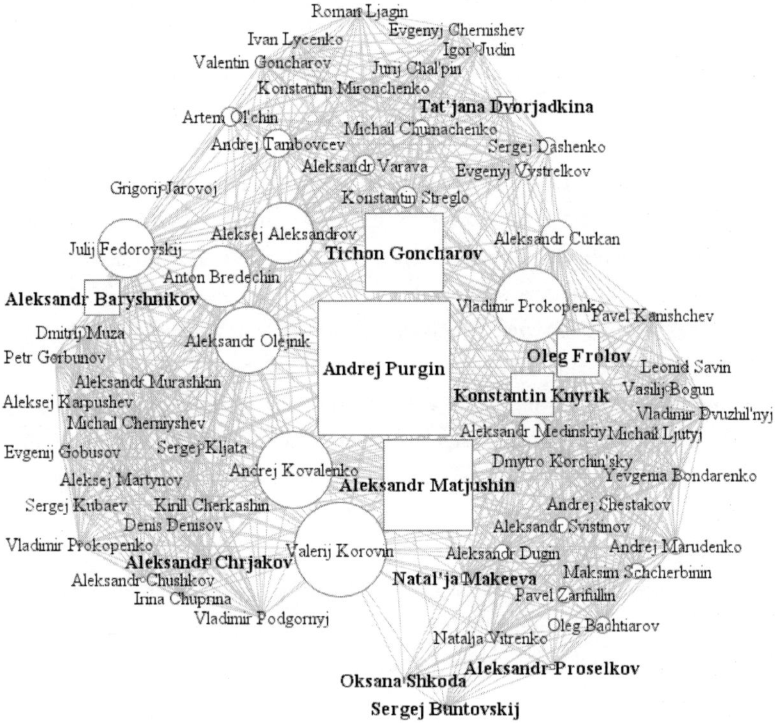

Roman Ljagin
Ivan Lycenko   Evgenyj Chernishev
Valentin Goncharov   Igor Judin
    Jurij Chal'pin
Konstantin Mironchenko
    Tat'jana Dvorjadkina
Artem Ol'chin   Michail Chumachenko
Andrej Tambovcev
    Sergej Dashenko
Aleksandr Varava   Evgenyj Vystrelkov
Grigorij Jarovoj
    Konstantin Streglo
Julij Fedorovskij   Aleksej Aleksandrov
    Tichon Goncharov   Aleksandr Curkan
Anton Bredechin
Aleksandr Baryshnikov
Dmitrij Muza   Aleksandr Olejnik   Vladimir Prokopenko
Petr Gorbunov   Pavel Kanishchev
    Andrej Purgin   **Oleg Frolov**   Leonid Savin
Aleksandr Murashkin
Aleksej Karpushev   **Konstantin Knyrik**   Vasilij Bogun
Michail Chernyshev   Vladimir Dvuzhil'nyj
    Aleksandr Medinskiy Michail Ljutyj
Evgenij Gobusov   Sergej Kljata
    Andrej Kovalenko   Dmytro Korchin'sky
Aleksej Martynov   **Aleksandr Matjushin**   Yevgenia Bondarenko
Sergej Kubaev   Kirill Cherkashin   Andrej Shestakov
    Denis Denisov   Aleksandr Svistinov
Vladimir Prokopenko   Andrej Marudenko
    Aleksandr Chrjakov Valerij Korovin   Aleksandr Dugin
Aleksandr Chushkov   **Natal'ja Makeeva**   Maksim Shcherbinin
Inna Chuprina   Pavel Zarifullin
Vladimir Podgornyj
    Natalja Vitrenko   Oleg Bashtiarov
    Aleksandr Proselkov
Oksana Shkoda
Sergej Buntovskij

Explanation illustration 2:

Aleksandr Olejnik — Actor of the network with no connection to DNR (symbol: ellipse)

Tichon Goncharov — Actor of the network with connection to DNR (symbol: rectangle, label bold)

- Size of symbols: The larger a symbol is, the higher the betweenness centrality value is
- Calculation and visualization by the program visone, using the following algorithm (Jansen, 2013: 137): $C_B(n_i) = \sum_{j<k}^{n} \sum^{n} b_{jk}(n_i)$

The most central actors are informal leading figures of the TAN and formal leading figures of neo-Eurasianist organizations and entities. Most of them have actively participated in separatist actions since 2014 and/or were actively involved in the establishment of the so-called DNR.[xvi] Their centrality inside the network is caused by their membership in many important organizations of the network and their participation at events.

Andrej Purgin (* 1976, Donetsk), the founder of the 'Doneckaja Respublika' (DR) in 2005, participated actively in the first separatist actions in Donbas in 2014, for example the storming of the Donetsk city administration. He also supported the separatists in Donbas financially and finds himself on the USA's and EU's sanctions lists. He was arrested in March 2014 by Ukrainian Security Services but was released shortly thereafter. Later in 2014, he became the first 'Vice Prime Minister' of the so-called DNR and the spokesperson of the 'People's council of the DNR' (Shekhovtsov 2016). However, he resigned from office as early as 2015, a step for which the reasons remain unclear.[xvii]

Aleksandr Matjushin (* 1984, Makeevka) has his activist roots in demonstrations and protests against the Orange Revolution in 2004. Since then, he has been campaigning for the secession of South-Eastern Ukraine in cooperation with the ESM, the National Bolshevik Party and DR. Since 2014, he has been a fighter in the Donbas where he commands the military unit 'Varjag', a combat unit that is directly subordinated to the DNR's 'Ministry of security'.[xviii] With regard to his network position, he links the members of the ESM and the DR among each other and to the conference 'Donbas within the Eurasian project'.

Tichon Goncharov is a professional musician and worked as a member of the Luhansk Symphony Orchestra. He is also a publicist, writing for the Novaja Zemlja, Russkoe Slovo, novorossia.su, and other sources. As the head of the Luhansk department of the 'Movement of Vladimir Monomach Rus', he also actively participated in separatist actions in the Donbas (Goncharov 2015). As an active member of the ESM and equally the ESM's representative at the Round Table 'The future of the Donbas', his network position links these members.

Oleg Frolov is, together with Purgin and Curkan, one of the founders of the organization 'Donetskaja Respublika'. In the so-called DNR, he first became a member of parliament. Being a combatant at the same time, he was seriously wounded in the battles at the Donetsk airport. Since then, he has worked in the DNR 'parliament'.[xix]

Konstantin Knyrik (*1989) has been the ESM's regional coordinator in Crimea since 2007 and participated in one of the ESM's summer camps in 2006. He was the head of the DNR information centre 'South-eastern front', but at the moment he works as the head of the political party 'Rodina' in Crimea.[xx] He has for a longer time publicly endorsed the separation of Crimea from Ukraine, and together with representatives of the 'DR', he published a convention to announce the 'Donetsk Federal Republic' (Shekhovtsov 2015: 10).

The network analysis shows not only the centrality of some actors but also the personal and organizational continuity of the separatist and neo-Eurasianist endeavors in Eastern Ukraine. The centrality of the actors and their 'Eurasian' biographies underline our argument that the separation and the proclamation of the so-called DNR have been prepared well in advance.

5. Conclusion

Since the Orange Revolution in 2004, a neo-Eurasian Transnational Advocacy Network has been created in Ukraine. Its actors either are part of an organization that promotes neo-Eurasian ideas in Ukraine or participate in neo-Eurasian conferences or summer camps. The ideological fundament of the network is Aleksandr Dugin's transnational ideology of neo-Eurasianism, which seeks a Eurasian territorial union under Russian domination and the simultaneous combat of 'Western values'. Furthermore, the Russian state indirectly supports the non-institutionalized and non-governmental network financially by giving presidential grants to the ESM. The empirical phenomenon, the neo-Eurasian transnational advocacy network, is clearly based on violence, non-democratic practices and illiberalism and therefore marks an interesting example of the 'dark side of transnational civil society'—an uncivil advocacy network.

Our analysis of the internal structures and power relations of the neo-Eurasian TAN leads to the following conclusions: First, the influence of the ESM on the neo-Eurasian TAN is quite high, as we can see from the centrality measures. Second, the TAN is a dense network, which implies that the communication channels between the actors are short and the network structures are well-functioning. Third, few actors play central roles and consequently control and influence the TAN. Fourth, the personal-biographical links between neo-Eurasian and separatist activism and establishment of the so-called DNR are obvious. This connection notes that the dense structures and the high possibilities of control and influence of some actors within the network created since 2005 favor separatist efforts and the building of the so-called DNR.

6. Bibliography

Bredechin, Anton. 2012. "Grazhdanskaja iniciativnaja gruppa 'Donbass za EAS' vyrazila zhelanie vstupit' v 'Internacional'nuju Rossiju." *Russkij Mir Zaporozh'ja*, 12 February 2012. Accessed 10 November 2016. https://rusmirzp.wordpress.com/2012/02/21/гражданская-инициативная-группа-до/.

Jansen, Dorothea. 2013. *Einführung in die Netzwerkanalyse: Grundlagen, Methoden, Forschungsbeispiele.* Opladen: VS Verlag für Sozialwissenschaften.

Freeman, Linton C. 1977. "A Set of Measures of Centrality Based on Betweenness." *Sociometry* 40(1): 35–41.

Freeman, Linton C. 1979. "Centrality in Social Networks. Conceptual Clarification." *Social Networks* 1(3): 215–39.

Friedkin, Noah E. 1991. "Theoretical Foundations for Centrality Measures." *American Journal of Sociology* 96(6): 1478–504.

Frank, Susi. 2003. "Eurasianismus: Projekt eines russischen 'dritten Weges' 1921 und heute." *Europa und die Grenzen im Kopf (= Themenband zur Wieser Enzyklopädie des europäischen Ostens),* 197–223.

Goncharov, Tichon. 2015. "'Donbass' ni v kakom vide ne zhelaet vozvrata na Ukrainu", *Regnum,* 27 April 2015. Accessed 10 November 2016. http://regnum.ru/news/1919344.html.

Hahn-Fuhr, Irene and Susann Worschech. 2014. "External Democracy Promotion and Divided Civil Society – the Missing Link." In *Civil Society and Democracy Promotion,* edited by Timm Beichelt, Irene Hahn-Fuhr, Frank Schimmelfennig and Susann Worschech, 11–41. Basingstoke, Hampshire: Palgrave Macmillan.

Jarzyńska, Katarzyna. 2014. "Russian nationalists on the Kremlin's policy in Ukraine." *OSW Commentary* 156: 1–8.

Keck, Margaret E. and Kathryn Sikkink. 1999. "Transnational advocacy networks in international and regional politics." *International Social Science Journal* 51/159: 89–101.

Kopecky, Petr. 2003. "Civil society, uncivil society and contentious politics in post-communist Europe." In *Uncivil Society? Contentious politics in post-communist Europe,* edited by Cas Mudde and Petr Kopecky, 1–17. London: Routledge.

Luks, Leonid. 2015. "Der Mythos vom Endkampf." *The European*, 3 May 2015. Accessed 10 November 2016. http://www.theeuropean.de/leonid-luks/8421-neoimperiale-revanche-in-der-ukraine.

Mitrokhin, Nikolay. 2014a. "Infiltration, Instruktion, Invasion. Russlands Krieg in der Ukraine." *Osteuropa* 64/8: 3–16.

Mitrokhin, Nikolay. 2014b. "Transnationale Provokation: Russische Nationalisten und Geheimdienstler in der Ukraine." *Osteuropa* 64/5-6: 157–174.

Pershin, Sergej. n.d. "Pervye vschody: rozhdenie novoj oprichenny", *rossia3.ru*. Accessed 12 November 2016. http://rossia3.ru/mer/lager1.

Rüb, Friedbert. 2000. "Von der zivilen zur unzivilen Gesellschaft: Das Beispiel des ehemaligen Jugoslawiens." In *Systemwechsel. 5. Zivilgesellschaft und Transformation,* edited by Wolfgang Merkel, 173–203. Opladen: Buske + Laden.

Ruzza, Carlo. 2011. "Identifying uncivil society in Europe: Towards a 'new politics of the enemy'?" In: *The new politics of European civil society*, edited by H. J. Trenz, 143–162. London: Routledge.

Shekhovtsov, Anton. 2008. "The Palingenetic Thrust of Russian Neo-Eurasianism: Ideas of Rebirth in Aleksandr Dugin's Worldview." *Totalitarian Movements and Political Religions* 9/4: 491–506.

Shekhovtsov, Anton. 2009. "Aleksandr Dugin's Neo-Eurasianism: The New Right à la Russe." *Religion Compass* 3/4: 697–716.

Shekhovtsov, Anton. 2014a. "Putin's Brain?" *New Eastern Europe* 4: 72–79.

Shekhovtsov, Anton. 2014b. "Is Putin a new Hitler (in making?)" *Anton Shekhovtsov's blog,* 4 March 2014. Accessed 11 November 2016. http://anton-shekhovtsov.blogspot.cz/2014/03/is-putin-new-hitler-in-making.html.

Shekhovtsov, Anton. 2016. "How Alexander Dugin's Neo-Eurasianists geared up for the Russian-Ukrainian war in 2005–2013." *Anton Shekhovtsov's blog*, 25 January 2016. Accessed 10 November 2016. http://anton-shekhovtsov.blogspot.cz/2016/01/how-alexander-dugins-neo-eurasianists.html.

Shekhovtsov, Anton. 2017. "Aleksandr Dugin's Neo-Eurasianism and the Russian-Ukrainian War." In *The Politics of Eurasianism,* edited by Mark Bassin and Gonzalo Pozo-Martin, 185–204. Lanham: Rowman & Littlefield Publishers, forthcoming.

Snow, David A., E. Burke Rochford, Steven K. Worden, and Robert D. Benford. 1986. "Frame Alignment Processes, Micromobilization, and Movement Participation." *American Sociological Review* 51(4): 464–81.

Terras, Victor. 1985. Handbook of Russian Literature. Binghamton: Yale University Press.

Umland, Andreas. 2007. "Post-Soviet 'uncivil society' and the rise of Aleksandr Dugin: a case study of the extra- parliamentary radical right in contemporary Russia." PhD diss., Trinity College Cambridge.

visone project team (2001–2014) Visone 2.9.2: Analysis and visualization of social networks. http://visone.info.

Zarifullin, Pavel. 2007. "Imperskij marsh", *zavtra.ru*. 28 March 2007. Accessed 10 November 2016. http://www.zavtra.ru/content/view/2007-03-2823/.

Zarovnaja, Tat'jana. 2014. "Gubarev smotrel na odnokursnikov napoleonom i vyrashchival konoplyu", *Obozrevatel*, 12 August 2014. Accessed 10 November 2016. http://obozrevatel.com/interview/32568-gubarev-smotrel-na-odnokursnikov-napoleonom-i-vyiraschival-konoplyu.htm.

List of sources of the network analysis

"Projekt 'DNR': "Respublika" desjat' let nazad." *112 UA*, 23 April 2015. Accessed 1 January 2017. http://112.ua/statji/proekt-dnr-respublika-desyat-let-nazad-223313.html.

"Grazhdanskaja iniciativa gruppa 'Donbass za EAC' vyrazila zhelanie vstupit' v 'Internacional'nuju Rossiju'." *Russkij Mir Zaporozh'ja*, 21 February 2012. Accessed 1 January 2017. https://rusmirzp.wordpress.com/2012/02/21/гражданская-инициативная-группа-до/.

"Nazvali sebja vlast'ju: novye nachal'niki Donecka." *Korrspondent.net*, 19 May 2014. Accessed 1 January 2017. http://korrespondent.net/ukraine/3365187-nazvaly-sebia-vlastui-novye-nachalnyky-donetska.

"V Donecke proshla mezhdunarodnaja nauchno-prakticheskaja konferencija 'Donbass v evrazijskom proekte'." *Russkij Mir. Ukraina*, 28 November 2012. Accessed 1 January 2017. http://russmir.info/pol/3362-v-donecke-proshla-mezhdunarodnaya-nauchno.html.

"Ukraina za Evrazijskij sojuz: novyj format rossijsko-ukrainskogo sotrudnichestva." *Russkaja narodnaja linija*, 14 March 2012. Accessed 1 January 2017. http://ruskline.ru/news_rl/2012/03/14/ukraina_za_evrazijskij_soyuz_n ovyj_format_rossijskoukrainskogo_sotrudnichestva/.

"Ukrainskie i rossijskie obshchestvennye organizacii vyskazalis' za evrazijskuju integraciju." *rossija 3.ru*, 13 March 2012. Accessed 1 January 2017. http://www.rossia3.ru/ideolog/nashi/ukr_eas.

"Letnij lager' ESM – avgust 2016." *rossija 3.ru*, 4 March 2005. Accessed 1 January 2017. http://rossia3.ru/foto2.

"Istorija Donbassa" (Sergej Buntovskij). *knigotopia.ru*. Accessed 1 January 2017. http://knigotopia.ru/book/item/5204/.

"Evrazijskij sojuz molodezhi." *Antikompromat*. Accessed 1 January 2017. http://www.anticompromat.org/esm/esm_spr.html.

"Pervye vschody: rozhdenie novoj oprichiny." *rossija3.ru*, 20 August 2005. Accessed 1 January 2017. http://rossia3.ru/mer/lager1.

"Prikljuchenija evrazijcev v Ukraine: interv'ju." *rossija3.ru*, 26 July 2006. Accessed 1 January 2017. http://rossia3.ru/prikl.

"Kto est' kto v DNR i LNR." *dsnews*, 7 December 2015. Accessed 1 January 2017. http://www.dsnews.ua/politics/kto-est-kto-v-dnr-i-lnr-07122015080600.

"Fotogalereja. Letnij lager' ESM po podgotovke kommandnogo sostava." *evrazija.org*, 30 August 2005. Accessed 1 January 2017. http://www.evrazia.org/m odules.php?name=News&file=article&sid=2640.

---

i   Originating in the Russian Emigration in Prague/Paris in the 1920 by pro-czarist intellectuals (Petr N. Savitskij, Petr P. Suvcinskij, Nikolaj S. Trubeckoj, Georgij V. Florovskij), Eurasianism has geoculturological and political aspects (Frank, 2003: 200).
ii Dugin's statement is cited from Shekhovtsov (2014b).
iii Photo of Dar'ja Dugina at the summer camp, [http://rossia3.ru/foto1], Accessed 10 November 2016.
iv MED was founded in 2003 in Moscow. It has approximately thirty-six regional representations in the Russian Federation and smaller branches in twenty-two countries. "Mezhdunarodnoe evrazijskoe dvizhenie", evrazia.org. [http://evrazia.org/modules.php?name=New s&file=article&sid=1575.] Accessed 10 November 2016.
v   "Evrazijskaja intellektual'naja molodezh' vybiraet jestetiku Arktiki", evrazia.org, 29 December 2004, [http://evrazia.org/modules.php?name=News&file=article&sid=2152]. Accessed 10 November 2016.
vi "Progressivnaja socialisticheskaja partija Ukrainy", wikipedia.org, [http://tinyurl.co m/gpdhnm9]. Accessed 10 November 2016.

vii Because these people associate themselves with Russianness, we have transliterated their names in Russian.
viii "'Doneckie' ne priznajut ukrainskuju naciju! – soobshchenie", KID. Jugo vostochnaja liga, 19 February 2008. Accessed 10 November 2016.
ix "V Char'kove zapritili "Evraziijskij sojuz molodezhi", podrobnosti.ua, 7 November 2008, [http://podrobnosti.ua/565016-v-harkove-zapretili-evrazijskij-sojuz-molodezhi.html]. Accessed 10 November 2016.
x See, for example, [http://evrazia.org/text/16] and [http://www.rossia3.ru/smi/kredoru]. Accessed 8 December 2016.
xi According to reports of the Moscow-based Centre for Economic and Political Reforms /Центр экономических и политических реформ (ЦЭПР), about 1054 non-governmental organizations have received financial support from the Russian state since 2006. The funds were awarded under the "Program for the support of civil society institutes and human rights" and had already been announced by President Vladimir Putin in 2005. "Prezidentskie granty NKO. Pooshchirenie lojal'nosti vmesto razvitija grazhdanskogo obshchestvo", Centr jekonomicheskich a politicheskich reform, 21 December 2015. [http://tinyurl.com/zo7xa82]. Accessed 10 November 2016.
xii "Prezidentskie granty NKO. Pooshchirenie lojal'nosti vmesto razvitija grazhdanskogo obshchestvo", Centr jekonomicheskich a politicheskich reform, 21 December 2015. [http://tinyurl.com/zo7xa82] .Accessed 10 November 2016.
xiii For a full list of our empirical sources, see the source list at the end of the text.
xiv Max. possible centrality-value (degree) is 1 (actor is connected to all other actors/organizations/events), min. centrality-value is 0 (Jansen, 2013: 132).
xv In a constellation with three connected actors, the shortest connection between two actors is looked at, whereby actors having this connection are designated as mediators. The more often an actor acts as mediator, the higher is his betweenness-centrality in the range of 0–1 (Jansen, 2013: 141).
xvi Other actors of the network with a proved link to the DNR: Oleg Frolov, Konstantin Knyrik, Aleksandr Proselkov, Oksana Shkoda, Natal'ja Makeeva, Sergej Baryshnikov, Aleksandr Chrjakov, Srgej Buntovskij, Roman Ljagin, Tat'jana Dvorjadkina.
xvii "Glava 'narodnogo soveta' DNR otpravlen v otstavku", russkaja sluzhba bbc, 5 September 2015. [www.bbc.com/russian/international/2015/09/150905_donbass_purhin_sacked]. Accessed 10 November 2016.
xviii "Aleksandr Matjushin komandir 'Varjag' o situacii v Novorossii", dnr-lnr.info, March 2015. [www.dnr-lnr.info/aleksandr-matyushin-komandir-varyag-o-situacii-v-novorossii/]. Accessed 10 November 2016.
xix "Oleg Frolov: Vlast' dolzhna byt' otvetsvennoj", Informacionnoe Agenstvo Newsfront, 20 July 2015. [http://news-front.info/2015/07/20/oleg-frolov-vlast-dolzhna-byt-otvetstvennoj/]. Accessed 1 January 2017.
xx "Konstantin Knyrik: Vse 24 goda krymchane oshchushchali sebja v okkupacii", Informacionnoe Agenstvo Newsfront, 19 March 2015. [http://news-front.info/2016/03/19/konstantin-knyrik-vse-24-goda-krymchane-oshhushhali-sebya-v-okkupacii/]. Accessed 1 January 2017.

Part V:
Conclusion

Ukraine and Beyond:
Concluding Remarks on Transnationalism

Susann Worschech and Timm Beichelt

This chapter offers a critical reflection of the case studies presented in this book, and reconnects the empirical analyses with the concept of transnationalism as outlined in the introduction. Socio-structural, symbolic and practice-related transnationalist approaches are related to different aspects of border-transgressing phenomena. The chapter discusses the dimensions of transnationalism and offers an attempt to systematize the results of the case studies. Based on this conceptual reflection, the authors outline the additional value of a transnationalist perspective to Ukrainian studies.

1. Transnationalism: an Appropriate Concept?

'Transnational Ukraine' is a daring and perhaps confusing book title. Is it legitimate to refer to a country as 'transnational', in particular if its frontiers are currently challenged and violated, inter alia by its neighboring state? In our introduction, we argued that contemporary Ukraine might be better understood if it is seen in a transnational rather than in a national context. This proposition is not theoretically induced but driven by the observation that many recent political events in Ukraine refer to border-transgressing elements.

Mainly and foremost, this is true for the protests and changes of 2013 and 2014 that came to be known as the *Revolution of Dignity*. The fact that the protests started with the aim to intertwine closer with the European Union already shows a dimension beyond the nation state. Additionally, the stage set up at Nezalezhnosti Square in Kyiv between December 2013 and February 2014 was constantly visited by non-Ukrainians—both politicians and civil society actors. Euromaidan in Kyiv was accompanied and supported by similar, albeit smaller, events in cities abroad with a Ukrainian diaspora. And the involvement of Russian citizens—both in official and non-official functions—in the annexation of Crimea in March 2014 and a few weeks later in the secession attempts in other cities of Eastern Ukraine displays a field of action that goes beyond the nation state but cannot be limited to the sphere of international relations.

Transnational elements also prevailed after spring 2014. In October of that year, a group of young Euromaidan activists gained parliamentary seats in the Verkhovna Rada. Common features of these young deputies—in addition to their civil society and Euromaidan background—were their high education, international working experience, and cosmopolitan attitudes (Worschech 2014). As genuine transnationalist activist-politicians, some of them became members of the Ukrainian delegations to the Organization of Security and Cooperation in Europe (OSCE) and the North Atlantic Treaty Organization (NATO). Another transnational feature of Ukrainian politics can be seen in the story of several non-Ukrainian citizens—partly with Ukrainian roots—who were granted Ukrainian citizenship and were appointed ministers of Ukraine or, as was the case for the former Georgian president Mikhail Saakashvili, governor.

However, we do not claim that the transnational perspective covers every recent development in Ukraine. A few parts of the Ukrainian experiment of forced transnational governance diffusion ended rather quickly. In November 2016, three of the young Euromaidan deputies were dismissed from Ukraine's delegations to OSCE and NATO. The 'external' ministers resigned or were thrown out in April 2016. Saakashvili, who had come into office as a decided fighter against corruption, withdrew from office in the fall of 2016, officially because of his frustration about a lack of presidential support for his fight against corruption in Ukraine.[i]

Still, we do not think that these examples indicate that the experiment of modernizing Ukraine with the help of transnational experiences and knowledge has failed. Rather, we argue that the transnationalist perspective is still relevant with regard to Euromaidan and its consequences. Maybe even more important, we have tried to show that transnational elements have dominated Ukraine over long periods. These include different regions and places, and they focus on multifold social spheres.

Our idea of 'Ukraine as a transnational entity' emerged from the discontent with certain shortcomings in the explanation of recent political and societal processes in Ukraine. Ukraine (and other countries of the EU's Eastern Partnership) cannot be understood properly as long as the respective framework of analysis remains strictly within categories that refer to nation states. It was our intention to acknowledge the 'in-between-ness' of Ukraine with regard to location and borders.

In that sense, Ukraine is situated between Western and Eastern Europe, between the EU and Russia, between Western and Eastern cultures, and between transitionist and post-transitionist developments—if these stereotyped distinctions are to be maintained at all. A quarter-century after the breakdown of the Soviet Union, it is high time to heed Ukraine's character of 'interdependent independence' also in scientific analysis.

Hence, methodological nationalism cannot not be the only answer with reference to an entity with frazzled social and cultural borders. The framework of the nation state has its limits in explaining Ukraine's bumpy path of societal and political modernization since 1991. In the 1990s, nation *building* presented a core interest of political scientists—a clear indicator that Ukraine's path was judged as development of a previously incomplete nation state. Many of the elected politicians of the first decade had in fact a hard time speaking the national language—Ukrainian. Additionally, the debate on origins and characteristics of Ukraine's *Orange Revolution* and the *'Colored Revolutions'* in the post-Soviet space revealed networks and practices that went beyond national borders. As only a very limited number of scholars (Bunce and Wolchik 2007) have taken up the concept of transnationalism in a serious way, we think it is necessary to play through that concept with regard to different objects of scholarly research.

Therefore, the aspiration of this volume was to pick up the threads of Ukraine's transnational embeddedness and to develop transnationalism as an analytical tool for nation building, democratization and the evolution of post-Soviet societies. In our introduction, we formulated two assumptions: First, we argued that contemporary Ukraine is better understood if we focus on transnational characteristics, and we designed a conceptual framework that encompasses symbols, practices and networks as elements of analytical transnationalism. Second, our reasoning implied that Ukraine can be considered an exemplary case for transnational nation building. Both conjectures require critical assessment, which will be provided in the following paragraphs.

Transnationalism is one of the catch-all and ever-present terms in contemporary social sciences. With the framework outlined in our introduction, we provided a matrix that transforms transnationalism into a concept that is valid both empirically and analytically. Transnationalism can be translated in border-crossing *social structures*, *symbols* and *practices* that are contextualized in specific *temporal*, *spatial* and *societal settings*. Our hope is that this frame would help to integrate border-crossing aspects systematically in the investigation of societies and politics when boundaries become permeable and affiliations become fluid. The different analyses presented in this volume show such patterns.

2. Temporal Dimension of Transnationalism

The empirical case studies assembled in this book investigate Ukraine's interdependencies from the early 20th century until 2016. Not surprisingly, temporal landmarks are Ukraine's formal independence in 1991 and, most recently, Ukraine's societal independence as expressed by the Euromaidan movement 2013/14 and its aftermath. The overlying time-related dimension of these analyses reveals certain regularities.

Networks, interactions and transnational agency are short- or medium-term phenomena that force scholars to conduct their research within rather narrow time windows. Clientelistic affiliations—as Simon Schlegel described them in his text on Southern Bessarabia—may be of a long-term nature, but the ways they are used reflect contingent regime structures. Supporting votes for 'patrons' and respective gifts to the supporting 'clients' change as the 'offers' provided by 'patrons' change or become less attractive. In a context of practices that transgress borders, the political stabilizing function of states diminishes and favors the establishment of fluid power relations. While we are able to identify transnational networks in given settings of time and space, we are not capable to make permanent assertions about their meanings and functions for longer time periods.

In contrast, network or group formation processes that aim at exploiting and/or escalating existing cleavages are both short and medium-term phenomena. The contributions from Susanne Spahn on Russian media in Germany as well as from Jonas Eichhorn, Mascha Brammer and Veronika Borysenko on uncivil transnational networks in the Donbas underline that mobilization in the form of realizing media campaigns or establishing activist units can be successful as long as favorable opportunity structures and a manageable temporal scope are given. However, it is another issue to establish long-term structures. If mobilization is planned to lead into larger political upheavals and to work for longer periods, state structures seem to be necessary after all. The stabilization of Crimea after Russia's annexation of the peninsula was successful (although under complete non-democratic circumstances), whereas the pure transnational (and uncivil) approach of the insurgents in the Luhansk and Donetsk regions led into unstable entities that manage only to establish unrestful power structures. The promises of the transnationalist perspective therefore bring added value only under certain circumstances. The transnationalist take is promising in historic situations of fluidity, uncertainty, and open-endedness.

The *emergence, persistence or transformation of symbols* cannot be understood and explained without deploying a broad time frame, as the two articles on symbolic transnationalism illustrate. Mikhail Minakov shows in his manuscript that the contemporary network around the issue of Novorossiya encompasses transnational roots, paths and effects with extremely long-lasting lines of development. The re-framing of Novorossiyan symbols can only be understood with a precise dissection of the relevant historic narratives and conflicts about interpretations. In Minakov's context, symbols usually refer to such grand historical lines. Not only Soviet narratives, but also many pre-Soviet Russian narratives play a central role in the thinking of the supporters of Novorossiya.

In addition, Yulia Yurchuk's text on the transformation of memory politics underlines the medium- or long-term temporality of transnational imaginations. Yurchuk shows how several symbols that represent World War II—or, as others would say, symbols representing the Great Patriotic War—have been reconfigured in deliberate actions by memory politicians of different camps. In the Ukrainian context, the remembrance of war(s) inevitably leads into the transnational arena as different powers have tried to incorporate territories inhabited by Ukrainians into their respective states. Practices of remembering transform underlying interpretations of symbols into action and therefore serve as a sort of 'hinge' between symbols and interactions.

As time can be grasped in objective or subjective terms, temporal assignments of action such as an 'era' or a 'societal epoch' hint at the social construction of symbols, practices, and interactions. Minakov and Yurchuk also show that different—and partly competing—concepts of 'eras', and related meaningful attributions can be discovered in contemporary Ukraine. One pertinent concept is the 'break' that the Euromaidan protests represent—a break that distinguishes the pre- and post-Maidan eras. This division of times and temporality is clearly conceptualized in Yurchuk's presentation of new symbols of national remembrance. Here, Ukraine's contemporary sense of time and societal re-building is described as accompanied by a content-related shift of selective history narratives. A 'post-Maidan era' is also constructed in the ideology of Novorossiya (again, see Minakov in this volume).

The two texts by Yurchuk and Minakov describe ideational references to the same objective past period—the time of the Soviet Union and World War II. Both construct the meaning of their respective contemporary action in historic symbols. However, the framing of this period and the use of this frame highly differ between both cases. On the one hand, politicians try to promote transnationally established cultures or styles of remembrance, including De-Sovietization and a firm departure from most Soviet symbols. The aim of this move is to set a new starting point for future interpretations of national identity. On the other hand, the proponents of Novorossiya—notably the group Minakov calls 'imperialists' —aim at a re-erection of Soviet symbols. Their aim consists in the preservation of an (imagined) past. Despite this difference, both empirical cases share the fact that symbolic transnationalism serves as a practice to establish specific 'eras' from which certain symbols are deducted.

The book further contains two contributions on what we call *practice related transnationalism*. These manuscripts by Alexander Clarkson and by Andriy Korniychuk, Magdalena Patalong and Richard Steinberg focus on the making of identities in the Ukrainian diasporas, be it in the large and long-standing Canadian Ukrainian diaspora or in the younger diasporic groups in Central Europe. These authors show that the 'implementation' of symbols in interaction and networks is based on narratives that emerge in longer-term periods, but the symbolic reference base may be switched or even suddenly readjusted.

In sum, we draw as a first conclusion that the temporal dimension of transnationalism is long-term oriented for symbolic transnationalism, rather short-term oriented for socio-structural transnationalism, and medium- or long-term oriented for practice related transnationalism. What does that mean for the time-related concepts of temporality and history within transnationalist studies? In his book on "Big Structures, Large Processes, Huge Comparisons", the historian and sociologist Charles Tilly (1984) stressed the relevance of macro- and microhistorical approaches for our understanding of the formation (or disintegration) of nations and other presumably stable entities with state-like functions. Whereas the macrohistorical perspective focuses on big structures, large processes, and their alternate forms within a given area, the microhistorical approach integrates encounters and interactions between individuals and groups into the analysis (Seitz 1986). In this view, the long-term relevance of transnational symbols is compatible with the macrohistorical perspective, whereas the microhistorical perspective goes along with a focus on the practices and interaction patterns of transnationalism.

3. Spatial Dimension of Transnationalism

Similar to time, space is a double-sided concept. It specifies the localization of social phenomena, but it also includes the aspect that social processes (re-)produce spatial structures and perceptions of space. Accordingly, the spatial dimension of transnationalism encourages the questions where symbols are affiliated to, where practices take place, and where structures and interactions are situated. The spatial perspective also allows us to ask which social spaces are constructed by transnational symbols, practices, and networks. Societal spaces do not exist per se, but are subjectively constructed by those who connect them to the enactment of symbols and the networks that arise from practices. Therefore, spatial constructions reflect units of sociation (Löw 2001; 2010).

Both papers in this volume that focus on *symbols* conceptualize Ukraine as a 'location' where such symbols come into operation. Yuliya Yurchuk argues in her contribution that memory in Ukraine gets 'glocalized': Ukraine as a nation or Ukrainian regions form the venue where transnationally embedded symbols are merged with local ones to form new interpretations in the local, regional or national context. The invention of new meaning patterns of spatial affiliation seems to be based on a targeted mingling of external and domestic symbols on the domestic territory. Notably, the alteration process is related singularly to the domestic space—symbolic systems beyond Ukraine appear to remain unaffected. Symbolic transnationalism, in other words, comprises a process of domestication and local alteration of transnationally rooted symbols.

In the introduction to this book, we have also distinguished symbolic from structural transnationalism. The divide between the two approaches is underlined by the different findings with regard to spatial patterns that are brought up by the case studies within the book. The analysis of transnational structures reveals *networks, agents, and social structures* that open trans-regional contexts between Ukraine and other countries or regions. The authors of the majority of texts within our volume observe bi- or multilateral social spaces. The study of Ukrainian transnational oligarchy by Heiko Pleines is an example. This analysis describes a transnational sphere of business relations between Ukraine, Russia, Cyprus, and a range of other countries that emerge around the oligarchic structures and form a system of corridors for specific business models. In the examples given by Pleines, this mainly concerns rent-seeking approaches. Unlike in the spatial manifestation of symbolic transnationalism, Pleines' approach to socio-structural transnationalism alters both sides of the process—domestic Ukrainian actors transform international ones and vice versa.

Similar to that case, Susanne Spahn's illustration of information and media interrelations describes a transnational corridor system between Russia, Germany, and Ukraine. However, we have to admit that Ukraine is not an equal participant of that network but rather an object of misinformation in a bilateral communication tube between Russia and Germany. In still another manuscript, the analysis of the making of the so-called DNR by Eichhorn, Brammer and Borysenko points at the forced emergence of new regions and new regional identities by spatially overlapping networks. Here, transnational ties and structures do not form a border-crossing 'social corridor system' but a flashpoint region where transnational connections are bundled and locally fixed. The case of Southern Bessarabia, described by Simon Schlegel, forms another impressive example of spatial transnationalism. The region stands for a multilateral social space below the formal-structural level of the nation-state.

Socio-structural transnationalism then appears to relate to a process of the emergence and structuring of new regions—be it in the form of rather narrow corridors spanning larger distances, or in the form of the establishment and demarcation of new transnational regions. Our hypothesis here is that socio-structural transnationalism comprises a process of transregionalization.

In this context, it is interesting to notice that the transnational *practices* of the Ukrainian diaspora bear a specific locus. Similar to symbolic transnationalism, practice-related transnationalism seems to affect only one side of the tie—in this case: the 'remote' one. As Alexander Clarkson shows in his text on diaspora reactions to Euromaidan, the Ukrainian diaspora in Canada passed a process of identity construction that was linked to but did not alter Ukraine itself. The same applies for the diaspora groups in Germany and Poland, as shown by Andriy Korniychuk, Magdalena Patalong, and Richard Steinberg. These two examples indicate that the making of a transnational space resembles a one-way-street: this spatial transnationalism is a process of merging and altering practices that takes place in remoteness, namely on foreign soil. Imagined and 'practice-related elements' of Ukraine are located on the diaspora's side, but this does not affect the making of Ukraine very much. We propose to call the spatial process presumably related to practice-oriented transnationalism conversion.

These three processes within the spatial dimension of symbolic, socio-structural and practice-related transnationalism—domestication and local alteration, transregionalization and conversion—can be understood as different modes for the (re-)structuration and (re-)production of new social spaces. Consequently, the social construction of space is a relational-communicative act of drawing boundaries that invents, alters and reinforces collective identity. These findings support an argument presented by the German sociologist Klaus Eder: that the communication of difference generates identity, but that the communication of identity generates difference (Eder 2007). Following this idea, we propose that further research in this field should focus on the question how 'Ukraineness' is constructed, forced or refused in the domestication of symbols, the transregionalization of networks, and the local conversion of practices.

4. Societal Dimension of Transnationalism

Transnationalism as an analytical perspective bears new insights into sociation beyond national boundaries. According to Georg Simmel (1992), sociation (*"Vergesellschaftung"*) consists of the interplay between individuals. In the context of our research, we can transform the concept of transnationalism into the long-term delimitation and alteration of symbols, the medium-term conversion of practices, and the short-term transregionalization of structures, which are all forms of transnational sociation. But how do transnational processes contribute in detail to the social interplay of individuals?

In our introduction, we have argued that *symbolic transnationalism* can be observed in cultural codes that lie at the basis of affiliations, belongings and communities. But what type of society emerges through symbolic-transnational interaction? One answer is provided by Yuliya Yurchuk. Her study of Ukrainian memory politics gives an idea on the central topics that specify symbolic transnational sociation. On the basis of videos that combine the Red Army's fight in World War II with the Ukrainian army's fight in the Donbas since 2014, a positively charged narrative of two Ukrainian struggles for freedom and justice is created—a narrative that is aimed to fit with narratives of ending tyranny, of a common fight for unity, and for a (presumed) adaptation to European values. Likewise, national remembrance seems to have changed the meaning of 'victory' from the idea of agonistic superiority to the protection of—again—European values. Obviously, the idea behind this creation of new narratives and meanings is to settle Ukraine in a European future instead of Soviet history and Russian hegemony.

Memory politics of the transnational network around the construction of Novorossiya pursue an opposite aim, as Mikhail Minakov illustrates. Here, the symbolic recourse on Novorossiya is intended to reactivate Russian and/or Soviet narratives that are positioned against Western or EU-integrationist positions. Minakov's insight is one of the many examples of a widespread pattern. Processes of symbolic transnational sociation are often characterized by antagonistic reasoning. Transnationalization is therefore not always—and probably not even in the majority of cases—inherently linked to cosmopolitan or other idealistic sets of awareness. The fact that national borders are overcome does not, at least not automatically, lead to a diminished relevance of all borders. Instead, memory politicians from the nationalist Ukrainian as well as from the anti-Ukrainian camp refer to border transgressing symbols that create new or reinforce formerly pale boundaries. Symbolic transnationalism with reference to sociation is an act of societal (re-)construction that maintains the difference of alter and ego on the collective level.

To a lesser degree, this insight is also mirrored in Simon Schlegel's text on loyalty networks in Southern Bessarabia. In this historically eventful region, the build-up and maintenance of local or regional affiliations include the establishment of networks of personal dependency and influence that rely on ethnicity. Through this backdoor, the nation as a category remains relevant despite the overarching context that makes low-barrier borders a functional necessity in an integrating Europe. Ukraine presents a paradigmatic example of a transnationalizing entity in which border transformations induce a simultaneous softening *and* re-consolidation of identities, affiliations, and cleavages.

Socio-structural transnationalism further focuses on new or broader paths of distribution and resource transfer, for example, with regard to money, goods, information, support, or ideas. Here, several case studies in our book present unexpected results: Heiko Pleines shows that the economic sector—where we would expect high levels of international connectedness because of the needs of a division of labor—is characterized by limited transnationalization. Pleines explains this with the rent-granting capacities of national institutions, in particular of licensing agencies and courts. On the contrary, as the media analysis of Susanne Spahn shows, communication has a tendency of transnationalization despite a media ownership that is clearly linked to the national sphere. Russian state media work on targeted transnational information distribution not only for Russian nationals in foreign countries (in Spahn's case in Germany) but also to influence the political publics of these countries.

One important question for further analysis of socio-structural transnational sociation concerns positions and roles within these structures. If interlinkages and interaction are seen as central, the relational analysis of informal hierarchies, power structures, positions of brokers, and information diffusion is necessary. In their manuscript, Eichhorn, Brammer, and Borysenko reveal the relevance and influence of single actors and positions in formation processes and groups and collective identities. Spahn's analysis of Russian-German media cooperation suggests an important role for information brokers but leaves open the question to which extent this brokerage is transformed into political influence. Only substantial network analyses would be able to find patterns of real power relations, and we do not know very much about them.

Finally, *practice-related transnationalism* is suited to identify new forms and aspects of sociation. Steinberg, Patalong, and Korniychuk describe how diasporic action emerges in Germany and (to a lesser extent) in Poland in the context of the Euromaidan events in Ukraine. Whereas in particular Ukrainians in Germany hardly organized or even met as a 'diaspora' before 2013, only the confrontation with the political struggle in Ukraine created a diasporic movement in German cities and helped to unify the fragmented network. Correspondingly, Clarkson writes that the intensity with which different groups and factions of Ukrainian diasporas supported the Maidan protests helped to reshape diaspora attitudes and hence, practices. Another example is the newly established acceptance of russophone Ukrainians within the diaspora in Canada or Europe. This de-fragmentation of diaspora in context with conflicts confirms one of the central arguments of sociology, namely that conflicts always bear integrative social functions (see Simmel 1992, Coser 2009). Consequently, practice-related transnationalism with reference to sociation consists of the increasing establishment of linkages and cooperation in diasporic sites that is brokered through the confrontation with conflicts in the homeland.

5. The Additional Value of Transnationalism in Ukrainian Studies

The aim of our volume consisted of critically assessing the approach of transnationalism with regard to the analysis of social processes in contemporary Ukraine.

We would like to suggest that this endeavor was successful at least in that several case studies dealing with spatial, temporal, and societal fluidity have found a common roof to help to understand Ukraine as an entity that resists many categorizations invariantly linked to nation states.

From this perspective, we would first like to suggest that Ukraine—despite the aggressive policies of Russia as well as the vast economic and social problems of the country—is a place that is not only characterized by crisis. Ukrainian society has, to a considerable extent, resisted threats, storms, and oblivion. Memory politics may have led to questionable results, but they displayed broad public discussions that may help to further strengthen civic consciousness. Some regions have seen deep crises, but others—like Southern Bessarabia—show stability that rests on more than one ethnicity and may well prove to be a source for transethnic understanding. Diasporas have upheld faith in civil contrariness to Russian hostility and further imported a readiness for compromise, which is needed for democratic consolidation. And even a part of the network that is favorable to Novorossiya has debated the virtues of societal autonomy and contrasted it with Russian hegemony. By revealing all of this, the transnational approach has brought to light that situations of fluidity, uncertainty, and open-endedness do not necessarily imply lostness, but mirror broader global tendencies of a dissolution of traditional borders.

However, second, the case studies in this book do not stop at this point. They do not argue for a complete shift of focus to get along better with the problems of Ukraine. In fact, not one text argues that the transnationalist perspective leads to a more positive evaluation of the situation in Ukraine. The diminishment of borders does not ease a country's problems, at least not as a general rule. Those authors who have discerned complex interaction patterns in the border zones of Ukraine (for example, Mikhail Minakov on Novorossiya, Yuliya Yurchuk on memory politics, or Simon Schlegel on Southern Bessarabia) have rather noticed that the growing porosity of old borders is accompanied by the establishment of new border lines. The discussion of the Novorossiyan myth brought up a line of division between 'imperialists' and 'transnationalists' (Minakov), the overconfident politics of desovietization brought back a certain consciousness for the values and virtues of that period (Yurchuk), and the discussion in the diasporas in Europe or North America brought to light divisions that had been covered up before (Clarkson and Korniychuk, Patalong and Steinberg).

Transnational shifts, then, do not simply dissolve pre-existing national entities and re-create transnational spaces. The texts of this volume draw a more complex picture. The results of transnational dynamism cannot be characterized as arenas of conflict between the national sphere on the one side and transnational elements on the other. This is our third conclusion. There is not simply a "growing disjuncture between territory, subjectivity and collective social movement" (Vertovec 2009: 12) of traditional state and new transnational inhabitants of a symbolic space. Rather, division and difference mark the transnational entities themselves. The stronger the historic impulse to overcome the state as a framework to contain and decommodify conflicts, the more likely is the re-establishment of contradictions and antagonism within the newly created spaces, especially if expectations are high that transnationalist settings will prevail for longer time horizons.

Another element that brings pessimism into the debate on transnationalism is, fourth, its inhabitation by uncivil actors. Eichhorn, Brammer, Borysenko, and Minakov have shown that symbolic and spatial conflicts can bring violence and also lead to a radicalization within the opposing camps. This radicalization marginalizes the impact of some formerly classic transnational actors: international non-governmental organizations. Transnationalization, then, is not a guarantee for the growing impact of political actors that operate beyond the nation state. The relevant entity to hold back uncivil transnational forces still seems to be the state, not other transnational (but civil) actors.

In sum, the additional value of transnationalism to the study of contemporary Ukraine is multi-layered. Transnationalism adds to our understanding by shifting the focus on previously underestimated phenomena and sheds new light on the emergence of symbols, practices, and structures. It helps in estimating the (potential) influence of non-state movements and actors on political, social, and economic life. As such, they do sometimes alter or diminish the sphere of influence of states. Under certain circumstances, transnational action challenges states to a degree that reactivates state action and even leads to what we can call a return of the state. As our final point, we argue that this is not surprising. After all, the recent history of Ukraine is accompanied by state failure—of the Soviet Union. Contemporary Ukraine is still marked by large-scale strategies to cope with the void this breakdown has left. These strategies are not grasped if we exclusively speak of nation-building, even if this concerns one of the largest states in Europe. However, it is also not sufficient to insist that the transnational take alone is relevant. Methodological Nationalism and transnationalism form complementary perspectives.

6. Bibliography

Bunce, Valerie and Sharon L. Wolchik. 2007. "Transnational networks, diffusion dynamics, and electoral revolutions in the postcommunist world." *Physica A: Statistical Mechanics and its Applications* 378 (1): 92–99. DOI: 10.1016/j.physa.2006.11.049.

Coser, Lewis A. 1956. *The Functions of Social Conflict.* New York: The Free Press of Glencoe.

Eder, Klaus. 2007. "Die Grenzen Europas. Zur narrativen Konstruktion europäischer Identität." In *Der europäische Raum. Die Konstruktion europäischer Grenzen*, edited by Petra Deger, 187–208. Wiesbaden: VS Verlag für Sozialwissenschaften.

Löw, Martina. 2001. *Raumsoziologie.* Frankfurt am Main: Suhrkamp.

Löw, Martina. 2010. "Raumdimensionen der Europaforschung: Skalierungen zwischen Welt, Staat und Stadt." In *Gesellschaftstheorie und Europapolitik*, edited by Monika Eigmüller and Steffen Mau, 142–152. Wiesbaden: VS Verlag für Sozialwissenschaften.

Seitz, Steven Thomas. 1986. "Big Structures, Large Processes, Huge Comparisons. By Tilly Charles." *American Political Science Review* 80 (1): 355–356. DOI: 10.2307/1957147.

Simmel, Georg. 1992 [1908]. *Soziologie. Untersuchungen über die Formen der Vergesellschaftung.* Suhrkamp Verlag.

Tilly, Charles. 1984. *Big structures, large processes, huge comparisons.* New York: Russell Sage Foundation.

Vertovec, Steven. 2009. *Transnationalism.* London, New York: Routledge.

Worschech, Susann. 2014. "Euromaidan goes Parliament: Wer sind 'die neuen' ParlamentskandidatInnen?" *Forschungsstelle Osteuropa Bremen (Ukraine-Analysen, 138).* http://www.laender-analysen.de/ukraine/pdf/UkraineAnalysen138.pdf.

---

i See [https://www.ft.com/content/22b7c2ca-a4f7-11e6-8b69-02899e8bd9d1], accessed 3 December 2016.

SOVIET AND POST-SOVIET POLITICS AND SOCIETY

Edited by Dr. Andreas Umland

ISSN 1614-3515

1   Андреас Умланд (ред.)
    Воплощение Европейской
    конвенции по правам человека в
    России
    Философские, юридические и
    эмпирические исследования
    ISBN 3-89821-387-0

2   Christian Wipperfürth
    Russland – ein vertrauenswürdiger
    Partner?
    Grundlagen, Hintergründe und Praxis
    gegenwärtiger russischer Außenpolitik
    Mit einem Vorwort von Heinz Timmermann
    ISBN 3-89821-401-X

3   Manja Hussner
    Die Übernahme internationalen Rechts
    in die russische und deutsche
    Rechtsordnung
    Eine vergleichende Analyse zur
    Völkerrechtsfreundlichkeit der Verfassungen
    der Russländischen Föderation und der
    Bundesrepublik Deutschland
    Mit einem Vorwort von Rainer Arnold
    ISBN 3-89821-438-9

4   Matthew Tejada
    Bulgaria's Democratic Consolidation
    and the Kozloduy Nuclear Power Plant
    (KNPP)
    The Unattainability of Closure
    With a foreword by Richard J. Crampton
    ISBN 3-89821-439-7

5   Марк Григорьевич Меерович
    Квадратные метры, определяющие
    сознание
    Государственная жилищная политика в
    СССР. 1921 – 1941 гг
    ISBN 3-89821-474-5

6   Andrei P. Tsygankov, Pavel
    A.Tsygankov (Eds.)
    New Directions in Russian
    International Studies
    ISBN 3-89821-422-2

7   Марк Григорьевич Меерович
    Как власть народ к труду приучала
    Жилище в СССР – средство управления
    людьми. 1917 – 1941 гг.
    С предисловием Елены Осокиной
    ISBN 3-89821-495-8

8   David J. Galbreath
    Nation-Building and Minority Politics
    in Post-Socialist States
    Interests, Influence and Identities in Estonia
    and Latvia
    With a foreword by David J. Smith
    ISBN 3-89821-467-2

9   Алексей Юрьевич Безугольный
    Народы Кавказа в Вооруженных
    силах СССР в годы Великой
    Отечественной войны 1941-1945 гг.
    С предисловием Николая Бугая
    ISBN 3-89821-475-3

10 Вячеслав Лихачев и Владимир
    Прибыловский (ред.)
    Русское Национальное Единство,
    1990-2000. В 2-х томах
    ISBN 3-89821-523-7

11 Николай Бугай (ред.)
    Народы стран Балтии в условиях
    сталинизма (1940-е – 1950-е годы)
    Документированная история
    ISBN 3-89821-525-1

12 Ingmar Bredies (Hrsg.)
    Zur Anatomie der Orange Revolution
    in der Ukraine
    Wechsel des Elitenregimes oder Triumph des
    Parlamentarismus?
    ISBN 3-89821-524-5

13 Anastasia V. Mitrofanova
    The Politicization of Russian
    Orthodoxy
    Actors and Ideas
    With a foreword by William C. Gay
    ISBN 3-89821-481-8

14 *Nathan D. Larson*
    Alexander Solzhenitsyn and the
    Russo-Jewish Question
    ISBN 3-89821-483-4

15 *Guido Houben*
    Kulturpolitik und Ethnizität
    Staatliche Kunstförderung im Russland der
    neunziger Jahre
    Mit einem Vorwort von Gert Weisskirchen
    ISBN 3-89821-542-3

16 *Leonid Luks*
    Der russische „Sonderweg"?
    Aufsätze zur neuesten Geschichte Russlands
    im europäischen Kontext
    ISBN 3-89821-496-6

17 *Евгений Мороз*
    История «Мёртвой воды» – от
    страшной сказки к большой
    политике
    Политическое неоязычество в
    постсоветской России
    ISBN 3-89821-551-2

18 *Александр Верховский и Галина
    Кожевникова (ред.)*
    Этническая и религиозная
    интолерантность в российских СМИ
    Результаты мониторинга 2001-2004 гг.
    ISBN 3-89821-569-5

19 *Christian Ganzer*
    Sowjetisches Erbe und ukrainische
    Nation
    Das Museum der Geschichte des Zaporoger
    Kosakentums auf der Insel Chortycja
    Mit einem Vorwort von Frank Golczewski
    ISBN 3-89821-504-0

20 *Эльза-Баир Гучинова*
    Помнить нельзя забыть
    Антропология депортационной травмы
    калмыков
    С предисловием Кэролайн Хамфри
    ISBN 3-89821-506-7

21 *Юлия Лидерман*
    Мотивы «проверки» и «испытания»
    в постсоветской культуре
    Советское прошлое в российском
    кинематографе 1990-х годов
    С предисловием Евгения Марголита
    ISBN 3-89821-511-3

22 *Tanya Lokshina, Ray Thomas, Mary
    Mayer (Eds.)*
    The Imposition of a Fake Political
    Settlement in the Northern Caucasus
    The 2003 Chechen Presidential Election
    ISBN 3-89821-436-2

23 *Timothy McCajor Hall, Rosie Read
    (Eds.)*
    Changes in the Heart of Europe
    Recent Ethnographies of Czechs, Slovaks,
    Roma, and Sorbs
    With an afterword by Zdeněk Salzmann
    ISBN 3-89821-606-3

24 *Christian Autengruber*
    Die politischen Parteien in Bulgarien
    und Rumänien
    Eine vergleichende Analyse seit Beginn der
    90er Jahre
    Mit einem Vorwort von Dorothée de Nève
    ISBN 3-89821-476-1

25 *Annette Freyberg-Inan with Radu
    Cristescu*
    The Ghosts in Our Classrooms, or:
    John Dewey Meets Ceauşescu
    The Promise and the Failures of Civic
    Education in Romania
    ISBN 3-89821-416-8

26 *John B. Dunlop*
    The 2002 Dubrovka and 2004 Beslan
    Hostage Crises
    A Critique of Russian Counter-Terrorism
    With a foreword by Donald N. Jensen
    ISBN 3-89821-608-X

27 *Peter Koller*
    Das touristische Potenzial von
    Kam''janec'–Podil's'kyj
    Eine fremdenverkehrsgeographische
    Untersuchung der Zukunftsperspektiven und
    Maßnahmenplanung zur
    Destinationsentwicklung des „ukrainischen
    Rothenburg"
    Mit einem Vorwort von Kristiane Klemm
    ISBN 3-89821-640-3

28 *Françoise Daucé, Elisabeth Sieca-
    Kozlowski (Eds.)*
    Dedovshchina in the Post-Soviet
    Military
    Hazing of Russian Army Conscripts in a
    Comparative Perspective
    With a foreword by Dale Herspring
    ISBN 3-89821-616-0

29 Florian Strasser
Zivilgesellschaftliche Einflüsse auf die
Orange Revolution
Die gewaltlose Massenbewegung und die
ukrainische Wahlkrise 2004
Mit einem Vorwort von Egbert Jahn
ISBN 3-89821-648-9

30 Rebecca S. Katz
The Georgian Regime Crisis of 2003-2004
A Case Study in Post-Soviet Media
Representation of Politics, Crime and
Corruption
ISBN 3-89821-413-3

31 Vladimir Kantor
Willkür oder Freiheit
Beiträge zur russischen Geschichtsphilosophie
Ediert von Dagmar Herrmann sowie mit
einem Vorwort versehen von Leonid Luks
ISBN 3-89821-589-X

32 Laura A. Victoir
The Russian Land Estate Today
A Case Study of Cultural Politics in Post-Soviet Russia
With a foreword by Priscilla Roosevelt
ISBN 3-89821-426-5

33 Ivan Katchanovski
Cleft Countries
Regional Political Divisions and Cultures in
Post-Soviet Ukraine and Moldova
With a foreword by Francis Fukuyama
ISBN 3-89821-558-X

34 Florian Mühlfried
Postsowjetische Feiern
Das Georgische Bankett im Wandel
Mit einem Vorwort von Kevin Tuite
ISBN 3-89821-601-2

35 Roger Griffin, Werner Loh, Andreas
Umland (Eds.)
Fascism Past and Present, West and
East
An International Debate on Concepts and
Cases in the Comparative Study of the
Extreme Right
With an afterword by Walter Laqueur
ISBN 3-89821-674-8

36 Sebastian Schlegel
Der „Weiße Archipel"
Sowjetische Atomstädte 1945-1991
Mit einem Geleitwort von Thomas Bohn
ISBN 3-89821-679-9

37 Vyacheslav Likhachev
Political Anti-Semitism in Post-Soviet
Russia
Actors and Ideas in 1991-2003
Edited and translated from Russian by Eugene
Veklerov
ISBN 3-89821-529-6

38 Josette Baer (Ed.)
Preparing Liberty in Central Europe
Political Texts from the Spring of Nations
1848 to the Spring of Prague 1968
With a foreword by Zdeněk V. David
ISBN 3-89821-546-6

39 Михаил Лукьянов
Российский консерватизм и
реформа, 1907-1914
С предисловием Марка Д. Стейнберга
ISBN 3-89821-503-2

40 Nicola Melloni
Market Without Economy
The 1998 Russian Financial Crisis
With a foreword by Eiji Furukawa
ISBN 3-89821-407-9

41 Dmitrij Chmelnizki
Die Architektur Stalins
Bd. 1: Studien zu Ideologie und Stil
Bd. 2: Bilddokumentation
Mit einem Vorwort von Bruno Flierl
ISBN 3-89821-515-6

42 Katja Yafimava
Post-Soviet Russian-Belarusian
Relationships
The Role of Gas Transit Pipelines
With a foreword by Jonathan P. Stern
ISBN 3-89821-655-1

43 Boris Chavkin
Verflechtungen der deutschen und
russischen Zeitgeschichte
Aufsätze und Archivfunde zu den
Beziehungen Deutschlands und der
Sowjetunion von 1917 bis 1991
Ediert von Markus Edlinger sowie mit einem
Vorwort versehen von Leonid Luks
ISBN 3-89821-756-6

44 *Anastasija Grynenko in Zusammenarbeit mit Claudia Dathe*
Die Terminologie des Gerichtswesens der Ukraine und Deutschlands im Vergleich
Eine übersetzungswissenschaftliche Analyse juristischer Fachbegriffe im Deutschen, Ukrainischen und Russischen
Mit einem Vorwort von Ulrich Hartmann
ISBN 3-89821-691-8

45 *Anton Burkov*
The Impact of the European Convention on Human Rights on Russian Law
Legislation and Application in 1996-2006
With a foreword by Françoise Hampson
ISBN 978-3-89821-639-5

46 *Stina Torjesen, Indra Overland (Eds.)*
International Election Observers in Post-Soviet Azerbaijan
Geopolitical Pawns or Agents of Change?
ISBN 978-3-89821-743-9

47 *Taras Kuzio*
Ukraine – Crimea – Russia
Triangle of Conflict
ISBN 978-3-89821-761-3

48 *Claudia Šabić*
"Ich erinnere mich nicht, aber L'viv!"
Zur Funktion kultureller Faktoren für die Institutionalisierung und Entwicklung einer ukrainischen Region
Mit einem Vorwort von Melanie Tatur
ISBN 978-3-89821-752-1

49 *Marlies Bilz*
Tatarstan in der Transformation
Nationaler Diskurs und Politische Praxis 1988-1994
Mit einem Vorwort von Frank Golczewski
ISBN 978-3-89821-722-4

50 *Марлен Ларюэль (ред.)*
Современные интерпретации русского национализма
ISBN 978-3-89821-795-8

51 *Sonja Schüler*
Die ethnische Dimension der Armut
Roma im postsozialistischen Rumänien
Mit einem Vorwort von Anton Sterbling
ISBN 978-3-89821-776-7

52 *Галина Кожевникова*
Радикальный национализм в России и противодействие ему
Сборник докладов Центра «Сова» за 2004-2007 гг.
С предисловием Александра Верховского
ISBN 978-3-89821-721-7

53 *Галина Кожевникова и Владимир Прибыловский*
Российская власть в биографиях I
Высшие должностные лица РФ в 2004 г.
ISBN 978-3-89821-796-5

54 *Галина Кожевникова и Владимир Прибыловский*
Российская власть в биографиях II
Члены Правительства РФ в 2004 г.
ISBN 978-3-89821-797-2

55 *Галина Кожевникова и Владимир Прибыловский*
Российская власть в биографиях III
Руководители федеральных служб и агентств РФ в 2004 г.
ISBN 978-3-89821-798-9

56 *Ileana Petroniu*
Privatisierung in Transformationsökonomien
Determinanten der Restrukturierungs-Bereitschaft am Beispiel Polens, Rumäniens und der Ukraine
Mit einem Vorwort von Rainer W. Schäfer
ISBN 978-3-89821-790-3

57 *Christian Wipperfürth*
Russland und seine GUS-Nachbarn
Hintergründe, aktuelle Entwicklungen und Konflikte in einer ressourcenreichen Region
ISBN 978-3-89821-801-6

58 *Togzhan Kassenova*
From Antagonism to Partnership
The Uneasy Path of the U.S.-Russian Cooperative Threat Reduction
With a foreword by Christoph Bluth
ISBN 978-3-89821-707-1

59 *Alexander Höllwerth*
Das sakrale eurasische Imperium des Aleksandr Dugin
Eine Diskursanalyse zum postsowjetischen russischen Rechtsextremismus
Mit einem Vorwort von Dirk Uffelmann
ISBN 978-3-89821-813-9

60 Олег Рябов
    «Россия-Матушка»
    Национализм, гендер и война в России XX века
    С предисловием Елены Гощило
    ISBN 978-3-89821-487-2

61 Ivan Maistrenko
    Borot'bism
    A Chapter in the History of the Ukrainian Revolution
    With a new introduction by Chris Ford
    Translated by George S. N. Luckyj with the assistance of Ivan L. Rudnytsky
    ISBN 978-3-89821-697-5

62 Maryna Romanets
    Anamorphosic Texts and Reconfigured Visions
    Improvised Traditions in Contemporary Ukrainian and Irish Literature
    ISBN 978-3-89821-576-3

63 Paul D'Anieri and Taras Kuzio (Eds.)
    Aspects of the Orange Revolution I
    Democratization and Elections in Post-Communist Ukraine
    ISBN 978-3-89821-698-2

64 Bohdan Harasymiw in collaboration with Oleh S. Ilnytzkyj (Eds.)
    Aspects of the Orange Revolution II
    Information and Manipulation Strategies in the 2004 Ukrainian Presidential Elections
    ISBN 978-3-89821-699-9

65 Ingmar Bredies, Andreas Umland and Valentin Yakushik (Eds.)
    Aspects of the Orange Revolution III
    The Context and Dynamics of the 2004 Ukrainian Presidential Elections
    ISBN 978-3-89821-803-0

66 Ingmar Bredies, Andreas Umland and Valentin Yakushik (Eds.)
    Aspects of the Orange Revolution IV
    Foreign Assistance and Civic Action in the 2004 Ukrainian Presidential Elections
    ISBN 978-3-89821-808-5

67 Ingmar Bredies, Andreas Umland and Valentin Yakushik (Eds.)
    Aspects of the Orange Revolution V
    Institutional Observation Reports on the 2004 Ukrainian Presidential Elections
    ISBN 978-3-89821-809-2

68 Taras Kuzio (Ed.)
    Aspects of the Orange Revolution VI
    Post-Communist Democratic Revolutions in Comparative Perspective
    ISBN 978-3-89821-820-7

69 Tim Bohse
    Autoritarismus statt Selbstverwaltung
    Die Transformation der kommunalen Politik in der Stadt Kaliningrad 1990-2005
    Mit einem Geleitwort von Stefan Troebst
    ISBN 978-3-89821-782-8

70 David Rupp
    Die Rußländische Föderation und die russischsprachige Minderheit in Lettland
    Eine Fallstudie zur Anwaltspolitik Moskaus gegenüber den russophonen Minderheiten im „Nahen Ausland" von 1991 bis 2002
    Mit einem Vorwort von Helmut Wagner
    ISBN 978-3-89821-778-1

71 Taras Kuzio
    Theoretical and Comparative Perspectives on Nationalism
    New Directions in Cross-Cultural and Post-Communist Studies
    With a foreword by Paul Robert Magocsi
    ISBN 978-3-89821-815-3

72 Christine Teichmann
    Die Hochschultransformation im heutigen Osteuropa
    Kontinuität und Wandel bei der Entwicklung des postkommunistischen Universitätswesens
    Mit einem Vorwort von Oskar Anweiler
    ISBN 978-3-89821-842-9

73 Julia Kusznir
    Der politische Einfluss von Wirtschaftseliten in russischen Regionen
    Eine Analyse am Beispiel der Erdöl- und Erdgasindustrie, 1992-2005
    Mit einem Vorwort von Wolfgang Eichwede
    ISBN 978-3-89821-821-4

74 Alena Vysotskaya
    Russland, Belarus und die EU-Osterweiterung
    Zur Minderheitenfrage und zum Problem der Freizügigkeit des Personenverkehrs
    Mit einem Vorwort von Katlijn Malfliet
    ISBN 978-3-89821-822-1

75   *Heiko Pleines (Hrsg.)*
     Corporate Governance in post-
     sozialistischen Volkswirtschaften
     ISBN 978-3-89821-766-8

76   *Stefan Ihrig*
     Wer sind die Moldawier?
     Rumänismus versus Moldowanismus in
     Historiographie und Schulbüchern der
     Republik Moldova, 1991-2006
     Mit einem Vorwort von Holm Sundhaussen
     ISBN 978-3-89821-466-7

77   *Galina Kozhevnikova in collaboration
     with Alexander Verkhovsky and
     Eugene Veklerov*
     Ultra-Nationalism and Hate Crimes in
     Contemporary Russia
     The 2004-2006 Annual Reports of Moscow's
     SOVA Center
     With a foreword by Stephen D. Shenfield
     ISBN 978-3-89821-868-9

78   *Florian Küchler*
     The Role of the European Union in
     Moldova's Transnistria Conflict
     With a foreword by Christopher Hill
     ISBN 978-3-89821-850-4

79   *Bernd Rechel*
     The Long Way Back to Europe
     Minority Protection in Bulgaria
     With a foreword by Richard Crampton
     ISBN 978-3-89821-863-4

80   *Peter W. Rodgers*
     Nation, Region and History in Post-
     Communist Transitions
     Identity Politics in Ukraine, 1991-2006
     With a foreword by Vera Tolz
     ISBN 978-3-89821-903-7

81   *Stephanie Solywoda*
     The Life and Work of
     Semen L. Frank
     A Study of Russian Religious Philosophy
     With a foreword by Philip Walters
     ISBN 978-3-89821-457-5

82   *Vera Sokolova*
     Cultural Politics of Ethnicity
     Discourses on Roma in Communist
     Czechoslovakia
     ISBN 978-3-89821-864-1

83   *Natalya Shevchik Ketenci*
     Kazakhstani Enterprises in Transition
     The Role of Historical Regional Development
     in Kazakhstan's Post-Soviet Economic
     Transformation
     ISBN 978-3-89821-831-3

84   *Martin Malek, Anna Schor-
     Tschudnowskaja (Hrsg.)*
     Europa im Tschetschenienkrieg
     Zwischen politischer Ohnmacht und
     Gleichgültigkeit
     Mit einem Vorwort von Lipchan Basajewa
     ISBN 978-3-89821-676-0

85   *Stefan Meister*
     Das postsowjetische Universitätswesen
     zwischen nationalem und
     internationalem Wandel
     Die Entwicklung der regionalen Hochschule
     in Russland als Gradmesser der
     Systemtransformation
     Mit einem Vorwort von Joan DeBardeleben
     ISBN 978-3-89821-891-7

86   *Konstantin Sheiko in collaboration
     with Stephen Brown*
     Nationalist Imaginings of the
     Russian Past
     Anatolii Fomenko and the Rise of Alternative
     History in Post-Communist Russia
     With a foreword by Donald Ostrowski
     ISBN 978-3-89821-915-0

87   *Sabine Jenni*
     Wie stark ist das „Einige Russland"?
     Zur Parteibindung der Eliten und zum
     Wahlerfolg der Machtpartei
     im Dezember 2007
     Mit einem Vorwort von Klaus Armingeon
     ISBN 978-3-89821-961-7

88   *Thomas Borén*
     Meeting-Places of Transformation
     Urban Identity, Spatial Representations and
     Local Politics in Post-Soviet St Petersburg
     ISBN 978-3-89821-739-2

89   *Aygul Ashirova*
     Stalinismus und Stalin-Kult in
     Zentralasien
     Turkmenistan 1924-1953
     Mit einem Vorwort von Leonid Luks
     ISBN 978-3-89821-987-7

90 Leonid Luks
    Freiheit oder imperiale Größe?
    Essays zu einem russischen Dilemma
    ISBN 978-3-8382-0011-8

91 Christopher Gilley
    The 'Change of Signposts' in the
    Ukrainian Emigration
    A Contribution to the History of
    Sovietophilism in the 1920s
    With a foreword by Frank Golczewski
    ISBN 978-3-89821-965-5

92 Philipp Casula, Jeronim Perovic
    (Eds.)
    Identities and Politics
    During the Putin Presidency
    The Discursive Foundations of Russia's
    Stability
    With a foreword by Heiko Haumann
    ISBN 978-3-8382-0015-6

93 Marcel Viëtor
    Europa und die Frage
    nach seinen Grenzen im Osten
    Zur Konstruktion ‚europäischer Identität' in
    Geschichte und Gegenwart
    Mit einem Vorwort von Albrecht Lehmann
    ISBN 978-3-8382-0045-3

94 Ben Hellman, Andrei Rogachevskii
    Filming the Unfilmable
    Casper Wrede's 'One Day in the Life
    of Ivan Denisovich'
    Second, Revised and Expanded Edition
    ISBN 978-3-8382-0044-6

95 Eva Fuchslocher
    Vaterland, Sprache, Glaube
    Orthodoxie und Nationenbildung
    am Beispiel Georgiens
    Mit einem Vorwort von Christina von Braun
    ISBN 978-3-89821-884-9

96 Vladimir Kantor
    Das Westlertum und der Weg
    Russlands
    Zur Entwicklung der russischen Literatur und
    Philosophie
    Ediert von Dagmar Herrmann
    Mit einem Beitrag von Nikolaus Lobkowicz
    ISBN 978-3-8382-0102-3

97 Kamran Musayev
    Die postsowjetische Transformation
    im Baltikum und Südkaukasus
    Eine vergleichende Untersuchung der
    politischen Entwicklung Lettlands und
    Aserbaidschans 1985-2009
    Mit einem Vorwort von Leonid Luks
    Ediert von Sandro Henschel
    ISBN 978-3-8382-0103-0

98 Tatiana Zhurzhenko
    Borderlands into Bordered Lands
    Geopolitics of Identity in Post-Soviet Ukraine
    With a foreword by Dieter Segert
    ISBN 978-3-8382-0042-2

99 Кирилл Галушко, Лидия Смола
    (ред.)
    Пределы падения – варианты
    украинского будущего
    Аналитико-прогностические исследования
    ISBN 978-3-8382-0148-1

100 Michael Minkenberg (ed.)
    Historical Legacies and the Radical
    Right in Post-Cold War Central and
    Eastern Europe
    With an afterword by Sabrina P. Ramet
    ISBN 978-3-8382-0124-5

101 David-Emil Wickström
    Rocking St. Petersburg
    Transcultural Flows and Identity Politics in
    the St. Petersburg Popular Music Scene
    With a foreword by Yngvar B. Steinholt
    Second, Revised and Expanded Edition
    ISBN 978-3-8382-0100-9

102 Eva Zabka
    Eine neue „Zeit der Wirren"?
    Der spät- und postsowjetische Systemwandel
    1985-2000 im Spiegel russischer
    gesellschaftspolitischer Diskurse
    Mit einem Vorwort von Margareta Mommsen
    ISBN 978-3-8382-0161-0

103 Ulrike Ziemer
    Ethnic Belonging, Gender and
    Cultural Practices
    Youth Identitites in Contemporary Russia
    With a foreword by Anoop Nayak
    ISBN 978-3-8382-0152-8

104 Ksenia Chepikova
,Einiges Russland' - eine zweite KPdSU?
Aspekte der Identitätskonstruktion einer postsowjetischen „Partei der Macht"
Mit einem Vorwort von Torsten Oppelland
ISBN 978-3-8382-0311-9

105 Леонид Люкс
Западничество или евразийство? Демократия или идеократия?
Сборник статей об исторических дилеммах России
С предисловием Владимира Кантора
ISBN 978-3-8382-0211-2

106 Anna Dost
Das russische Verfassungsrecht auf dem Weg zum Föderalismus und zurück
Zum Konflikt von Rechtsnormen und -wirklichkeit in der Russländischen Föderation von 1991 bis 2009
Mit einem Vorwort von Alexander Blankenagel
ISBN 978-3-8382-0292-1

107 Philipp Herzog
Sozialistische Völkerfreundschaft, nationaler Widerstand oder harmloser Zeitvertreib?
Zur politischen Funktion der Volkskunst im sowjetischen Estland
Mit einem Vorwort von Andreas Kappeler
ISBN 978-3-8382-0216-7

108 Marlène Laruelle (ed.)
Russian Nationalism, Foreign Policy, and Identity Debates in Putin's Russia
New Ideological Patterns after the Orange Revolution
ISBN 978-3-8382-0325-6

109 Michail Logvinov
Russlands Kampf gegen den internationalen Terrorismus
Eine kritische Bestandsaufnahme des Bekämpfungsansatzes
Mit einem Geleitwort von Hans-Henning Schröder
und einem Vorwort von Eckhard Jesse
ISBN 978-3-8382-0329-4

110 John B. Dunlop
The Moscow Bombings of September 1999
Examinations of Russian Terrorist Attacks at the Onset of Vladimir Putin's Rule
Second, Revised and Expanded Edition
ISBN 978-3-8382-0388-1

111 Андрей А. Ковалёв
Свидетельство из-за кулис российской политики I
Можно ли делать добро из зла?
(Воспоминания и размышления о последних советских и первых послесоветских годах)
With a foreword by Peter Reddaway
ISBN 978-3-8382-0302-7

112 Андрей А. Ковалёв
Свидетельство из-за кулис российской политики II
Угроза для себя и окружающих
(Наблюдения и предостережения относительно происходящего после 2000 г.)
ISBN 978-3-8382-0303-4

113 Bernd Kappenberg
Zeichen setzen für Europa
Der Gebrauch europäischer lateinischer Sonderzeichen in der deutschen Öffentlichkeit
Mit einem Vorwort von Peter Schlobinski
ISBN 978-3-89821-749-1

114 Ivo Mijnssen
The Quest for an Ideal Youth in Putin's Russia I
Back to Our Future! History, Modernity, and Patriotism according to *Nashi*, 2005-2013
With a foreword by Jeronim Perović
Second, Revised and Expanded Edition
ISBN 978-3-8382-0368-3

115 Jussi Lassila
The Quest for an Ideal Youth in Putin's Russia II
The Search for Distinctive Conformism in the Political Communication of *Nashi*, 2005-2009
With a foreword by Kirill Postoutenko
Second, Revised and Expanded Edition
ISBN 978-3-8382-0415-4

116 Valerio Trabandt
Neue Nachbarn, gute Nachbarschaft?
Die EU als internationaler Akteur am Beispiel ihrer Demokratieförderung in Belarus und der Ukraine 2004-2009
Mit einem Vorwort von Jutta Joachim
ISBN 978-3-8382-0437-6

117 Fabian Pfeiffer
Estlands Außen- und Sicherheitspolitik I
Der estnische Atlantizismus nach der
wiedererlangten Unabhängigkeit 1991-2004
Mit einem Vorwort von Helmut Hubel
ISBN 978-3-8382-0127-6

118 Jana Podßuweit
Estlands Außen- und Sicherheitspolitik II
Handlungsoptionen eines Kleinstaates im
Rahmen seiner EU-Mitgliedschaft (2004-2008)
Mit einem Vorwort von Helmut Hubel
ISBN 978-3-8382-0440-6

119 Karin Pointner
Estlands Außen- und Sicherheitspolitik III
Eine gedächtnispolitische Analyse estnischer
Entwicklungskooperation 2006-2010
Mit einem Vorwort von Karin Liebhart
ISBN 978-3-8382-0435-2

120 Ruslana Vovk
Die Offenheit der ukrainischen
Verfassung für das Völkerrecht und
die europäische Integration
Mit einem Vorwort von Alexander
Blankenagel
ISBN 978-3-8382-0481-9

121 Mykhaylo Banakh
Die Relevanz der Zivilgesellschaft
bei den postkommunistischen
Transformationsprozessen in mittel-
und osteuropäischen Ländern
Das Beispiel der spät- und postsowjetischen
Ukraine 1986-2009
Mit einem Vorwort von Gerhard Simon
ISBN 978-3-8382-0499-4

122 Michael Moser
Language Policy and the Discourse on
Languages in Ukraine under President
Viktor Yanukovych (25 February
2010–28 October 2012)
ISBN 978-3-8382-0497-0 (Paperback edition)
ISBN 978-3-8382-0507-6 (Hardcover edition)

123 Nicole Krome
Russischer Netzwerkkapitalismus
Restrukturierungsprozesse in der
Russischen Föderation am Beispiel des
Luftfahrtunternehmens "Aviastar"
Mit einem Vorwort von Petra Stykow
ISBN 978-3-8382-0534-2

124 David R. Marples
'Our Glorious Past'
Lukashenka's Belarus and
the Great Patriotic War
ISBN 978-3-8382-0574-8 (Paperback edition)
ISBN 978-3-8382-0675-2 (Hardcover edition)

125 Ulf Walther
Russlands "neuer Adel"
Die Macht des Geheimdienstes von
Gorbatschow bis Putin
Mit einem Vorwort von Hans-Georg Wieck
ISBN 978-3-8382-0584-7

126 Simon Geissbühler (Hrsg.)
Kiew – Revolution 3.0
Der Euromaidan 2013/14 und die
Zukunftsperspektiven der Ukraine
ISBN 978-3-8382-0581-6 (Paperback edition)
ISBN 978-3-8382-0681-3 (Hardcover edition)

127 Andrey Makarychev
Russia and the EU
in a Multipolar World
Discourses, Identities, Norms
With a foreword by Klaus Segbers
ISBN 978-3-8382-0629-5

128 Roland Scharff
Kasachstan als postsowjetischer
Wohlfahrtsstaat
Die Transformation des sozialen
Schutzsystems
Mit einem Vorwort von Joachim Ahrens
ISBN 978-3-8382-0622-6

129 Katja Grupp
Bild Lücke Deutschland
Kaliningrader Studierende sprechen über
Deutschland
Mit einem Vorwort von Martin Schulz
ISBN 978-3-8382-0552-6

130 Konstantin Sheiko, Stephen Brown
History as Therapy
Alternative History and Nationalist
Imaginings in Russia, 1991-2014
ISBN 978-3-8382-0665-3

131 Elisa Kriza
Alexander Solzhenitsyn: Cold War
Icon, Gulag Author, Russian
Nationalist?
A Study of the Western Reception of his
Literary Writings, Historical Interpretations,
and Political Ideas
With a foreword by Andrei Rogatchevski
ISBN 978-3-8382-0589-2 (Paperback edition)
ISBN 978-3-8382-0690-5 (Hardcover edition)

132 Serghei Golunov
The Elephant in the Room
Corruption and Cheating in Russian Universities
ISBN 978-3-8382-0570-0

133 Manja Hussner, Rainer Arnold (Hgg.)
Verfassungsgerichtsbarkeit in Zentralasien I
Sammlung von Verfassungstexten
ISBN 978-3-8382-0595-3

134 Nikolay Mitrokhin
Die "Russische Partei"
Die Bewegung der russischen Nationalisten in der UdSSR 1953-1985
Aus dem Russischen übertragen von einem Übersetzerteam unter der Leitung von Larisa Schippel
ISBN 978-3-8382-0024-8

135 Manja Hussner, Rainer Arnold (Hgg.)
Verfassungsgerichtsbarkeit in Zentralasien II
Sammlung von Verfassungstexten
ISBN 978-3-8382-0597-7

136 Manfred Zeller
Das sowjetische Fieber
Fußballfans im poststalinistischen Vielvölkerreich
Mit einem Vorwort von Nikolaus Katzer
ISBN 978-3-8382-0757-5

137 Kristin Schreiter
Stellung und Entwicklungspotential zivilgesellschaftlicher Gruppen in Russland
Menschenrechtsorganisationen im Vergleich
ISBN 978-3-8382-0673-8

138 David R. Marples, Frederick V. Mills (eds.)
Ukraine's Euromaidan
Analyses of a Civil Revolution
ISBN 978-3-8382-0660-8

139 Bernd Kappenberg
Setting Signs for Europe
Why Diacritics Matter for European Integration
With a foreword by Peter Schlobinski
ISBN 978-3-8382-0663-9

140 René Lenz
Internationalisierung, Kooperation und Transfer
Externe bildungspolitische Akteure in der Russischen Föderation
Mit einem Vorwort von Frank Ettrich
ISBN 978-3-8382-0751-3

141 Juri Plusnin, Yana Zausaeva, Natalia Zhidkevich, Artemy Pozanenko
Wandering Workers
Mores, Behavior, Way of Life, and Political Status of Domestic Russian Labor Migrants
Translated by Julia Kazantseva
ISBN 978-3-8382-0653-0

142 David J. Smith (eds.)
Latvia – A Work in Progress?
100 Years of State- and Nation-Building
ISBN 978-3-8382-0648-6

143 Инна Чувычкина (ред.)
Экспортные нефте- и газопроводы на постсоветском пространстве
Анализ трубопроводной политики в свете теории международных отношений
ISBN 978-3-8382-0822-0

144 Johann Zajaczkowski
Russland – eine pragmatische Großmacht?
Eine rollentheoretische Untersuchung russischer Außenpolitik am Beispiel der Zusammenarbeit mit den USA nach 9/11 und des Georgienkrieges von 2008
Mit einem Vorwort von Siegfried Schieder
ISBN 978-3-8382-0837-4

145 Boris Popivanov
Changing Images of the Left in Bulgaria
The Challenge of Post-Communism in the Early 21st Century
ISBN 978-3-8382-0667-7

146 Lenka Krátká
A History of the Czechoslovak Ocean Shipping Company 1948-1989
How a Small, Landlocked Country Ran Maritime Business During the Cold War
ISBN 978-3-8382-0666-0

147 Alexander Sergunin
Explaining Russian Foreign Policy Behavior
Theory and Practice
ISBN 978-3-8382-0752-0

148 Darya Malyutina
     Migrant Friendships in
     a Super-Diverse City
     Russian-Speakers and their Social
     Relationships in London in the 21st Century
     With a foreword by Claire Dwyer
     ISBN 978-3-8382-0652-3

149 Alexander Sergunin, Valery Konyshev
     Russia in the Arctic
     Hard or Soft Power?
     ISBN 978-3-8382-0753-7

150 John J. Maresca
     Helsinki Revisited
     A Key U.S. Negotiator's Memoirs
     on the Development of the CSCE into the
     OSCE
     With a foreword by Hafiz Pashayev
     ISBN 978-3-8382-0852-7

151 Jardar Østbø
     The New Third Rome
     Readings of a Russian Nationalist Myth
     With a foreword by Pål Kolstø
     ISBN 978-3-8382-0870-1

152 Simon Kordonsky
     Socio-Economic Foundations of the
     Russian Post-Soviet Regime
     The Resource-Based Economy and Estate-
     Based Social Structure of Contemporary
     Russia
     With a foreword by Svetlana Barsukova
     ISBN 978-3-8382-0775-9

153 Duncan Leitch
     Assisting Reform in Post-Communist
     Ukraine 2000–2012
     The Illusions of Donors and the Disillusion of
     Beneficiaries
     With a foreword by Kataryna Wolczuk
     ISBN 978-3-8382-0844-2

154 Abel Polese
     Limits of a Post-Soviet State
     How Informality Replaces, Renegotiates, and
     Reshapes Governance in Contemporary
     Ukraine
     With a foreword by Colin Williams
     ISBN 978-3-8382-0845-9

155 Mikhail Suslov (ed.)
     Digital Orthodoxy in the Post-Soviet
     World
     The Russian Orthodox Church and Web 2.0
     With a foreword by Father Cyril Hovorun
     ISBN 978-3-8382-0871-8

156 Leonid Luks
     Zwei „Sonderwege"? Russisch-
     deutsche Parallelen und Kontraste
     (1917-2014)
     Vergleichende Essays
     ISBN 978-3-8382-0823-7

157 Vladimir V. Karacharovskiy, Ovsey I.
     Shkaratan, Gordey A. Yastrebov
     Towards a New Russian Work Culture
     Can Western Companies and Expatriates
     Change Russian Society?
     With a foreword by Elena N. Danilova
     Translated by Julia Kazantseva
     ISBN 978-3-8382-0902-9

158 Edmund Griffiths
     Aleksandr Prokhanov and Post-Soviet
     Esotericism
     ISBN 978-3-8382-0903-6

159 Timm Beichelt, Susann Worschech
     (eds.)
     Transnational Ukraine?
     Networks and Ties that Influence(d)
     Contemporary Ukraine
     ISBN 978-3-8382-0944-9

160 Mieste Hotopp-Riecke
     Die Tataren der Krim zwischen
     Assimilation und Selbstbehauptung
     Der Aufbau des krimtatarischen
     Bildungswesens nach Deportation und
     Heimkehr (1990-2005)
     Mit einem Vorwort von Swetlana
     Czerwonnaja
     ISBN 978-3-89821-940-2

161 Olga Bertelsen (ed.)
     Revolution and War in
     Contemporary Ukraine
     The Challenge of Change
     ISBN 978-3-8382-1016-2

162 Natalya Ryabinska
     Ukraine's Post-Communist
     Mass Media
     Between Capture and Commercialization
     With a foreword by Marta Dyczok
     ISBN 978-3-8382-1011-7

163 *Alexandra Cotofana,*
    James M. Nyce (eds.)
    Religion and Magic in Socialist and
    Post-Socialist Contexts
    Historic and Ethnographic Case Studies of
    Orthodoxy, Heterodoxy, and Alternative
    Spirituality
    With a foreword by Patrick L. Michelson
    ISBN 978-3-8382-0989-0

164 *Nozima Akhrarkhodjaeva*
    The Instrumentalisation of Mass
    Media in Electoral Authoritarian
    Regimes
    Evidence from Russia's Presidential Election
    Campaigns of 2000 and 2008
    ISBN 978-3-8382-1013-1

165 *Yulia Krasheninnikova*
    Informal Healthcare in Contemporary
    Russia
    Sociographic Essays on the Post-Soviet
    Infrastructure for Alternative Healing
    Practices
    ISBN 978-3-8382-0970-8

166 *Peter Kaiser*
    Das Schachbrett der Macht
    Die Handlungsspielräume eines sowjetischen
    Funktionärs unter Stalin am Beispiel des
    Generalsekretärs des Komsomol
    Aleksandr Kosarev (1929-1938)
    Mit einem Vorwort von Dietmar Neutatz
    ISBN 978-3-8382-1052-0

167 *Oksana Kim*
    The Effects and Implications of
    Kazakhstan's Adoption of
    International Financial Reporting
    Standards
    A Resource Dependence Perspective
    With a foreword by Svetlana Vlady
    ISBN 978-3-8382-0987-6

168 *Anna Sanina*
    Patriotic Education in
    Contemporary Russia
    Sociological Studies in the Making of the
    Post-Soviet Citizen
    ISBN 978-3-8382-0993-7

ibidem-Verlag

Melchiorstr. 15

D-70439 Stuttgart

info@ibidem-verlag.de

www.ibidem-verlag.de
www.ibidem.eu
www.edition-noema.de
www.autorenbetreuung.de